The Fall of the Iron Curtain and the Culture of Europe

The end of communism in Europe has tended to be discussed mainly in the context of political science and history. This book, in contrast, assesses the cultural consequences for Europe of the disappearance of the Soviet bloc. Adopting a multi-disciplinary approach, the book examines the new narratives about national, individual and European identities that have emerged in literature, theatre and other cultural media, investigates the impact of the re-unification of the continent on the mental landscape of Western Europe as well as Eastern Europe and Russia, and explores the new borders in the form of divisive nationalism that have reappeared since the disappearance of the Iron Curtain.

Peter I. Barta is Professor of Comparative Literature at Texas Tech University, USA, and Professor Emeritus at the University of Surrey, UK, where he held the Chair in Comparative Literature between 2000 and 2012.

Routledge Contemporary Russia and Eastern Europe Series

1 Liberal Nationalism in Central Europe
Stefan Auer

2 Civil-Military Relations in Russia and Eastern Europe
David J. Betz

3 The Extreme Nationalist Threat in Russia
The growing influence of Western Rightist Ideas
Thomas Parland

4 Economic Development in Tatarstan
Global markets and a Russian Region
Leo McCann

5 Adapting to Russia's New Labour Market
Gender and employment strategy
Edited by Sarah Ashwin

6 Building Democracy and Civil Society East of the Elbe
Essays in honour of Edmund Mokrzycki
Edited by Sven Eliaeson

7 The Telengits of Southern Siberia
Landscape, religion and knowledge in motion
Agnieszka Halemba

8 The Development of Capitalism in Russia
Simon Clarke

9 Russian Television Today
Primetime drama and comedy
David MacFadyen

10 The Rebuilding of Greater Russia
Putin's Foreign Policy towards the CIS Countries
Bertil Nygren

11 A Russian Factory Enters the Market Economy
Claudio Morrison

12 Democracy Building and Civil Society in Post-Soviet Armenia
Armine Ishkanian

13 NATO-Russia Relations in the Twenty-First Century
Aurel Braun

14 Russian Military Reform
A failed exercise in defence decision making
Carolina Vendil Pallin

15 The Multilateral Dimension in Russian Foreign Policy
Edited by Elana Wilson Rowe and Stina Torjesen

16 Russian Nationalism and the National Reassertion of Russia
Edited by MarlÒne Laruelle

17 The Caucasus An Introduction
Frederik Coene

18 Radical Islam in the Former Soviet Union
Edited by Galina M. Yemelianova

19 Russia's European Agenda and the Baltic States
Janina leivyte

20 Regional Development in Central and Eastern Europe
Development processes and policy challenges
Edited by Grzegorz Gorzelak, John Bachtler and Maciej Smetkowski

21 Russia and Europe
Reaching agreements, digging trenches
Kjell Engelbrekt and Bertil Nygren

22 Russia's Skinheads
Exploring and rethinking subcultural lives
Hilary Pilkington, Elena Omel chenko and Al'bina Garifzianova

23 The Colour Revolutions in the Former Soviet Republics
Successes and failures
Edited by Donnacha Æ BeachÃin and Abel Polese

24 Russian Mass Media and Changing Values
Edited by Arja Rosenholm, Kaarle Nordenstreng and Elena Trubina

25 The Heritage of Soviet Oriental Studies
Edited by Michael Kemper and Stephan Conermann

26 Religion and Language in Post-Soviet Russia
Brian P. Bennett

27 Jewish Women Writers in the Soviet Union
Rina Lapidus

28 Chinese Migrants in Russia, Central Asia and Eastern Europe
Edited by Felix B. Chang and Sunnie T. Rucker-Chang

29 Poland's EU Accession
Sergiusz Trzeciak

30 The Russian Armed Forces in Transition
Economic, geopolitical and institutional uncertainties
Edited by Roger N. McDermott, Bertil Nygren and Carolina Vendil Pallin

31 The Religious Factor in Russia's Foreign Policy
Alicja Curanovic

32 Postcommunist Film Russia, Eastern Europe and World Culture
Moving images of postcommunism
Edited by Lars Lyngsgaard Fjord Kristensen

33 Russian Multinationals
From regional supremacy to global lead
Andrei Panibratov

34 **Russian Anthropology After the Collapse of Communism**
Edited by Albert Baiburin, Catriona Kelly and Nikolai Vakhtin

35 **The Post-Soviet Russian Orthodox Church**
Politics, culture and Greater Russia
Katja Richters

36 **Lenin's Terror**
The ideological origins of early Soviet State violence
James Ryan

37 **Life in Post-Communist Eastern Europe after EU Membership**
Edited by Donnacha O Beachain, Vera Sheridan and Sabina Stan

38 **EU Border Security**
Challenges, (mis)perceptions, and responses
Serghei Golunov

39 **Power and Legitimacy – Challenges from Russia**
Edited by Per-Arne Bodin, Stefan Hedlund and Elena Namli

40 **Managing Ethnic Diversity in Russia**
Edited by Oleh Protsyk and Benedikt Harzl

41 **Believing in Russia Religious Policy After Communism**
Geraldine Fagan

42 **The Changing Russian University**
From State to Market
Tatiana Maximova-Mentzoni

43 **The Transition to National Armies in the Former Soviet Republics, 1988–2005**
Jesse Paul Lehrke

44 **The Fall of the Iron Curtain and the Culture of Europe**
Peter I. Barta

45 **Russia After 2012**
From Putin to Medvedev to Putin Continuity, Change, or Revolution?
Edited by J.L. Black and Michael' Johns

The Fall of the Iron Curtain and the Culture of Europe

Edited by
Peter I. Barta

LONDON AND NEW YORK

First published 2013
by Routledge

Published 2014 by Routledge
2 Park Square, Milton Park, Abingdon, Oxfordshire OX14 4RN

Simultaneously published in the USA and Canada
by Routledge
711 Third Avenue, New York, NY 10017

Routledge is an imprint of the Taylor and Francis Group, an informa business

First issued in paperback 2015

© 2013 selection and editorial material, Peter I. Barta; individual chapters, the
contributors

The right of the editor to be identified as the author of the editorial material,
and of the authors for their individual chapters, has been asserted in
accordance with sections 77 and 78 of the Copyright, Designs and Patents Act
1988.

All rights reserved. No part of this book may be reprinted or reproduced or
utilised in any form or by any electronic, mechanical, or other means, now
known or hereafter invented, including photocopying and recording, or in any
information storage or retrieval system, without permission in writing from
the publishers.

Trademark notice: Product or corporate names may be trademarks or
registered trademarks, and are used only for identification and explanation
without intent to infringe.

British Library Cataloguing in Publication Data
A catalogue record for this book is available from the British Library

Library of Congress Cataloging in Publication Data
The fall of the iron curtain and the culture of Europe / edited by
Peter I. Barta.
pages ; cm. -- (Routledge contemporary Russia and Eastern Europe series ; 44)
Includes bibliographical references and index.
1. Post-communism--Europe. 2. Europe--Civilization--21st century. I. Barta,
Peter I. II. Series: Routledge contemporary Russia and Eastern Europe series ; 44.
D2021.F35 2013
940.56--dc23
2012039690

ISBN 978-0-415-59237-6 (hbk)
ISBN 978-1-138-95640-7 (pbk)
ISBN 978-0-203-55002-1 (ebk)

Typeset in Sabon
by Taylor & Francis Books

"To the memory of Dr Otto von Habsburg, last Crown Prince of Austria-Hungary"

Contents

Contributors		xi
Foreword		xiv
KATALIN BOGYAY		
	New paradigms in changing spaces: an introduction	1
	PETER I. BARTA	
1	The Wall has fallen on all of us	12
	DUBRAVKA UGREŠIĆ	
2	Twenty years after the Curtain fell: a personal account by an Austrian	17
	GABRIELE MATZNER-HOLZER	
3	The rediscovery of Central Europe in the 1980s	24
	CATHERINE HOREL	
4	Gulfs and gaps – Prague and Lisbon – 1989 and 2009	40
	WOLFGANG MÜLLER-FUNK	
5	Borders in mind or how to re-invent identities	48
	RÜDIGER GÖRNER	
6	The Iron Curtain, the Wall and performative *Verfremdung*	58
	ANNELIS KUHLMANN	
7	The re-emergence of national cultures following independence in the Baltic states	70
	CHARLES DE CHASSIRON	
8	Explosions, shifts and backtracking in post-Soviet fiction	77
	HÉLÈNE MÉLAT	

x   *Contents*

9 Neither East nor West: polyphony and deterritorialization in
   contemporary European fiction   92
   MARIA RUBINS

10 The fall of the Iron Curtain and the new linguistic landscape of
   East-Central Europe   104
   MICHAEL MOSER

   Index   118

Contributors

Peter I. Barta held the Chair in Comparative Literature at the University of Surrey until August 2012 and is now Professor of Comparative Literature at Texas Tech University. He is author/editor of nine books and has published over 100 articles/chapters. His main research interests lie in the study of intercultural ties, especially in the literature of Russia, Western and Central Europe and Classical Antiquity.

Katalin Bogyay is the President of the General Conference of UNESCO. A former journalist, she was Director of the Hungarian Cultural Centre in London between 1999 and 2006 and served as State Secretary for International Affairs at the Hungarian Ministry of Education and Culture between 2006 and 2009. Since 2009 she has been Hungary's Ambassador to UNESCO in Paris. She has published four books to date.

Charles de Chassiron was educated at Rugby School and Cambridge, where he studied history, before undertaking postgraduate studies at Harvard. He was a member of the British Diplomatic Service from 1972 to 2000 and served in six countries, including Sweden, Italy and Estonia. In the latter he was British Ambassador from 1994 to 1997. He finished his career as Director of Protocol. He was later chairman of Spencer House in London (2006–11) and since 2006 he has been chairman of the British-Italian Society.

Rüdiger Görner is Professor of German with Comparative Literature and Founding Director of the Centre for Anglo-German Cultural Relations at Queen Mary, University of London. He also founded the Ingeborg Bachmann Centre for Austrian Literature. He is Corresponding Fellow of the Deutsche Akademie für Sprache und Dichtung. His recent monographs include *Gewalt und Grazie: Heinrich von Kleists Poetik der Gegensätzlichkeit* (Heidelberg: Winter, 2011); *Goethes geistige Morphologie* (Heidelberg: Winter, 2012); *Sprachrausch und Sprachverlust. Essays zur österreichischen Literatur von Hofmannsthal bis Mayröcker* (Wien: Sonderzahl, 2011).

Catherine Horel is Professor of Central European History at the University of Paris I. She specialises in social and political structures, and urban and Jewish studies. Her latest books are *Soldaten zwischen nationalen Fronten. Die*

xii *Contributors*

Auflösung der Militärgrenze und die Entwicklung der königlich-ungarischen Landwehr (Honvéd) in Kroatien-Slawonien: 1868–1914 (Vienna: Austrian Academy of Sciences, 2009); Cette Europe qu'on dit centrale. Des Habsbourg à l'intégration européenne (1815-2004) (Paris: Beauchesne, 2009; Prix Guizot of the French Academy 2010).

Annelis Kuhlmann earned her PhD at the University of Aarhus in Denmark in 1997. She teaches dramaturgy and performance analysis at the Department of Aesthetics and Communication at Aarhus. Her doctoral thesis studied Stanislavsky's theatre. More recently her published research has focused on theatre directors who, after World War II, have given artistic representation of the politically divided space in Europe.

Gabriele Matzner-Holzer is a senior Austrian diplomat who has specialised in international law. She served, among other places, in Moscow, Washington DC and Berlin and was Austrian Ambassador in Bratislava, Tunis and London. She was a member of the cabinet of Bruno Kreisky, the Austrian Prime Minister, in the 1970s. Her books to date have addressed Austro-German relations, the cultural and political history of Slovakia, and the intellectual and political contributions of Egon Matzner to Austrian social democracy.

Hélène Mélat is Maître de Conferences in Russian Literature at Paris-4 Sorbonne. A leading expert in contemporary Russian culture, she has been seconded to the Embassy of France in Moscow where she currently holds the post of Chargée de Mission pour le Livre et l'Ecrit. Her published research includes *Samovar lexique alphabétique français-russe/russe-français*, *Le premier quinquennat de la prose russe du XXIe siècle* and 'Andrei Makine: Testament francais ou Testament russe?'.

Michael Moser is Professor of Slavonic Languages at the University of Vienna, at the Ukrainian Free University in Munich and at the Pázmáneum Catholic University in Budapest/Piliscsaba. His eight monographs and more than 250 articles and reviews include *Prychynky do istoriyi ukrayin movy* (Vinnytsia, 2012) and *Taras Shevchenko i suchasna ukrayinska mova: sproba hidnoyi ocinky* (Lviv, 2012).

Wolfgang Müller-Funk holds the Chair in Cultural Studies at the Department of European and Comparative Literature and Language Studies at the University of Vienna. His research has been in Austrian and Central European studies, romanticism, modernism, cultural theory and narratology. His recent publications include *The Architecture of Modern Culture* (2012), *Joseph Roth* (2nd edition, 2012), *Kulturtheorie* (2010), *Komplex Österreich* (2009) and *Die Kultur und ihre Narrative* (2nd edition, 2008).

Maria Rubins has published over 100 articles and a monograph, *Crossroad of Arts, Crossroad of Cultures: Ecphrasis in Russian and French Poetry* (Palgrave, 2000; Russian edition, 2003). Her edited volumes have focused on Russian émigré authors, including Irina Odoevtseva and Vasily Yanovsky.

Contributors xiii

She has translated Judith Gautier's memoirs on Wagner and several novels by Irène Némirovsky and Arnaud Delalande from French into Russian.

Dubravka Ugrešić is the author of novels, essays and short stories, including *Fording the Stream of Consciousness*, *Lend Me Your Character*, *The Culture of Lies*, *The Museum of Unconditional Surrender*, *The Ministry of Pain*, *Nobody's Home*, *Baba Yaga Laid An Egg*, and *Karaoke Culture*. Her books have been translated into more then twenty languages. She has received several esteemed European literary awards, including the Österreichischer Staatspreis für Europäische Literatur, the Heinrich Mann Preis and the Prix Européen de l'Essai Charles Veillon. She was born and educated in Zagreb and lives in Amsterdam.

Foreword

Katalin Bogyay[1]

The fall of the Iron Curtain heralded the beginning of a new phase in human history marked by fundamental transformations in the political and economic realities of the newly liberated societies. Volumes of scholarly work have been dedicated to the study of the events and conditions that led to the demise of authoritarian regimes in Central and Eastern Europe, bringing to light the weakening legitimacy of the state, the failures of the centralized economy and the burden of military competition with the West.

In November 2009 I had the pleasure of participating in a most exciting conference on this topic organized by Professor Peter I. Barta of the University of Surrey at the Austrian Cultural Forum and the Hungarian Cultural Centre in London. The latter, symbolizing cultural collaboration in a new, undivided Europe, had been set up under my directorship ten years earlier, in 1999, at the time of the tenth anniversary of the end of Soviet occupation and the communist dictatorship in Hungary. Our aim was to provide a platform for different views, ideas and forms of artistic expression to meet and inspire each other. The conference commemorating the twentieth anniversary of forcing open the barbed wired barrier between Austria and Hungary lived up to these aspirations admirably and served as inspiration for the present volume of essays. Literature, philosophy and the arts are often overlooked in their role as catalyst in social, economic and political change. In the state-socialist regimes of Eastern Europe, culture fed the liberation movements that culminated in popular uprisings against the ruling regimes. Equally importantly, the long and tedious process of state-building that has followed the fall of the Iron Curtain in the region – now integrated within a united Europe – both underpins, and is mediated by, cultural production. Hence this book fills in a gap in scholarship on the subject that tends to focus on politics and the economy, not infrequently to the detriment of giving appropriate consideration to the essential importance of the humanities.

The collapse of communist regimes in the Eastern Bloc unravelled a system that had previously imposed an identity on the citizens of the Soviet Union and its erstwhile 'satellite's' and elicited reassessments of historical legacies, cultural heritage, predominant systems of epistemology and figures of style within the discourse of newly independent nations. The multi-ethnic character of most of these countries and the long-term legacy of conflicts, border disputes and population

Foreword xv

migrations presented complex challenges to the sovereign states. The triumph of freedom over totalitarianism is associated with shifts in cultural landscapes where age-old regimes of oppression thwarting people's desire to articulate their sense of identity now gave way to outbursts of self-expression. Some of this took the form of artistic creativity and genuine celebration of the richness of historical heritage and traditions, mobilizing people around positive ideas and values of democratic citizenship. At the same time, we have witnessed the emergence of explosive and narrow-minded nationalism that has kindled ethnic conflicts of extreme intensity and destructive power.

The shape of Western, Central and Eastern European civilization after decades of enforced division now is evolving freely. Unrestrained cultural expression represents perpetual motion, like a river viewed from a great distance – the top of a mountain or the window of an aeroplane – as it carves out a distinctive shape in the landscape below. From afar it resembles a fixed structure. But once you step into it, you feel the dynamic flow of water rushing forcefully around your body, removing all obstacles in its way. Just like a river, culture is dynamic, adaptive and transformative while at the same time it carves out a structure that defines who we are: our common values and shared identities at any moment in time and space. The countries that have shed the oppressive weight of autocratic communism will have to find ways to realize the tremendous potential of cultural diversity that characterizes their societies. Europeans, East and West of the former Iron Curtain, will have to embrace cultural pluralism as an essential element for averting negative societal trends of prejudice, stereotyping, xenophobia, discrimination and exclusion in the globalizing world. When the wall – physical as well as ideological – came down, and people-to-people encounters started to accelerate, the stereotypes that had existed among the groups living on either side of the divide also began gradually to break down. It is this tradition of dialogue and understanding the 'other' that we need to cherish and sustain in years to come

For the last two decades, the leaders of the post-communist countries have had to reconcile two seemingly divergent aspirations. On the one hand, most governments have adopted a strategic agenda of close integration into the economic, political and social fabric of the European Union. At the same time, countries have had to build identities based on the common history and shared experiences of their people, often representing mixed ethnic and cultural backgrounds. This dichotomy between the desire to adopt a wider European identity and the wish simultaneously to be identified with a historically marked region, continues to influence domestic political discourse in Central and Eastern European countries today. In this context, education assumes a pivotal role: it enables citizens, and especially young people, to acquire knowledge that empowers them to relate to their cultural heritage and to look beyond their borders to appreciate what other cultures have to offer. Only when one understands one's own culture will she or he be able successfully to adopt a pan-European identity and accept diversity and difference with respect and pragmatism.

xvi *Katalin Bogyay*

The end of the bi-polar world of the Cold War and the subsequent rise of a new, multi-polar international system has shed light on the significance of cross-cultural dialogue as a modality of inter-state relations. Cultural diplomacy will assume an important role for channeling culture and its expressions towards peaceful ends and away from conflicts. In various parts of the world cultural diplomacy has proven its capacity to bring about understanding and to promote conciliation. It can play a similarly positive role among the ethnically and culturally diverse societies in the Central and Eastern European countries by way of language teaching, educational exchanges and other forms of cultural contact, leading to long-lasting and stable cooperation. Culture will be necessary to understand and to be understood, to build meaningful links between ethnically and socially different communities and to work together in order to protect our shared European values and diverse national traditions. *The Fall of the Iron Curtain and the Culture of Europe*, brought about in close collaboration between academic scholars and diplomats committed to advancing intercultural dialogue, will make a significant contribution towards the realization of these ambitions.

Note

1 H.E. Katalin Bogyay is President of the General Conference of UNESCO and Hungary's Ambassador to UNESCO. She founded the Hungarian Cultural Centre in London in 1999 and served as its director between 1999 and 2006.

New paradigms in changing spaces: an introduction

Peter I. Barta

Jüri võitlus lohega (George's fight with the dragon), one of Jüri Arrak's most famous paintings, disappeared without trace in the early 1990s from a gallery in Estonia. Produced in Soviet times (1979), it has never been found but, surprisingly, its disappearance has never been properly investigated. Mr Arrak has graciously agreed to our using a reproduction of the painting for the cover of this volume.[1] The painting depicts the dragon that has apparently prevailed over George. But George continues the fight from inside the monster even as he is being swallowed. By driving his spear through the dragon's body, he presumably inflicts a mortal wound. The monster's death, however, is merely implied. In addition to the two main figures, those of St George and the dragon, we see other semi-human creatures staring out of the painting with scary red eyes. George's left eye, conveying the same expression as the other nine eyes, is visible from inside the monster's body. Inspired by psychoanalysis and the theatre of the absurd, Arrak maintained that his paintings represented the reality of life in the Soviet Union (Rosenfeld 2002: 93). Arrak himself summarized the meaning of his work as follows:

> The motif of St George conveyed a political hint in my interpretation. The dragon was huge and red; its claws inflicted wounds from which people underneath were bleeding. Besides, George did not kill the dragon with a sword or spear but instead he leapt into its mouth and destroyed it from inside: the spear and one of his hands were already visible sticking out of the rear side of the monster's body. Ten years ago, this is exactly what happened: the Red Empire collapsed from inside. As my name is Jüri [George in English, PIB] I was able to tell them [i.e. the censors, translator's comment] back then that the painting was depicting my struggle with my own shortcomings.
>
> (Arrak 2005)[2]

It is beyond doubt that Arrak, who was never allowed to leave the Soviet Union, was viewed with considerable suspicion by the state (Rosenfeld 2002: 94). It is not so surprising that his own comments should have led some scholars to impose too rigid an interpretation on the painting.[3] Great art, however, never

2 Peter I. Barta

relies on the all too unambiguous, straightforward linearity of mono-discourse. Not only is its stuff polyvalent but its creator's intentions do not solely control its meaning. The iconography of St George extends across many European civilizations; while he is patron saint of England, he is no less venerated by the Orthodox Church. St George and the dragon appear on the coat of arms of the city of Moscow and among the many cultures that venerate him, Estonians also observe St George's Day. This is perhaps not unconnected to a peasant uprising in 1343 that was crushed on this day by the Teutonic Order, as the Germans, Swedes and Danes were fighting over control of Estonians.

Cultural communication relies heavily on figurative language. Metaphorical imagery, allegory, irony, symbols and especially myths signify within multiple codes, and their ability to configure meaning depends on the narrative within which they find accommodation (Barthes 1977: 79). Arrak's lost painting and the controversy surrounding it capture the spirit of this book about European culture after communism. The two decades following the end of totalitarian rule in the Eastern half of Europe and the division of the continent have been marked by taking stock of still open wounds left by two world wars and the Cold War and by attempts to find redress. In culture the period has witnessed the articulation of individual, national and European forms of 'new' identities, the intensified production and consumption of published and audio-visual texts and the unprecedented expansion of intercultural communication. This volume aims to illuminate characteristic trends in culture and in the humanities as they have emerged within interactions between Eastern and Western Europe over the last quarter of a century. We understand culture in this context as artistic and literary activity as well as an essential gauge with which to study social and political communication. Politics and history predominate in scholarship on the Berlin Wall and the 'Iron Curtain': the latter is a metaphor coined by Winston Churchill in reference to the physical barriers being built on the borders of Soviet-dominated Eastern European states to prevent people from fleeing to the Western, democratic countries of post World War II Europe.[4] Argumentative writing of an explicitly ideological content is unavoidably underpinned by overtly politicized judgement. Michel Foucault has argued that the values of culture are hierarchical and thus never unencumbered by power politics.[5] The essays in this book represent ideologically diverse, albeit informed and balanced, views by an international team of scholars, diplomats and writers hailing from Western, Central and Eastern Europe, addressing the entanglement of ideology, culture and communication with a view to events that preceded and succeeded 1989, East as well as West. We do not lose sight of the predominant political, social and cultural importance for Europe of the reunification of Germany and the fall of the Soviet Union. Yet we also focus on a selection of 'smaller' cultures: shifting identities in the re-emerging Baltic states, whose very statehood had been lost prior to the changes initiated in 1989 (Berglund and Dellenbrant 1994: 238; Kotkin 2009: 138); the role of Austria and the legacy of 'Mitteleuropa', linguistic developments in the Slavonic languages of post-Soviet Europe, innovations in European theatre and the changing

Introduction: new paradigms 3

concepts of 'diaspora' and 'émigré' culture. We wish to offer specific and original insights into general problems in the hope that these will advance understanding of European culture today.

The photographic images of cheering crowds mounting the Berlin Wall and the cutting of the barbed-wire fence in the summer of 1989 on the Austro-Hungarian border have become emblematic of the end of communism and the division of the continent. The champions of the pro-Western, liberal 'velvet revolutions' of this period – mainly writers, artists and philosophers – however, gradually fell out of favour with the electorates of the new democracies and were among others transposed by 'neo-liberal' entrepreneurs, jingoistic nationalists and 'anti-communists' (Gati 2006: 226; Bozoki 1999: 7). Expectations of an easy transition from communism to liberal democracy in the countries of the former Warsaw Pact were premature and proved to be short-lived (Blokker 2010: 1). The 'new' Europe – the former East – did not, of course, overnight cease to be, or be perceived as, less civilized and economically less stable than the 'old' Europe – the former West (Hoffman 1994: xi). Cultural representation of social change conveys new anxieties about new forms of intolerance: the days of the émigré writer leaving her/his homeland and even native language for a life and artistic career in Western Europe appear not to be over: the Croatian Dubravka Ugrešić (The Netherlands), the Hungarian Imre Kertész (Germany) and the Czech Milan Kundera (France) are some of the names that come most immediately to mind. The former dissident writers and philosophers of the East have, since the late 1980s, been steadily losing their hold of the intellectual centre ground. As Vladimir Tismaneanu puts it:

> [O]nce revolutionary fever subsided, people looked for politicians and ideas they could feel akin to. Dissidents … had to fail because their values did not belong in the post-communist order. Equally opposed to technocratic pragmatism and to populist demagogy, dissidents cultivated democratic individualism, a political choice dramatically unpopular in the region.
>
> (Tismaneanu 1998: 143)

There has been a rise of new millionaires and also of distortive accounts of the past – easily seen as a store for topical, usable and often mendacious narratives to occupy undeveloped minds. Dissemination has been unproblematic and efficient by way of cheaply produced publications and via the new electronic media tied to advocates of populist ideologies and their attached commercial interests (Kubik 2003: 319). Simultaneously, high culture has also located new consumers for its products thanks to great advances in the dissemination of works in translation, satellite television and the increased visibility of large groups of ethnic, gender-identified or disability-based diasporas.

The seemingly smooth binary opposites of East and West, communist autocracy and capitalist democracy, oppression and freedom, poverty and wealth had become troubled by the time Europe's division ended. Not that the dichotomy of the 'civilized' West and the 'barbaric' East was ever anything other than the

4   Peter I. Barta

result of stereotypical thinking. Lumping has characterized many studies of the world seen from the Western metropolis: specific and closely observed aspects of the non-Western 'other' have tended to be measured against an unchanging, 'ideal model of the West' (Hayoz *et al.* 2011: 19). However, it is indisputable that Eastern Europe's liberal artists and intellectuals have to a varying extent – depending on prevailing relations of power in the given historical period – felt threatened in their native countries, and especially so since the fall of the Austro-Hungarian monarchy and the rise of Bolshevism after World War I.[6] They have tended to contrast the civilizational backwardness of their native societies with an idealized, socially, politically and economically advanced Europe, always understood to be Western and metropolitan (Bozoki 1999: 1) The lines of the Hungarian poet, Attila József, in a poem entitled 'Welcoming Thomas Mann', produced for the occasion of the writer's visit to Budapest in 1937, illustrate this point. The voice of the subject in the poem, using the first person plural in clear reference to the community of like-minded friends around him, assumes the position of subservient children waiting to be reassured by the reliable, trusted, knowledgeable and decent adult, the Noble prize laureate, the world famous writer who emigrated from his native Germany as soon as the Nazis came to power in 1933. He is seen as the prototypical European – a category to which the states in the hands of boorish and murderous autocrats do not belong. Thus 'Europe' becomes endowed with the values of tolerance and fairness, and ceases to designate a geographical area. The last three lines of the poem read:

> We are listening to you and some of us will
> just keep looking at you, happy to see today
> a European, conspicuous among the crowds of white-skinned people.[7]

Quixotic he or she may be, but as Sir Philip Sydney argues in *The Defence of Poesy*, 'the poet … never lies'. József articulates with rare clarity the sense of isolation and vulnerability of the Eastern European intellectual, always already out of touch with his country's backward-looking and potentially violently intolerant social and political practices.

The populations in the new democracies in the East exhibit numerous similarities: in addition to having, with few exceptions, been invaded by Nazi Germany before or during World War II, they were also subsequently subjected to autocratic communist police states for several decades prior to 1989. The region contains ethnic diversity and ethnic tensions both within and between countries (Batt 2007: 2). In addition, a tradition of intellectual argumentation and persuasion in addressing conflicts has generally failed to take hold in public life to date across the region.[8] Because of the stereotypical and orientalist associations of the term 'Eastern' with backwardness, inefficiency, corruption and the lack of civilized values, the concept of 'Central Europe' has become the preferred self-designation for many individuals and institutions both in countries that used to form Habsburg 'Mitteleuropa' and also elsewhere, further East, North and South.[9]

Introduction: new paradigms 5

The West, however, has not remained immune from the jolts that shook the continent after the end of communism. Symbolic as well as financial economies have had to adjust to today's changed situation, even as much of the continent is moving towards political and economic integration amidst banking crises, rising uncertainty about the mission of the EU and the growing momentum of the new nationalist right (Binder 2010: 342). The contributors to this volume have undertaken to negotiate new concepts and renegotiate old ones, worrying the clichés of the present and the past as they go.

In 'The Wall has fallen on all of us', Dubravka Ugrešić, the Amsterdam-based Croatian writer from former Yugoslavia, returns to the literary genre of the essay whose present-day 'rediscovery' she initiated in her famous piece, 'Kultura laži' (The Culture of Lies, 1996). This form enables literary authors to use creative writing in addressing social problems on their own behalf and to voice their anxiety about intolerant trends in politics without the need to employ fictional characters in a narrative (Müller 2011: 611–13).[10] In the first chapter of this volume Ugresic illuminates themes that recur later on: the problems surrounding the brand of Eastern European culture; the autonomy of the writer and the legacy of societal expectations of her/him in Eastern Europe; the implications for culture today to have to fight for dominance in a battle against new mono-discursive ideologies, such as xenophobic nationalism and racism; the status of the émigré writer vis-à-vis the post-1989 nation state; Eastern European culture and the Western European metropolitan centres in each other's gaze. As the provocative title of the essay implies, the removal of barbed wire fences and minefields from international borders did not result in instantaneous epistemological changes. The troubling image of the 'Wall' collapsing on those in its shadow suggests that liberation from one form of oppression can just as easily unleash other, new forms of violence.

The political dimensions of culture are in the focus of Gabriele Matzner-Holzer's essay, 'Twenty Years after the Curtain Fell: A Personal Account by an Austrian'. A published author on intercultural matters and an accomplished painter, Matzner-Holzer is one of the most senior Austrian diplomats serving in the period on which this volume concentrates. During a career spanning four decades, she had postings in Moscow and New York, then she served as Consul General in West Berlin before and after the removal of the Berlin Wall in 1989 and, subsequently as Ambassador in Bratislava, Tunis and London. Having been a member of the foreign policy advisory team of Bruno Kreisky, the author draws upon personal insights into Austrian involvement with prominent writers and artists unwilling to be mouthpieces of the Communist Parties of the Eastern Bloc. Her years in the Austrian Embassy in the Soviet capital in the 1970s had acquainted her with the conflict between individual desire for self-expression and the struggle by the Communist Party autocracy to stifle any signs of dissent or dissatisfaction with the regime. Matzner-Holzer analyses unofficial communication between people driving, involved in, or shaken by such a sweeping shift of paradigms as the end of Soviet power in Germany and in most of the lands of the former Habsburg Empire. With the benefit of

6 Peter I. Barta

combining the gaze both from inside and outside civilisations affected by the Iron Curtain, the essay produces a balanced view of expectations of freedom ahead of, and socio-cultural realities following, the arrival of democracy in East-Central Europe.

The concept of 'Mitteleuropa' – specifically a shared sense of identity in the countries of the former Austro-Hungarian Empire – is interrogated in Catherine Horel's article entitled 'The Rediscovery of Central Europe in the 1980s'. In her investigation, Horel takes 1971 as her point of departure when Croatian intellectuals began problematizing the legacies of cultural identity in the successor states of the Habsburg monarchy. The analysis considers the series of meetings in the 1980s of writers and intellectuals from Austria, Italy, Yugoslavia and the 'socialist' countries of East-Central Europe (including among others, well-known politicians, historians, émigré and dissident writers such as Bruno Kreisky, Alois Mock, Claudio Magris, Eugène Ionesco, György Konrád and Danilo Kiš). Horel considers the renewed interest in pre-World War I Vienna as centre of Empire, even as the funeral of Empress and Queen Zita (widow of Karl IV and mother of Otto von Habsburg) and the Pan-European picnic on the Austro-Hungarian border dominated headlines in the spring of 1989. She assesses French and German attitudes, in addition to Austro-Italian sensitivities, amidst the rapidly changing political situation in the countries of the Warsaw Pact as she delineates the steady disappearance in the region of the writers' and intellectuals' 'dream' of recreating the lost 'Mitteleuropa'. The article traces the trajectory of events leading away from ideas of Central European regional integration towards NATO and EU membership.

The hiatus left by the rejection of a possible new Central European cultural and economic union and the eventual filling of this space by re-emerging nationalism and concomitant intercultural hostilities is the main concern in Wolfgang Müller-Funk's chapter. 'Gulfs and Gaps – Prague and Lisbon – 1989 and 2009' assesses the promises of the leaders of the 'velvet revolutions' in Warsaw, Berlin, Budapest and Prague. Müller-Funk considers with the benefit of hindsight of more than two decades, the intellectual stakeholders in Central Europe – discussed in Horel's chapter – and their struggle for liberal democracy that culminated in the events of 1989. Owing to their intellectual elitism, such individuals as Václav Havel, Jiři Dienstbier, Péter Esterházy or Imre Kertész, in the changed circumstances after communism (the rise of market capitalism, the very real possibilities of economic failure, the banking crisis), gradually lost their appeal even as right-wing isolationism and populism were gaining momentum with electorates. Müller-Funk compares the transition from right-wing dictatorship to democracy in Greece, Spain and Portugal with the aftermath of the fall of the communist dictatorships in the countries of Eastern Europe. In the latter, he concludes, neither a credible left wing nor a credible right wing has emerged to maintain the system of cheques and balances, crucial for political dialogue in democracies predicated upon the commitment to respect human rights.

Physical barriers put in place to divide and imprison people can be removed in space when the time comes to do so but the mental damage for those who

Introduction: new paradigms 7

survive them poses problems stretching into the indefinite future. Rüdiger Görner's 'Borders in Mind or How to Re-invent Identities' delves into German literary texts representing the trauma of coping with the presence and eventual fall of the Berlin Wall and the Iron Curtain that had split city and country apart, converting Germany into the forefront of Europe's Cold War. Such phenomena as free West-Berlin surrounded by a wall to keep citizens of the surrounding state out (and also a 'CIA-protected haven of extreme leftism' showcasing political pluralism and offering an unambiguous symbol of liberal democracy), West German writers applying for East German citizenship, or the literature of 'borderliners' mark essential stages in Görner's analysis of the complex German narrative of shattered identities. The frontier becomes conceptualized in this essay in a phenomenological sense in contexts complementing that of German (dis)unification: Hadrian's Wall, the Great Wall of China, the US-Mexico frontier as well as the one in the West Bank between Israelis and Palestinians or the EU's 'Schengen' border as seen by those securely inside as well as by those outside, unavoidably serve as eloquent literary figures of meaning in addition to their political, historical or military significance. The cultural products giving voice to the trauma caused by Germany's Iron Curtain form analogies in Görner's argumentation with a wide range of texts in such languages as English, Hungarian, Serb or Croatian, confirming that it is the voice of those kept outside fences whose stories fill in the void in the narratives of those feeling safe and superior inside.

Divided space in dramatic production, the theatre which gave birth to the metaphor of Europe's geo-political 'Iron Curtain', is the subject of Annelis Kuhlmann's 'The Iron Curtain, the Wall and "Performative Verfremdung"'. Similarly to the previous piece, Kuhlmann also provides a wide historical and cultural context from which to view European theatre's mediation of division and exclusion. The language of literature and especially that of theatre creates its effect by forcing the reader or viewer to consider the familiar in a new and different light. In this essay, Bertolt Brecht's experimental device of 'making strange' serves as a point of departure and reference to extend the analogy of barriers responsible for containing (un)freedom to the historical experimentation with artistic space and time that theatre elicits. Specifically the playhouse gives rise to performance within which actors and stage merge with, or are separated from, the audience. Considering significant moments in the history of theatre in Europe during the decades of the division of the continent after World War II, Kuhlmann discusses the work of directors across the continent that mediated desire by way of drama to remove oppressive hegemony restricting the expression of subjectivity. The essay illustrates, through its focus on collaboration in producing theatre, that art can only survive in a free exchange between cultures and languages. Drama cannot serve dogma because the very medium is predicated upon illuminating hidden aspects of daily life or upon eliciting new meaning from events and objects whose habitual perception is dulled by tedious repetition and the drabness of routine. Without lifting the iron curtain, no show can ever begin.

8   *Peter I. Barta*

Performance has a potentially therapeutic effect and Charles de Chassiron's essay 'The Re-Emergence of National Cultures Following Independence in the Baltic States' draws attention to the role the arts had to play in the rebirth of the three states. As British Ambassador in Tallinn during the 1990s, he had the opportunity to witness the creation of cultural processes essential for the building of a new sense of post-communist identity in this region, which unlike other European countries in the former Eastern bloc, had been part of the Soviet Union and thus deprived even of a semblance of independence. The opera houses in the three capitals became endowed with special significance as symbols of cultural independence within the European historical frame. But more than opera, it was choral music that succeeded in reaching out to extensive segments of the population. De Chassiron shares details of private conversations he had with the Estonian president (1992–2000), Lennart Meri. A published writer, film director and literary translator, Meri had an exceptional sense of the importance for Estonia to master information technology and he was thereby responsible for establishing his country as a market leader in this crucial area for the decades to come. Bearing witness to the three countries' determination to re-integrate into mainstream European civilisation are the impressive post-modernist buildings in the capitals. But like elsewhere in the new EU nations, both Western consumerism and Eastern European neo-nationalism have appeared in the Baltic states. The essay concludes by assessing writers' reactions to these trends.

Hélène Mélat's 'Explosions, Shifts and Backtracking in Post-Soviet Fiction' traces Russian literary history following the collapse of the Soviet Union. In a systematic manner, Mélat analyses the main trends of especially literary prose. Both the Iron Curtain and its removal were initiated from the centre of Eastern European state socialism in Moscow. Because the redrawing of borders between new states created, at least numerically, the largest upheaval in the Soviet successor states, the socio-cultural phenomena foregrounded in the texts Mélat analyses reveal trends that have affected the other countries of the Central and Eastern European region. Owing to its remarkable heritage in the production of prose and poetry, Russian literature has represented the mental attitudes of large groups of Eastern European populations perhaps most extensively of all. Hence, in the wake of the essentially unpredicted collapse of the state and empire, the discovery of the untold past of the country and its culture, the great and unrealistic expectations of prosperity and opportunities, disillusionment and the search for alternative realities and new forms of meaning amidst the rise of new types of populist and intolerant demagoguism have supplied an abundance of themes for writers. Mélat, as do the other authors in this volume, elaborates upon changing social expectations of literary texts and their creators in conditions following the disappearance of censorship and the restrictions on the movement of people, ideas and cultural products.

The work of Eastern Europe's émigré authors in Western democracies and the 'underground' texts produced and circulated illegally during the decades of oppression have had to be reassessed and re-evaluated during the recent two decades of freedom. In 'Neither East nor West: Polyphony and Deterritorialization in Contemporary European Fiction', Maria Rubins complicates such concepts as 'exile', 'diaspora', 'homeland', 'mother tongue', 'adopted tongue', 'national literature' and the like. Again, owing to its size and prominence, the case of literature in Russian produces the most characteristic and prominent data for analysis. Rubins considers how the appearance in Russia of formerly banned works, first published abroad, by authors from the Soviet Union, the output by the large numbers of Russian writers in Israel, Western Europe and the United States, not to mention a truly global readership of publications in Russian have changed the conditions of literature over the past twenty years. Rubins also discusses a different kind of growing trend: the production of culture in the language of the country to which writers and artists move from the civilizations in which they were born and brought up. She takes a close look at Germany and especially France where French language literature by non-native writers has become a relevant cultural phenomenon. Milan Kundera is by no means the first prominent writer to switch languages yet his choice of acquiring a French identity, his disposition towards his Czech origins and especially the post-communist Czech state illustrate the re-emergence of old Eastern European hostilities between the artist and the Establishment.

Identity manifests itself by way of social discourse, and monitoring changes in linguistic communication provides an indispensable tool for its study. With notable exceptions (Albanian, Estonian, Hungarian, Latvian, Romanian to name just the largest groups) the Eastern European bloc that emerged around 1989 from one-party state socialist dictatorships comprises the peoples of the Southern, Eastern and Western Slavonic world. The final piece in our volume by Michael Moser considers 'The Fall of the Iron Curtain and the New Linguistic Landscape of East-Central Europe'. The redrawn borders and the emergence of new states in the wake of the dissolution of Yugoslavia, Czechoslovakia and the Soviet Union, the replacement of Russian chiefly by English as the compulsory foreign language to study at school in most of Eastern Europe, and the extensive exposure to the English language owing to new commercial and military ties and to English-dominated electronic communication networks have had profound consequences on language use. In addition to these crucial issues Moser also addresses the status of 'variants' or 'dialects', the changing status of related languages, points of political correctness, the role of colloquialisms and non-standard features mainly of the spoken languages, not losing sight of social attitudes towards loan words from other languages and especially English.

I would like to take this opportunity to express my gratitude to individuals and organizations without whose support this book could not have been produced. Thanks are firstly due to Mr Peter Mikl, Director of the Austrian Cultural Forum in London, whose exceptional support and organizational skills were vital in planning the conference in 2009 which created the foundations for this volume. I am also grateful to the Hungarian Cultural Centre, the Austrian and the Hungarian Embassies in London, Erste Stiftung and Austrian Airlines for their support. I would like to thank the University of Surrey, and especially Professor Sir

10   *Peter I. Barta*

Christopher Snowden, the Vice-Chancellor, for essential financial, technical and moral support. May I hereby acknowledge with a deep sense of gratitude the selfless and demanding work of colleagues who very kindly undertook the task of refereeing submissions to the volume.

Notes

1 I am grateful to Ms Tiina Randviir, the editor of the *Estonian Literary Magazine*, for this information and all her help. I would also like to express my gratitude to Mr Charles de Chassiron for drawing my attention to Arrak's painting in the first place and for introducing me to Ms Randviir.
2 Jüri Arrak, 'Kunstniku pildiilm. Kunstniku maailmapilt', *Mäetagused* (29) 2005, http://www.folklore.ee/tagused/nr29/arrak.pdf (accessed on 13 October 2012), English translation by Tiina Randviir.
3 'Jüri obviously refers to the artist himself and the red dragon is the Soviet system, which has incorporated the struggling national figure' (Trossek 2012: 392).
4 Winston Churchill's 'Sinews of Peace', delivered at Westminster College, Fulton, Missouri, USA, 5 March 1946.
5 Foucault, M. (2001). *L'herméneutique du sujet*. Cours au Collège de France, 1981–82. Paris: Gallimard Seuil, p. 173. See also Kubik 2003: 321.
6 Such attitudes were not isolated. The first president of the Second Polish Republic, Gabriel Narutowicz, said about his country and its people on his deathbed in 1922 to Jozef Pilsudski, the first Marshal of the Republic: 'You are right, this is not Europe. These people would feel better under somebody who wrings their neck and smacks them in the face' (quoted in Michnik 2011: 97).
7 My translation from the Hungarian (PIB).
8 See Judit Friedrich (2011) 'Blaming versus Healing: Facing Communist Informers of the Past and a Literary Example in Peter Esterhazy's *Revised Edition*', in Hayoz *et al.* 2011: 630–46.
9 See Endre Bojtar (1988) 'Eastern or Central Europe', *Cross Currents*, 7: 253–69; Robert Evans (2002) 'Great Britain and East-Central Europe, 1908–48: A Study in Perceptions', King's College London; Catherine Horel (2009) *Cette Europe qu'on dit centrale: des Habsbourg à l'intégration européenne, 1815–2004*, Paris: Beauchesne.
10 See also Wachtel's (2006) comments about the phenomenon of writers (specifically Slavenka Draculić, Dubravka Ugrešić and Tatyana Tolstaya) directly addressing their readers in 'journalistic' writings.

Works Cited

Barthes, R. (1977) 'Introduction to the Structural Analysis of Narratives', in *Image-Music-Text*, London: Fontana.

Batt, J. (2007) 'Introduction: Defining Central and Eastern Europe', in White, S., Batt, J. and Lewis, P. G. (eds), *Developments in Central and Eastern European Politics*, Vol. 4, New York: Palgrave Macmillan, 1–19.

Berglund, S. and Dellenbrant, J. A. (1994) 'Prospects for the New Democracies in Eastern Europe' in Berglund, S. and Dellenbrant, J. A. (eds), *The New Democracies in Eastern Europe*, Second Edition, Aldershot: Edward Elgar, 238–52.

Binder, M. (2010) 'Changes in the Images of "Gypsies" in Slovakia and Hungary after the Post-Communist Transition', in Csaplar-Degovics, K., Mitrovits, M. and Zahoran, C. (eds), *After Twenty Years. Reasons and Consequences of the Transformation in Central and Eastern Europe*, Berlin: Osteuropa-Zentrum, 319–49.

Introduction: new paradigms 11

Blokker, P. (2010) *Multiple Democracies in Europe*, London: Routledge.

Bozoki, A. (ed.) (1999) *Intellectuals and Politics in Central Europe*, New York: Central European University Press.

Friedrich, J. (2011) 'Blaming Versus Healing: Facing Communist Informers of the Past and a Literary Example in Peter Esterhazy's Revised Edition', in Hayoz, N., Jesien, L. and Koleva, D. (eds) (2011) *20 Years after the Collapse of Communism*, Bern: Peter Lang, 630–46.

Gati, C. (2006) *Failed Illusions*, Stanford: Stanford University Press.

Hayoz, N., Jesien, L. and Koleva, D. (eds) (2011) *20 Years after the Collapse of Communism*, Bern: Peter Lang.

Hoffman, E. (1994) *Exit into History*, London: Minerva.

Kotkin, S. with a contribution by Gross, J. T. (2009) *Uncivil Society*, New York: The Modern Library.

Kubik, J. (2003) 'Cultural Legacies and State Socialism. History Making and Cultural-Political Entrepreneurship in Post-Communist Poland and Russia', in Ekiert G. and Hanson, S. E. (eds), *Capitalism and Democracy in Central and Eastern Europe*, New York: Central European Press, 317–52.

Müller, M. (2011) 'Essays and Travelogues. Two Literary Genres That Have Been Rediscovered during the Debate on the Yugoslavian Collapse', in Hayoz, N., Jesien, L. and Koleva, D. (eds) (2011) *20 Years after the Collapse of Communism*, Bern: Peter Lang, 609–27.

Michnik, A. (2011) *In Search of Lost Meaning*, Roman S. Czareny (trans.), Berkeley: University of California Press.

Rosenfeld, A. and Dodge, N. T. (eds) (2002) *The Struggle for Freedom of Artistic Expression under the Soviets*, New Brunswick: Rutgers University Press.

Tismaneanu, V. (1998) *Fantasies of Salvation*, Princeton: Princeton University Press.

Trossek, A. (2012) 'A Comparative Study: Rein Raamat's *Big Tõll* and Priit Pärn's *Luncheon on the Grass*' in Imre, A. (ed.) *A Companion to Eastern European Cinema*, Chichester: Wiley-Blackwell.

Ugrešić, D. (1996) 'Kultura laži', Zagreb: Arkzin.

Wachtel, A. B. (2006) *Remaining Relevant after Communism: The Role of the Writer in Eastern Europe*, Chicago: University of Chicago Press.

1 The Wall has fallen on all of us

Dubravka Ugrešić

> The Wall has fallen. It has fallen on everyone, on all of us.
> (Anonymous commentator)

Upton Sinclair, author of the novel *Oil!*, would have stayed half-forgotten as a classic of American literature had there not been a film adaptation of the novel called *There Will Be Blood*, which momentarily blew the dust off Sinclair's name. Having seen the movie, I recalled the bookshelf in my mother's flat and the book cover of the first Yugoslav edition of *Oil!*, entitled *Petrolej*. There were pencil drawings all over the cover: these, my mother said, were my first childish scribblings. It was just after World War II, a time of poverty, and the covers of books doubled as drawing pads. Upton Sinclair's novel *Oil!*, Maxim Gorky's *Mother* and Theodore Dreiser's *American Tragedy* were some of the first titles in the home library of my young parents.

I do not remember whether I have ever actually read *Oil!* Probably not, but if I did back when I was a student – earnestly dedicated to comparative literature – I dare not have said so. At that time, defense of the 'autonomy of the literary text' (or that of any work of art) was sacred to every student of literature, and I certainly saw myself battling on the front line. In my student days 'literary autonomy' was closely tied to literary taste. In simple terms, we felt that good writers did not embark on politics and did not write about life in overly realistic terms. Real life was left to bad writers and those who flirted with politics. The fashion of the day was the 'literariness' of literature.

Yugoslav writers were never seriously infected with the virus of socialist realism, which of course does not mean to say that there were not those who made compromises. But resistance to the tendency to ideologize and politicize literature, despite the occasional line penned to glorify Tito, lasted unusually long after the enemy, socialist realism, was dead and buried. As a result, there were many good writers who wrote fine books; there were bad writers, on the other hand, who were labeled 'good' because they 'did not get caught up in politics', just as many good writers were deemed bad because they had no bone to pick with the regime, or at least did not do so publicly; and then again there were bad writers who were deemed good only because they had taken a public

The Wall has fallen on all of us 13

stand against the regime. The fine Croatian writer, Miroslav Krleža, long since dead and buried, bears a stigma to this day for his friendship with Tito.

Today, of course, I know that the connection between literature and 'ideology' has been around since the beginnings of literacy. The Bible is not only a grandiose literary work, but also a grandiose ideological work. The history of the bond between literature and ideology is long, complex and dramatic. Writers have paid with their lives for the written word. The history of relations between emperors and poets, kings and court jesters, those who commission literature and those who comply with the commissions is too gory, episodes of book burning and censorship too frequent, the number of writers' lives sacrificed for the freedom of speech, for an idea, or even just for a dream is too vast to allow us to take this fatal liaison too lightly. The notion of literary autonomy served too often as an alibi for it to enjoy full validity: when they thought they had something to gain by it, there were writers who stepped into politics; others took on politics even when doing so led to symbolic or real suicide. Some, when they looked to save their skins, sought the shield of literary autonomy, while others paid for their literary autonomy with their skins.

The tension between the two opposing poles – the political engagement of a writer and a writer's autonomy – was particularly dramatic in the literatures of the former Eastern Europe, and even today, surprising as this may seem, it has still not been relieved, although the context has changed in terms of politics, ideas and culture. Eastern European literary environments were much more rigid than Western European ones. In the Eastern European literary zones, careers were destroyed because of the written word, or conversely the writer was elevated to such high offices of state as president, minister, or ambassador. This is no different today, though it may seem to be different: state institutions continue to play the part of literary patron, albeit a bad and stingy patron, but there is barely any independent territory left. The writer in small post-communist states is still treated as the 'voice of his people' or as a 'traitor'. Why? For the simple reason that communism in transitional countries has been replaced by nationalism and both systems have their eyes on writers. The literary marketplace is too small for the writer to maintain a belief in independence.

There were many Eastern European writers who were not fortunate enough to survive the shift from socialism to nationalism, to reposition themselves nationally, thereby insuring themselves a place on the bookshelves of the national literature. Some tried, and survived a year or so longer, slipping through the needle's eye. Many of the losers, along with their collected works and mountains of scribbled pages, however, sank into the dust of oblivion. Young writers, and with them the young literary critics and scholars, showed no compassion; they must have figured out that this was not their story. Today, after all, is another age, life is proceeding at a rapid clip and literature is a long-term investment in time, which for most of us does not provide anything more than aching joints and bankruptcy. But it is a kind of lottery that brings the lucky winner the jackpot. The young rush out to buy the lottery tickets and do not ask too many questions.

14   *Dubravka Ugrešić*

How is it, for instance, that writers who were dissidents in their communist states are so quick to accept posts in ministries, embassies, or elsewhere in the new democracies? How is it that today, in one way or another, everyone continues to live on government handouts? How is it that those who once pressed so fiercely for autonomy in literature are now demanding that their state institutions finance culture (hence literature), thereby implicitly agreeing that they will not bite the hand that feeds them? Overall, culture in small countries was never viable on the market, nor could it be. That is why writers of small countries, whether they like it or not, are condemned to act as representatives for their country, whether the state be Croatia, Serbia, Estonia, or Latvia. Either that or they are labeled 'traitors' and live abroad. One often goes hand in hand with the other. Even international literary stars, who have long since left their home literatures behind and have, along the way, changed the language in which they write, are not immune to the righteous fury of the homeland. The recent incident with Milan Kundera only confirms that the Czech Republic is a small country, and that the model for the traumatic back-and-forth between literature and ideology is unchanged.

Exile is a change of context in the literal sense. Exile implies the personal experience of every exiled writer, which would be difficult to subsume under the binary opposites stubbornly endorsed by literary critics: the writer's native civilization versus the hosting environment of the country of exile. The terms – émigré, immigrant, exile, nomad, minority, ethnic – are discriminatory, but also affirmative. With these terms, the home base expels the writer, while the same terms are used by the host environment to thrust the writer into an ethnic niche in order to affirm his or her existence. The home base makes assumptions of mono-culturalism, xenophobia, and exclusivity, while the host environment makes assumptions of multiculturalism, cosmopolitanism, and inclusivity, but both essentially work with the dusty labels of ethnicity and the politics of otherness.

Even if I were to write a text about the desolation of frozen landscapes at the North Pole, I would still be generally labeled a Croatian writer, or a Croatian writer in exile writing about the desolation of the frozen landscapes at the North Pole. Reviewers would promptly populate the frozen wasteland of my text with concepts such as exile, Croatia, ex-Yugoslavia, post-communism, the Balkans, Eastern Europe, the Slavonic world, Balkan feminism or perhaps Balkan eco-feminism, while journalists would ask me whether I had the opportunity while up in the frozen wasteland to run into the Yugoslav diaspora, and how I perceived the situation in Kosovo from the frozen point of view. If an English author writes his or her version of a visit to the North Pole, Englishness will not be likely to serve as the framework within which his or her text is read.

This attitude of the host environment to writer-newcomers springs from a subconscious colonial attitude, just when the larger literary world is doing its best to reject this; from a market that relishes any form of the profitably exotic; from always vital relations between the periphery and the centre. Periphery and

The Wall has fallen on all of us 15

centre, however, are elastic; I am sure that Serbs feel closer to the centre than Bulgarians, and that Bulgarians feel closer to the centre than the Turks. Feelings, however, are one thing and real relations of power are something else. The real centre of cultural power is America, or rather Anglo-American culture, whose domination marked the twentieth century. We are still looking to that centre with the same fascination today. Anglo-American culture is the dominant field of reference, while, at the same time, it is the most powerful, if not the fairest, mediator of cultural values. In other words, if Chinese writers are not translated into English, it is unlikely that any Serbian or Croatian reader, with the exception of the occasional lone Sinologist, will ever hear of them.

The relationship to a literary text changes, of course, with the change of language. There are many examples of writers who embraced the language of their host-country, yet even by doing so they did not manage to protect their texts from misreading. There is an even larger number of writers who, writing in the language of the host country, seek a special 'cultural' (which basically means ethnic or religious) status because only thanks to this will they attain visibility. Overall, an opposition asserts itself here: between the autonomy of the literary text and its critical reception and market evaluation (the market not being without its political aspirations) in the new context of the internationalization of literary texts and transnational literature. This is still the realm of literature as we know it with its traditions, canons, apparatus and institutions, with its system of values. This is a realm where literature (and the same holds true for other cultural texts) is read and evaluated within gender and post-colonial frames; within still existing bits and pieces of theoretical schools and approaches; within cultural geo-politics and its coordinates, such as the Eastern European and the Western European zones, or within the global cultural market dominated by American or Anglo-American language and culture. Here we still know, or at least we know approximately, what it is we are talking about when we speak of literature or culture.

As it leaps from the national to the international level, literature enters its third, unavoidable context: a new epoch of digital revolution and globalization. In that context literature, or, rather, assumptions about it, dissolves, vanishes, or transmutes into something else. True, the bookstores are full of books, the chains are reminiscent of supermarkets, there are more translations of books than ever before, more literary awards than ever, there are writers being lauded like pop stars, there are rich networks of EU cultural institutions, managers, mediators and cultural bureaucracy, there are numerous cultural projects and events. All of this suggests that things have never been better for culture. However, the switch from Gutenberg to the digital era caused a tectonic shift, and the impact is much more serious and complicated than it seems, or than we are able to see, predict and articulate. The whole system, with its codes, meanings and languages disappeared or transmuted into something else. Cultural values and their hierarchy have been destroyed, differentiations and differences between popular and mass culture, and consequently high culture, do not exist today. Intellectuals and experts as arbiters have been pushed to the margins.

16   *Dubravka Ugrešić*

Authors of works of art are disappearing together with the notion of authorship. A commonly known and often-quoted fact is that the most consulted source of reference has become Wikipedia, an internet-based encyclopaedia, controlled by anonymous kids. There is a parallel culture on the Internet with millions and millions of consumers, people who are not passive but ready to create, interact, change, compile, produce and exchange and, thanks to technology, they do so. Their main source of reference is the vast industry of popular culture. And here is the paradox: thanks to sophisticated high-tech devices we can observe the rapid process of regression and barbarization of culture. This is why new consumers are not able to read classical works of art any more (that the majority of us still consider culture), even if they should like to explore them. That is why we, on the other hand, are not able to communicate with the anonymous artistic product presented mostly on the Internet or TV, but also in the written word, in books. The fact that the celebrated David Hockney uses his iPhone to draw sketches does not slow down but rather speeds up this process.

So, what do we mean when we talk about culture? Are we equipped to answer that question? Add to this that we live in a new, self-centred epoch in which there is a premium on being heard rather than listening, being seen rather than watching and on being read rather than reading. This new status of an author can be best explained by the image of a person who suffers both from autism and exhibitionism at the same time.

Thus we are living in the ruins of the old cultural system. The crash of the system produced a terrible noise to which we are constantly exposed. We can no longer distinguish what it is we are hearing, and even if we hear something, we dare not say and define it. Our language belongs to the old system. There is a vast army of facilitators of that noise – cultural critics, professors, educators, teachers, the cultural bureaucrats, and many others – but nobody knows yet what the gist of the noise is.

The hardest job after the fall of the Wall is not done yet – and this is the competent and relevant evaluation of what has been gained in the process and what has been lost. For this job, we need scholars and thinkers who refuse to think within widely accepted stereotypes, political, ideological, cultural and otherwise. This job should be done on all the 'sides': the Wall has fallen on everyone, on all of us, as an anonymous commentator noticed a long time ago, with a tinge of melancholy in his voice.

2 Twenty years after the Curtain fell

A personal account by an Austrian

Gabriele Matzner-Holzer[1]

For forty years, until 1989, Europe, and particularly Central Europe, had lived in the shadow of the Iron Curtain, divided into hostile and heavily armed ideological blocs, more than once on the brink of hot war. Austria, where I grew up, had the good fortune to end up on the right side, that is to say, to the west of the dividing line that had been drawn though Europe by Allied agreements during and at the end of World War II. It remained occupied by the four major Allies until 1955 but it was spared the fate of becoming incorporated into the Soviet empire. This may have been at least partially owing to the deep hostility of many Austrians to communism: even under Soviet occupation Austrian communists could not get a foot in the door. More likely though were geo-strategic considerations responsible for this outcome.

In 1955 the Allies left Austria and the country declared its permanent neutrality. This option was not open to, or acceptable for, occupied and divided Germany. It seemed attractive to many Hungarians a year later though, in 1956: they too proposed neutrality for their country as a way to escape from the Soviet camp. But we know how that revolution ended. Neutrality was not only a useful tool to maintain independence. It also corresponded to Austria's historical experience of subservience to stronger neighbours and of fighting and losing wars on their side. This is why, even twenty years after the implosion of the Soviet empire, most Austrians still cherish neutrality. They do not want to join military alliances, such as NATO, with which Austria, nevertheless, cooperates very closely.

Neutral states have always been viewed with suspicion, especially by those who are at war. In terms of ideology, economics and politics, Austria has always been firmly on the Western side. Being neutral, the country could and did contribute to easing East-West tensions and to making life more bearable for many citizens in the Eastern bloc. It served as the first port of refuge for Hungarians in 1956 and for Czechs and Slovaks in 1968. Austrian politicians also managed to obtain the release and transit of hundreds of thousands of East Germans and Soviet Jews to West Germany, Israel, the United States and elsewhere. Overall, probably about two million people from the communist East were able to leave their countries and start new lives thanks to Austria. As part of the team of the Austrian prime minister Bruno Kreisky in the early 1980s, it was my task to draft letters to communist rulers asking them to exercise

18   *Gabriele Matzner-Holzer*

restraint, release prisoners and allow people to emigrate. This was called 'quiet diplomacy'; had it been 'loud', it would surely have been less successful. Kreisky would, for example, draw the attention of Erich Honecker, the East German leader, to the plight of an East German musician incarcerated for his unruly lyrics, and politely ask for his release on humanitarian grounds. Austrian politicians would, on occasion, request information from the Soviet leader, Leonid Brezhnev, about the confinement of a Russian poet in an insane asylum. Such enquiries signalled to rulers in the Communist world that acts of intimidation and mistreatment did not go unnoticed on the other side of the Iron Curtain. Coming from a small and neutral country, not suspected of potentially harbouring aggressive or hostile intentions, such messages often succeeded, at least in the longer run, to ease the suffering of innocent individuals. In the same manner, even before Kreisky's term of office, Austria had been instrumental in enabling the emigration of many Czech and Slovak intellectuals and artists after the crushing of the 'Prague Spring' in 1968. Many of them settled in Austria, enriching its cultural life and continuing to annoy the communist regime in nearby Prague.

From early on, Austrians established and maintained close ties both with the officials, but also with representatives of civilian society in the Eastern bloc: dissidents, writers, academics and church leaders. Austrian intellectuals, artists and clergy visited, or invited, their dissident counterparts or supplied them with information unavailable to them at home. All this had to be done more or less clandestinely and some Austrian diplomats and politicians were complicit in such activity. The aim was not to overthrow any regimes but to improve conditions for creative and critical people who had to live under communist rule. In doing so, old familial and cultural relations, originating in centuries of shared history within the Habsburg Empire, were being put to good use. This access endowed Austria with special expertise that is valuable to this day. The role the country played over the decades earned it respect on both sides of the Iron Curtain.

With effect from 1968, when the Czechoslovak experiment in democratic communism was eliminated by Warsaw Pact troops, it was evident for the more clearsighted that the Soviet system was fundamentally doomed. It had largely lost hearts and minds. The commitment of the Soviets in 1975, in the Final Acts of the Conference on Security and Cooperation in Europe, to respect human rights and permit humanitarian cooperation, was a clear signal of their waning power. Around that time I had my first personal experiences in a communist country, namely the Soviet Union, where I served as a junior diplomat. It was quite obvious that this regime of central planning was economically dysfunctional and democratically inadequate. Living permanently under such conditions required citizens to equip themselves with special skills of craftsmanship, improvisation and social networking. Beneath the official socio-economic system, there were several other layers of informal interaction, especially, of course, a vast black market of goods and services. I recall reading in one of the newspapers one day that thousands of rare and popular galoshes had arrived in Moscow shops – for left feet only. Galoshes for right feet had been delivered to Leningrad. But it seemed to be no problem for many buyers in the two cities to arrange for the appropriate exchanges.

Twenty years after the Curtain fell   19

It was also in Moscow that I think I understood the many aspects, forms and meanings that the concept of freedom signifies. The obvious restrictions of freedom of thought and expression and the ban on creating political organizations, as well as all the ensuing negative consequences for individuals and society as a whole, became to me more than a theory: it became a personal experience. I was nevertheless fortunate enough to meet individuals who were freer in heart and soul than any I had known in the West. They had survived years in Soviet concentration camps and seemed unbroken and completely fearless. They were not addicted to Western consumerism either. But craving for goods from market-based societies outside the Eastern bloc generated a great deal of frustration and unhappiness for many people both in the Soviet Union and its satellite countries. At the Austrian Embassy in Moscow I was in charge of consular affairs, which included issuing transit visas for many thousands of Soviet Jews allowed to emigrate to Israel. Occasionally I met some of these applicants in person. Under Soviet rules they could not take with them personal items such as doctoral theses, musical or literary manuscripts or objects of worship, and I am pleased to report that I managed to 'export' such belongings to many a rightful owner inside the diplomatic bag. There was even a Torah among this contraband which ended up in Israel. Occasionally I smuggled manuscripts by Soviet authors not allowed to publish their work inside the country. In doing so I was motivated by a sense of indignation about the primitive, barbaric regime and by a sense of sympathy with, and respect for, the courage and efforts of intellectuals and artists.

The signs of decline of the Soviet system multiplied. This brings me to Berlin, which always functioned as a seismograph of the status of East-West-relations. I served as Austrian Consul-General in West Berlin from 1986 to 1991. As in Moscow before, I had a special interest in the life and work of East German intellectuals and artists. Again, I took it upon myself to take manuscripts and other personal belongings across the border. Meanwhile, the Austrian Embassy in East-Berlin was involved in assisting citizens of the GDR to emigrate to West Germany via Austria and in facilitating contacts and visits by artists and academics between East Germany and Austria. Keeping open borders and minds, at least on the Austrian side, was part of a wider political scheme aimed at inspiring hope and trust. In 1989, I witnessed the Fall of the Wall and the 'Wende', the turn of the tide, that was to end the Cold War.

Of course, nobody could have predicted this astonishing turn of historical events. Both in the East and in the West most politicians, experts and observers had settled with the status quo for their lifetime. Western officials as well as experts later claimed they had no clue about the internal weaknesses in the East. They appeared, for instance, to be genuinely surprised by the dismal condition of the East German economy, which previously had received such good marks from them. It seems astonishing that they should have ignored the obviously poor quality of East German housing, infrastructure, production and services, that they should not have been aware of the widespread hatred that so many of the citizens felt towards the communist state. The vast majority of

20 *Gabriele Matzner-Holzer*

people in the German Democratic Republic were disgruntled and alienated, just waiting for an opportunity with little risk to life and limb to abolish the political system. Their moment arrived when it became apparent that the Soviet Union under Gorbachev would not 'shoot' any more; it would not, as on earlier occasions, save unpopular 'brotherly' regimes by military force. The regimes thus collapsed one after the other like so many houses of cards, fortunately in most cases without bloodshed.

Some time before the events of 1989, signs of change in Berlin became evident and in retrospect they fall into place. I recall the official annual celebration of the end of the Berlin Blockade in May 1989. For the first time ever, a high-ranking Soviet diplomat participated at this event. He told his baffled colleagues, including me, that his presence was in acknowledgement of the fact that the Soviet blockade of 1948–49 had been a mistake. In early 1989 rumours circulated in West Berlin that officials from the two sides of the divided city were meeting in secret to negotiate the technicalities of reconnecting streets and canals disrupted for decades by the Wall. People were also talking about the sale of real estate in East Berlin by intermediaries in West Berlin coffee shops. In retrospect, the reason for the announcement by US president Ronald Reagan in Berlin in June 1987 that the Berlin Wall would not exist for much longer became clear. Reports were indicating that Gorbachev had informed the West that East Germany was bankrupt.

Years later I had an opportunity to see the files that the East German secret service, the Stasi, had compiled on me. I was in a way disappointed that there was so little. It came to me as no surprise, however, to find the record of my alleged remarks to a man I had always suspected to be working for the Stasi and filing reports on me. I had purposely used our conversations to tell him what I thought he should feed back to the GDR secret service. He duly reported that I had said East Germany would not survive much longer unless it reformed itself along the lines of Gorbachev's 'glasnost' and 'perestroika' initiatives. Normally agents would not wish to include embarrassingly evident and unwelcome news in reports, presumably for their own protection from the wrath of irate spymasters. This man nevertheless did just that. The reason may have been that by this stage even some senior members within the hierarchy of the Stasi intelligence operation shared my view.

Surprisingly though, some direct contacts between Westerners and GDR citizens were of minor importance to the regime. I frequently used to visit distant relatives of ours in Dresden. These academic people were opponents of the regime not so much for political reasons but mainly on religious grounds. Their children, as a consequence, were refused admission to university and the couple were not able to obtain the books on mathematics and physics they needed for their research in their fields of specialization. Luckily, their secret service files also make it clear that their son was banned from military service on the border with the Federal Republic because of mysterious visits by an Austrian diplomat. But the Stasi never found out – in case they bothered at all – why these visits took place in the first place. It seems that the allegedly almighty secret service was already losing its total grip or interest.

Twenty years after the Curtain fell 21

Austria played a substantial role in spurring on events that led to the fall of the Iron Curtain. Foreign minister Alois Mock and his Hungarian counterpart Gyula Horn had publicly announced the disbanding of the impassable fortifications separating the two countries. This sensational step had a significant impact. In the summer of 1989 many thousands of East Germans took refuge in West German embassies in Budapest, Prague and Warsaw or attempted to cross the border to enter Austria. Some of them were successful. I recall a conversation in East Berlin with dissident writers in late 1988, prior to these turbulent events. According to these friends the authorities were beleaguered and no longer felt able to prevent their citizens from going to Hungary for their summer holidays in spite of facing the possibility of desperate attempts on a large scale to escape to Austria.

The euphoria of 1989 in Berlin and the expectations of a better life were enormous. Disappointment though set in rather soon. Catching up with living standards in the West would take a long time and a great deal of effort. All too soon, and not only in East Germany, the dissident intellectuals of the recent past were sidelined or discredited for having collaborated with the communist regime. 'Realpolitik', political business as usual, took over, often furnished by parts of the former communist elites. Secret services and other former pillars of the crumbled regimes speedily, and in many cases successfully, made attempts to destroy crucial evidence against them. Many of these individuals turned into entrepreneurs and some reappeared on the political scene in different guises. At the start, East Germans just wanted to be, or at least live like, West Germans. They were eager to discard all vestiges of the former regime, good or bad. I remember that in early 1990, the streets of East Berlin were littered with 'communist' furniture thrown out of windows. Fruit trees were cut down and farm animals slaughtered: they no longer met consumer expectations. East German markets had been swamped with mostly West German goods, and agricultural and industrial products of the erstwhile GDR had lost their buyers. The famously infamous East German cars, the 'Trabis', were abandoned throughout the country: the 'Ossis' – as they were nicknamed in the West – aspired to replace their unattractive vehicles with Audis and the like. Over time, people discovered the hurdles along the way to prosperity and some even developed feelings of GDR-nostalgia.

Certain schemes pursued by the new rulers were detrimental to confidence, cohesion and progress, such as the principle of 'restitution before compensation'. This meant in effect that large parts of East German territory were subject to restitution claims. The resulting sense of insecurity infuriated many innocent home owners as they had never personally dispossessed anyone. I recall the desperate fury with which the owner of an attractive little cottage near Dresden was attacking me for having stopped my car to admire her modest property. I could not convince her that I was not preparing to lay claims on it. Resentment also emerged on the Western side as it became clear how much and for how long every citizen of the former Federal Republic would have to pay to enable the East to catch up with the West. This feat to date has still not been achieved in

22   *Gabriele Matzner-Holzer*

spite of the great effort that has been made. Dismantling mental borders also takes time and good will. But progress is evident and encouraging.

The demise of the Soviet Empire drew many Western economic experts – most of them devotees of pure market ideology – to the region.They saw their task in converting centralized commando economies into market economies as fast as possible, in line with prevailing theories: liberalization, rapid privatization and deregulation. As experts flocked to Moscow and the other capitals of the former alliance of states under the 'Evil Empire' they met the emerging new local capitalists. These were in part members of the old elite who knew enough to exploit the old as well as the new system. In collaboration with Western investors many of them became exceedingly wealthy.

Warnings had been voiced about this foreseeable development that favoured profiteers in East and West and led to a steep fall in productive investment and in the living standards of the majority of affected populations, at least temporarily. These non-mainstream economists expressed concern in the early nineties about the potential of social upheavals and political instability resulting from 'shock-therapy'. One of these people was my late husband, Egon Matzner. Together with other Eastern and Western economists he presented alternative approaches to transformation in the early nineties. They pointed out that markets do not emerge automatically by themselves or by way of such simplistic methods as rapid privatization. Markets need other institutions, such as regulations and functioning legal systems. This sounds like common sense, but it was often disregarded in many of the new economies that had opted to follow mainstream market ideology.

The consequences of this shock-transformation were considerable and some are still with us. Most Eastern European economies and societies fell into a deep hole, some to the level of countries in the developing world. When their GDP started to rise, merely a small minority of the population benefitted while inequality and misery rose to unprecedented levels for many. This has had and will continue to have political consequences in the countries concerned and beyond. Commercial and political manipulation of power resources such as oil and gas, deep-seated resentment over lost, former greatness and hostilities in the wake of rising nationalism are some of the issues that come most immediately to mind.

I had my next glimpse at post-communism during the years I spent as Austrian Ambassador in Slovakia, formerly a part of the Austro-Hungarian monarchy and then, until 1992, of Czechoslovakia. My work there enabled me to understand the many similarities in culture and mentality between Austrians and Slovaks. This common heritage probably helped a great deal in gradually scrapping the mental borders and in renewing ties. Trade and Austrian investments in Central, Eastern and, subsequently, South-Eastern Europe have boomed to an unprecedented extent. In several of these countries, Austria comes top, or very close, in terms of economic and cultural involvement.

Slovak political history also offered an example of how former dissidents fared under the new circumstances. The building of the Austrian Embassy in

Bratislava had formerly been the headquarters of the 'Movement Against Violence', which had spearheaded the demise of the communist regime and took the first steps towards democracy. In 1999, I invited veterans of this movement to revisit the premises that used to accommodate them. Most of them were no longer in politics. They told me how at an early stage they were being offered ministerial posts. None of them, however, was willing to head up the Ministry of Internal Affairs. A little known provincial lawyer came forward to apply for the job. He was successful and subsequently appointed. His name was Vladimir Mečiar and later he rose to become prime minister, sadly with rather questionable democratic qualities. How strange and somehow telling, I thought, that the best and also the most trustworthy people, who had possessed the initial revolutionary impetus, should have shied away from taking on the crucially important Ministry of the Interior.

Soon after the fall of the Iron Curtain, most Eastern European states regarded joining the European Union and NATO as top priority. The 'old' Western EU states, to which Austria too had belonged since 1995, were keen to see them prepare thoroughly. This required a lengthy process of adjustment and it was not until 2004, fifteen years after the turn of the tide, that the first former communist countries could join. A British official once told me that the Eastern Europeans had had a 'bonanza', that they had received preferential treatment in being allowed to join this rich men's club. This perception is flawed. The process of fulfilling all criteria was highly demanding for the states involved. Austria, out of self-interest, assisted in this process.

It is short-sighted to ignore or belittle the experiences of peoples in the former communist countries, cut off from the rest of Europe by the Iron Curtain. Many of them fought a long and often courageous struggle against the regimes imposed on them. Most people tried to live a decent life under difficult circumstances. We in the former West of Europe should look at them with respect, be grateful to them for their resilience and courage, and learn from their experiences.

Note

1 Gabriele Matzner-Holzer was the Ambassador of the Republic of Austria to the United Kingdom between 2005–10. In 2009, at the conference entitled 'The Fall of the Iron Curtain and the Culture of Europe Twenty Years On', exercising her right of freedom of opinion as guaranteed by the Austrian Constitution, she gave one of the plenary lectures that was the basis for this essay. At present she is retired and lives in Vienna.

3 The rediscovery of Central Europe in the 1980s[1]

Catherine Horel[2]

This essay will address the build-up to the democratic transitions in 1989 and the subsequent debates that have exercised Central European societies since then. The 1980s revealed deep changes on many levels: the police surveillance became looser in some countries like, for example, Hungary, which even started to redirect the focus of its foreign policy towards the European Community and transformed gradually into a mixed economy. The process was less easy for Poland but there, too, a changed mentality was emerging. After the death of Marshall Tito, Yugoslavia split up: Slovenes and Croats led the protests. As early as 1971, the 'Croatian Spring' had raised economic as well as identity-related questions. In the meantime, intellectuals and historians began to revaluate the Habsburg past of these countries. Writers of the former Empire met regularly and their discussions addressed the question of reconstructing the community of Central Europe. In the West, turn-of-the-century Vienna came to be considered no more as a Völkerkerker – the prison of the peoples – but as a creative melting pot of nationalities: Viennese and Hungarian authors of this period were becoming fashionable.

Three types of protest were emerging from the countries of the region: 1) the demand for extensive religious freedom, reinforced by the election of a Polish pope; 2) anger about the destruction of the environment, specifically the nuclear accident in Chernobyl as well as the indifference of the authorities; 3) the question of Hungarian ethnic minorities, ignored in official relations between the region's socialist states but not any more in the Western media.

Immediately after 1989 the question arose whether to join the European Community as soon as possible or to proceed through an intermediate phase of regional integration. The latter solution seemed to be privileged for a while with the creation of the Visegrád group, together with many other regional initiatives that brought together the countries of Central Europe, Western Europe and, on occasion, even countries of the former Soviet Union.[3] But the Visegrád group showed its limitations very quickly and the split of Czechoslovakia weakened the entire initiative, even for its members who now wanted to proceed directly to Euro-Atlantic integration. Even if regional integration of the model of the Visegrád group did not work out as expected, the heads of government of the group did join forces on such major issues as accession to NATO. The Hungarian debate on

The rediscovery of Central Europe in the 1980s   25

neutrality that surfaced in 1956 did not come up again this time, even though it did in Austria where opponents of the country's neutrality presented their case again in the changed geopolitical circumstances.[4]

The integration of 2004 was the largest ever made in the European Union and it concerned most of Central Europe.[5] At the beginning of the process, the three most advanced candidates hoped for quick accession whereas the less prepared countries would have joined later. This period was characterised by the return of old nationalistic hostilities, each nation pretending to be more European, that is, more civilized, than its neighbours. The separation between the Czechs and the Slovaks was dominated by this rhetoric. The headline '[a]lone towards Europe or together towards the Balkans' in July 1992 in the Czech weekly *Respekt* revealed the full extent of the survival of old nationalistic cliches. The Czechoslovak divorce resurrected Slovakia, which only ever existed, highly problematically, as an 'independent' state between 1939 and 1945. The same difficulty arose for Croatia: it existed as an independent state before 1102, which was such a long time ago that its memory could hardly have been expected to sustain momentum for the formation of national identity. It was the dubious history of the Ustaša State of 1939-45 that Tuđman, president of the new state, took for his point of reference. The idea of Central Europe has its origin in the Habsburg Empire. The unavoidable scale of values associated with a formerly 'socialist' country's proximity to Austria has kept on generating frustration for Eastern Europeans, refuelling old and well known complexes of inferiority.[6]

1. The Role of the Dissidents

The relative liberalisation in the 1980s enabled intellectuals in Central Europe to meet and also to make contact with exiled compatriots. The Czechs generally stayed away from these gatherings: Prague increased its vigilance owing to the threat represented by the more liberal regime in Hungary and the Polish trade union movement. The favoured place for meetings was often Yugoslavia where visiting intellectuals could stay at residences for writers in Istria or on the Dalmatian coast (especially Korčula), as well as attend such international gatherings as those of the Pen Club or the World Congress of Historical Sciences. At their meetings, the history of the region was being reassessed and Habsburg rule largely rehabilitated in the light of historical events subsequent to the collapse of the Austro-Hungarian dual monarchy.

The history of these gatherings has yet to be researched and this should be done while many of the participants are still alive (Konrad 1986: 87–98; Dalos 1988: 154–56).[7] The Austrian contributions to these debates were particularly important: intellectuals and such politicians as for example Bruno Kreisky for the socialists or Alois Mock for the Conservatives took part in them. In addition, the Italians Claudio Magris, the Hungarian György Konrad and György Dalos, the Polish Adam Michnik and the Yugoslavs Danilo Kiš were some of the well-known figures whose names come most immediately to mind. Their discussions considered the problem of identity in the Central European region, its borders

26 *Catherine Horel*

and its relations with neighbours in Western Europe, the Balkans and the Soviet Union. Not only did these gatherings aim to abolish taboos and fill the pages of history left blank by the communist regimes, but they also problematized the term 'Mitteleuropa' by considering the geographical vagueness of the area it designates and its potential to allude to German expansionism.

Asking questions about the existence and possible unity of Central Europe constituted an alternative for the intellectuals of the countries belonging to the Soviet bloc; it challenged the global approach that the West had adopted by differentiating between the Soviet Union and its satellites but ignoring differences between the satellites. The Central European references and models were moreover rooted in a historic reality condemned by the official historiographies of the regimes. If the Austrians, the Hungarians, the Croats, the Slovenes and even the Italians reassessed the Habsburg Empire, each nation would be able to resuscitate its historical memories: the Czechs for their part could glorify the Czechoslovak First Republic and the Poles could recall their independence in the eighteenth century and during the two decades between the two world wars. In all cases, the prerequisite for these reflections was the existence of the region: the first publications issued by these groups gave geographical, historical and geopolitical definitions. Central Europe thus very quickly becomes contrasted to the Russian sphere of influence. The states of the Balkans were also seen as victims of Sovietisation and thus frequently associated with Central Europe, most notably in the case of Romania.

Exiles were generally less interested than dissidents in the issue of Central Europe and favoured the overthrow of the socialist system, the establishing of democracy and the reunification of the continent. Opponents of these regimes living at home aimed for less: some form of regional unity and solidarity. These positions confronted each other more and more during the course of the 1980s. The liberalization that took place in Hungary and Poland, the peculiar case of Yugoslavia and the active intermediary role played by Austria facilitated the circulation of ideas and a greater sense of freedom of speech than ever before. Samizdat publications reached the West and, in turn, many texts entered Eastern Europe illegally.

The first Central European conference was held in Duino in 1983 in the presence mostly of writers both from Western and Eastern Europe. Attending the event, Eugène Ionesco said: 'Mon écriture appartient, intellectuellement, à la France, mais aussi, culturellement, à ce vaste espace mental du milieu' (quoted in Reszler 1991: 106). Ionesco expressed his wishes at this conference for Hungarian-Romanian reconciliation even as the regime of Nicolae Ceaușescu was attempting to destroy all traces of Transylvanian identity. Ionesco contemplated the creation of a Central European confederation grouping these two countries as well as Croatia, Austria and Czechoslovakia. This original and utopian idea did not correspond to any historical model, combining the Central European and Danubian options, and leaving Yugoslavia and the Balkans without a clear vision for the future.

In Gorizia (Gorica, Görz), on the Italian-Slovenian border, an institute was created to facilitate the cultural exchanges in Central Europe (Istituto per gli

The rediscovery of Central Europe in the 1980s   27

incontri culturali mitteleuropei). Such initiatives as this one were often initiated by Austria. Here, at the beginning of the 1970s, the review *Pannonia* – with the eloquent subtitle 'magazine for Mitteleuropa' – was launched. Founded in Eisenstadt, the capital of Austria's Easternmost province, Burgenland, the periodical opened branches in Bratislava, Budapest, Ljubljana, Zagreb and Gorizia. The original issue in German was followed in 1979 by a Hungarian edition. The review welcomed contributions by politicians, writers and scientists of all disciplines. In the years to come bilateral activities emerged involving Austrian-Yugoslav (mainly Slovenian and Croatian) and Austrian-Hungarian partners. The small town of Mogersdorf in Burgenland became the centre during the summer months for meetings of *Pannonia's* intellectuals. The discussions concerned matters considered taboo in the 'peoples' democracies', most notably the issues of ethnic minorities (Jaworski 1988: 547). Events organized at Gorizia focused on cosmopolitan and supranational dimensions. Invited participants represented intellectual circles on a very broad basis from Italy, Slovenia, Croatia, Serbia, Austria and both countries making up Czechoslovakia. The Jewish component of erstwhile Central Europe was also kept in mind. All ideological and political concepts could be expressed freely (Konstantinović, 1994: 50), but the Italian orientation was obvious from the start: after 1989 the Italians proposed a regional union called Alpe-Adria, later to be referred to as the Pentagonal and then the Hexagonal union.[8]

The contributions of Italian historiography to the rediscovery of Central Europe are significant, and even if the generation of Italian specialists of the inter-war period has by now ceased to be active, the schools they started are still alive today. The multicultural particularity of Istria greatly contributed to the renewal of interest in Central Europe, which was apparent in particular in the work of Claudio Magris from Trieste. His doctoral dissertation published in 1966 did not at first provoke any reactions but by the 1980s it had become the reference work for those who considered former as well as contemporary Austria the decisive player in the Central European region (Magris 1991a). Magris was largely overtaken by his own success and felt uncomfortable about it; his book ended up contributing to the propagation of the Habsburg 'myth' in spite of its detached, scholarly approach. Inspired by this book as well as the arguments of those who initiated Austria's Ostpolitik, Erhard Busek, a member of ÖVP (The Austrian People's Party) launched in 1986 his Projekt Mitteleuropa, which he then developed in a considerable number of publications before and after the fall of the Iron Curtain (Busek and Brix 1986; Busek and Wilflinger 1986; Busek and Stourzh 1990). Thus, Austrian Mitteleuropa corresponds to the former Habsburg Empire, which Busek sees as a model of European integration *avant la lettre*. Its recreation it was argued, should not only be a political objective but also an intellectual project activating existing links between the respective countries and Vienna at the region's natural crossroads. Such an understanding of Mitteleuropa was intended as a beacon of hope for the future once the region became democratic.

28 *Catherine Horel*

2. The Habsburg Nostalgia

Working for the rebirth of Central Europe mounted a challenge for the political reality of the Soviet bloc. Above all the Czechs, Poles and Hungarians, but also the Baltic peoples, the Slovenes and the Croats positioned themselves in the centre rather than in the East of Europe. In Yugoslavia, speaking of Mitteleuropa and putting forward the Habsburg Empire as a model meant not only an aspiration to break away from state socialism but also from the Balkans. As Danilo Kiš said: 'Being conscious of belonging to the culture of Central Europe is already dissidence' (Kiš 1987: 299). For many people, unhappy memories of the Habsburg Empire and the German hegemony were progressively put aside to help along the re-emergence of the concept of Central Europe. If such an entity should not end up playing a significant role, at least it could become a political myth (Kende 1991: 463–71). Even if one considers the Habsburg monarchy as a model for successful integration, it nevertheless cannot be denied that its collapse was caused by its lack of capacity to reform and, most surely, to federalize. In the middle of the 1980s enthusiasm about the Habsburg model in France (but also elsewhere in Western Europe) culminated in the vogue of fin-de-siècle Vienna: the Centre Pompidou in Paris put on an excellent exhibition, accompanied by a catalogue of the highest quality (Clair 1986). In France, new translations appeared of Stefan Zweig but also of Arthur Schnitzler, seen as representatives of this 'world of yesteryear'. The biography of Emperor Franz Joseph by the French historian Jean-Paul Bled also contributed to the 'Habsburg revival' (Bled 1987). The old emperor and king acquired an emblematic stature, which his long reign emphasized all the more.

The funeral in Vienna on 1 April 1989 of Empress Zita, the long-surviving widow of Karl, the last Habsburg on the throne, marked the peak of this period and coincided with the changes that were taking place one after the other in the course of this year. Two weeks earlier, the Hungarians had commemorated freely, for the first time since the start of communist rule, the anniversary of 15 March 1848, the uprising against Habsburg rule, and a few days later the remains of the victims of the 1956 repression were exhumed. The concomitance of these events is striking in the Austro-Hungarian context: in late June the barbed wire of the Iron Curtain between the two countries was symbolically cut by the Austrian Vice-Chancellor, Alois Mock, and the Hungarian Foreign Minister of a still communist government, Gyula Horn. In the process, the head of the Habsburg family, the former crown prince Archduke Dr Otto von Habsburg-Lothringen (1912–2011) – at the time a senior member of the European Parliament – reappeared in the limelight. He led the debate on the democratic transition and became involved in discussions about the future of these countries, above all Hungary. He involved actively the Pan-European movement, of which he was President, and advocated quick integration into the European Union (Habsburg *et al.* 1997: 3).[9]

Starting from an Italian-Austrian initiative, the 'rebirth' of Central Europe went far beyond the region itself. As we said before, in Western Europe it was

The rediscovery of Central Europe in the 1980s   29

essentially France that resuscitated an old interest in the area. Incomprehensible for the French *esprit* as this world may have been, it lost none of the fascinating aura of mystery surrounding it. The excessive use of the term Mitteleuropa in France made it into a synonym for the Habsburg Empire. The disappearance of this entity in 1918 in the context of the subsequent rise of fascist, Nazi and communist totalitarian dictatorships now came to be seen as a major catastrophe. The emerging sense of nostalgias depicted the late monarchy as a multicultural paradise destroyed by the irresponsibility of the great powers and by nationalism.[10] The rehabilitation of the former 'Völkerkerker' was nevertheless exaggeratedly idealised. After all, most of the rediscovered writers and artists, the leaders of the intellectual life in Vienna around 1900, were very often extremely critical of the system. But it was nevertheless the famous line from František Palacký's letter to the Frankfurt Parliament that was repeatedly being quoted: 'Indeed, had the Austrian Empire not existed for a long time, we should promptly have brought it about in the interest of Europe, even in the interest of humanity' (Busek and Brix 1986: 82–83). The industry of tourism lost no time in taking advantage of the trend and the advertisements praising the beauties of Vienna, Budapest and Cracow made numerous references to the Habsburgs.

The dissidents and intellectuals of Central Europe displayed no nostalgia but acknowledged instead the stability of the erstwhile Habsburg Empire. In the years following the transition, many of them – backed by public opinion – were certainly attracted to the Austrian model, albeit to its contemporary form of neutrality and *modus vivendi* between the two blocs (Mlynář 1988: 51). They rejected the plans for regional union proposed during the years of transition and chose integration into the European Union as the only viable alternative for prosperity and, above all, collective security for the region.

At the beginning of the 1990s Péter Kende made a negative but clear-sighted assessment of the chances of federalism in Central Europe. He underlined the heterogeneity of the region in terms of political systems and raised five issues: 1) Is there or not between these states a community as well as economic complementarity? The answer is no partly because of the historical diversification aggravated by the Soviet system. 2) Is there homogeneity of leadership? Again, the answer is no. Czechoslovakia and Romania for instance have practically nothing in common; cultural and political institutions are heterogeneous and territorial unity of the region does not exist either – some borders in fact are disputed, for example the Oder-Neisse Line. 3) The national rivalries prevent the constitution of a community of values. 4) The linguistic diversity is also a problem: the unification through the German language and culture is no longer an option and Russian was not only unable to impose itself but, what is more, it was universally rejected in the end. 5) Finally, there is a lack of momentum and leaders willing to launch a federal project comparable to the French-German process of reconciliation in Western Europe. Hence, the only possible choice is made available by the European Union (Kende 1994: 121–25). Hungarian, Czech or Polish intellectuals adopted different positions towards

30   Catherine Horel

Central Europe. But, in any case, they tended to think of Europe in global terms, using Mikhail Gorbachev's metaphor of the 'common house'. This term broke away from the East-West binary. Adam Michnik warned in 1983 that Polish intellectuals should not turn systematically towards the West, from which no concrete help was to be expected. Instead he proposed as follows: 'either listen to the echo of the Parisian cafés and the goings-on in America – digesting out of this a pseudo-patriotic porridge, or instead examine closely underground culture in Russia, Czech and Slovak literature, Hungarian cinema, Lithuanian, Belorussian and Ukrainian intellectual productions' (Michnik 1983: 183). The board of editors of the Polish review *Krytyka* welcomed contributions from dissidents like Václav Havel or émigrés like Miklos Haraszti who lived beyond the Iron Curtain. *Krytyka* published special editions dedicated to the opposition in the other countries of the bloc (Michnik 1983: 17; Ash 1990).[11] At the end of the 1980s Milan Kundera, Adam Michnik, György Konrad, Danilo Kiš and many others were able to have a dialogue thanks to the mediation of the journals and met at gatherings we have already discussed. For dissidents, the monopolization of politics by the socialist regimes triggered not exactly the rejection of politics in order to be apolitical but instead an alternative that needed to be, according to Konrad, anti-political (Konrad 1987a).[12]

Konrad's thoughts differs from Kundera's for a very simple geographical reason: Budapest is situated east of Prague.

> From Budapest I am trying to reconcile East and West; as a paradoxical go-between, I am trying to defuse the bellicose exaggerations. This is where dissensions must be eased. The peoples in Central Europe have also something to say. We are different from Westerners; we observe them, we approve of them and as soon as we are among ourselves, Eastern Europeans, we look at each other and laugh. We go back to our macabre humour, to our moral ardour, to our inconsistency, to our gloom and to the sublime joy of sacrifice.
>
> (Konrad 1990: 89–90)

If Kundera is an advocate for a Western orientation for Central Europe, Konrad grants Hungary a resolutely median position between East and West. But in 1987 the region was politically still Eastern, culturally Western and geographically in the middle of Europe. Like other intellectuals of this particular moment of Central-European thinking, Konrad calls in history to justify progress: 'In Central Europe, modernity means recognition of lasting tendencies in our history and the ability intuitively to project them into the future' (Konrad 1990: 107). In order to achieve this, the prerequisite is to free oneself from the historiographical diktats enforced by the regimes that have distorted historical reality. That is why the emergence of the more objective approach of the Habsburg Empire was of so much importance in this context. Out of the three major attempts to overthrow Soviet domination – Hungary 1956, Czechoslovakia 1968 and Poland 1980 – Konrad builds a common past and a Central-European

The rediscovery of Central Europe in the 1980s   31

historical fraternity. He sees defeat as the single common denominator that becomes an asset and a milestone on the road towards victory in the long run. He sees this as one of the characteristics of Central Europe (Konrad 1990: 110). Just like others, Konrad wants to believe in a process of democratization coming from inside and his sarcasm is prophetic in foreseeing that 'colonizing' Russia would become 'infected' by the ideas formulated first in Central Europe. This attitude also explains why he did not want to leave Hungary where he was actually not under the same kind of threat as were many of his colleagues for example in more hard-line Czechoslovakia. He preferred to be a Westerner in Hungary instead of becoming an Easterner in the West – a fate, in his view, that befalls all Central Europeans (Konrad 1990: 119). Up until 1989, Konrad, more than others, managed to distribute his ideas about Central Europe in a considerable number of publications. He became for Western intellectuals one of the main sources of reference in every book dealing with the question. Similarly to what happened to Kundera, his words have been quoted and interpreted without having been understood by his readers as a result of their insufficient knowledge of Central Europe's complex realities.

On various occasions Konrad commented on the arguments discussed in *L'Antipolitique* (1987) but they were never reassessed or modified. He thus defined Central Europe as corresponding to the Habsburg imperial model: a unified inner space, left deliberately multicultural – a 'Europe of the middle' that is perfectly functional. 'Belonging to Central Europe is an attitude, a vision of the world, an aesthetical sensibility to the complicated, the diverse – to multiple ways of thinking and to different languages. ... For belonging to Central Europe means to consider plurality as a value' (Konrad 1987b: 29). But there is an issue where Konrad before 1989 displays naivety: he dismisses nationalism and in fact attributes its supposed absence to one of Central Europe's valuable qualities. As we have seen though, the democratic transition brought nationalism to the foreground in spite of integration into the European Union.

The 'misery' of the Central European nations is abundantly transformed by Konrad: the smallness of these states drives them to intellectual hyperactivity.[13] Similar views were expressed by many of his contemporaries in the region, who observed that the Central Europeans must liberate themselves from Soviet control without expecting assistance from the West: the latter would not act as long as the Soviet Union was not considered overtly aggressive. Liberation is not supposed to be achieved through violence but through the superiority of available cultural models and political alternatives. Konrad noted the awakening and the maturation of civilian society, the returning of history and the demand for the truth: these concepts represented for him the foundations of the 'anti-politics' that he had formulated a few years earlier. It is precisely the presence of civilian society and the shared heritage of the Middle Ages, the Renaissance and the Enlightenment that make Central Europe a constitutive part of Western and not Eastern Europe, as Antonin Liehm, a Czech exile in Paris, rightly asserted. The communist regimes attempted to eradicate this heritage, having derisively

32   Catherine Horel

labelled it 'bourgeois', and it had to be preserved and defended by the intellectuals (Liehm 1991: 125).

The mainly cultural approach leads Konrad to 'dream' of a Central Europe (Konrad 1986: 87–97) recreated irrespective of existing political divisions and American and Soviet imperialism (Konrad 1989). Before 1989 this 'dream' was a highly subversive one: the origin of its terms of reference rested with the former social elite and historical memories denied by the regimes. For example, questions were asked about the fate of the Jews and about the decline of the German language and culture. Konrad refused to accept that many centuries of common history in the region drew to a close in 1918 and that after 1945 this heritage became completely banished with forced integration into the Soviet system. After 1989 the Central European 'dream' was dealt another blow in the great rush towards the West and suddenly it became the symbol of conservatism; its cultural components were being appropriated by Habsburg loyalists. It is ironical in the extreme that it was rebels, some of them even coming from the far left, who had initially rekindled aspirations under Soviet occupation to recreate Mitteleuropa. They were in fact the true heirs of the most acerbic critics of the Empire at the turn of the century (Konstantinović 1991: 205–6). This important part of dissident thought – so crucial for the democratic transition – has been distorted by the Western media and by some unscrupulous intellectuals for reasons of their own. Such figures as Kundera and Konrad have become silent on the subject, opting instead to return to the writing of literary texts and less overtly politically essays.

3. The Western interpretations

The debate on Central Europe rapidly reached not only France but Germany, too. Intellectual and geopolitical interests in the old Mitteleuropa had been relegated to a distinctly secondary position because of the partition of the country and the resolutely Western orientation of the Federal Republic. Inspired by dissident intellectuals, the German historian Karl Schlögel also came to understand Central Europe as a means by which to challenge East-West bipolarity (Schlögel 1986). He echoed Konrad and others who had referred to the common cultural and historical heritage of the region. But Schlögel added a specific German twist, looking beyond the division of the country, and endowing the Central European project with political ambition. Notwithstanding historical memories that disqualify straight away any German initiative in the region (the extermination of the Jews – once one of the main carriers of German culture; the expulsion of German nationals from various parts of the region; the sharp decline of the German language) some scholars, like for instance Peter Glotz, wished for Germany to play a constructive role again. He stressed the 850 years of fruitful German presence in Centre of Europe, compared to the last 150 years of domination (Brechtefeld 1996: 82). Schlögel suggested that Germany had to rediscover its 'lost East' that once informed its sense of identity but was to do so without abandoning its *Westbindung* inaugurated by Konrad Adenauer. Conjuring

The rediscovery of Central Europe in the 1980s 33

up Mitteleuropa looked like a provocation for many reasons both in the East and in the West where 'the wall in the mind' was yet to be overthrown (Rupnik 1991: 247).

Paradoxically, Peter Glotz, the Social Democrat originally from the Sudeten-land, and the Conservative Karl Schlögel joined the Central European intellectuals rejecting the Americanization of Western Europe and appealed for Mitteleuropa to save the whole of Europe. By 1989 the entire West German political spectrum, from the Greens to the Christian Democrats, became affected by the debate on Central Europe. In 1988, two historians – Bernard Willms and Paul Kleinewefers – incorporated it into a model for German reunification (Willms and Kleinewefers 1988). They proposed to reunify the two German states within a Central European federation comprising Austria and Czechoslovakia, too (Brechtefeld 1996: 86). Such a symbiosis between the socialist and liberal-pluralist systems would have represented an incarnation of new political thinking in the region: federalism and the third way, an alternative both to communism and capitalism. The idea of reunification to be followed by neutrality in Germany and the Central European region did not survive for too long in the face of the Soviet bloc's disintegration and the increasing appeal of the European Union. Simultaneously, the intellectuals of Central Europe had ceased to view German reunification as a threat while the division of the continent and stockpiles of weapons seemed much more dangerous to them. The process of eliminating old taboos now faced up to reassessing the German question. Czech and Polish dissidents did raise it cautiously yet with a great deal of frankness. That was precisely the meaning of the Prague Call published in 'Charta 77' in 1985 (Rupnik 1991: 254).

The Austrians were partly responsible for the re-introduction of the term Mitteleuropa, which had acquired an unfortunate reputation since World War I. They managed to extrapolate it from its purely German context. In fact, their overall success in this endeavour exceeded all expectations thanks to the media, giving rise to new fantasies about what Mitteleuropa was or should be. One of the first Austrians to use the word in public in 1968 was none other than Bruno Kreisky. He was not yet Chancellor but had already served in prominent public office, notably as Foreign Minister. In an article written for *Neues Forum*, Kreisky used the term in order to challenge the binary logic of the two blocs. He defined Mitteleuropa, however, as an entity made up of Germany, Austria, Switzerland and Italy, containing two neutral states. Kreisky's Central Europe would be a bridge between cultures and, above all, between two antagonistic political systems. The nations of the Soviet bloc that 'longed' to join Mitteleuropa were in his view the Croats, Serbs, Czechs, Slovaks, Hungarians, Poles and Romanians (curiously he forgot about neighbouring Slovenes). Austria's mission was to facilitate this *rapprochement*, but not only on the economic level; Kreisky seemed to consider the latter to be less ideologically sensitive and thus easier to address. Austria should concentrate its efforts on culture instead, but not in the manner of a crusade; there was no need to be arrogant with the communist regimes and thereby thwart the entire initiative, nor was it wise to upset people with too many German references (Kreisky 1968: 145). Kreisky

34   Catherine Horel

warned the Germans straight away lest they think that this peculiarly Austrian way of promoting an *Ostpolitik* along the Danube is some kind of reconfiguration of Friedrich Naumann's idea of a 'victorious alliance between Germany and Austria' (Kreisky 1968: 147; Naumann 1915).[14] The success of Kreisky's policy was obvious during the 1980s and several scholars saw in it the revival of a Central European community able to circumvent the prevailing bipolar ideology. This achievement was indeed partly thanks to the traditions inherited from the Dual Monarchy (Löser and Schilling 1984: 194). Hungarian intellectuals called this period ironically the 'new K und K', referring to liberalisation under the Kádár regime and the policy of Kreisky (Hanák 1995: 230). The ensuing Habsburg nostalgia was, by necessity, centred in Vienna but it branched out to Budapest, Trieste, and even far beyond, to Paris. Vienna in this Mitteleuropa revival gradually lost its German connotations, came to face again the Habsburg myth, extolling the turn of the twentieth century – the *Jahrhundertwende* – as its paradigm (Busek and Brix 1986: 80).

Kreisky's Mitteleuropa drew upon Austria's past and present as a neutral state able to make improvements with regard to human rights and collective security (Busek and Brix 1986: 129). The practice of granting political asylum and welcoming immigrants from the communist world since well before 1956, in addition to the introduction of visa waivers in the late 1970s for Poles and Hungarians, demonstrate the continuity and consistence of this policy (Rovan 1988: 11). The Eastern Europeans seemed to prefer this idea of Central Europe to the 'common house' proposed by Gorbachev. As we said earlier, when they eventually escaped from the Soviets, however, Austria was forgotten in the great rush to the European Community (of which Austria was not even a member at the time) (Hobsbawm 1989: 17). Yet again, Mitteleuropa did not mean the same thing for everybody: there were the old supporters of the Pan-Germanic dream, awakened by the reunification of Germany; there were those who bemoaned with nostalgia the passing of the Austro-Hungarian Empire; the anti-communists saw in it the means for overthrowing the Soviet yoke; and finally it came to signify a great deal for those who aimed to reconstruct their sense of identity during the years preceding the transition (Pelinka 1990: 133).

As we have seen, in the 1970s Italy rediscovered Central Europe well before France did. The simple reason for this is that the Italian state incorporates a small but crucial region whose Central European identity is obvious: Trieste. The journal *Itinerari*, published in Genova, started putting out articles about Trieste, Istria and Dalmatia (the latter two regions then part of Yugoslavia) and devoted an entire double issue to Central Europe in 1975–76. Its editor, Francesco C. Rossi, even spoke of 'triestinità' to emphasize the significance of the Istrian capital in Italian culture (Rossi 1975, 1976). Joining Venice in this function, Trieste as a gateway to the Adriatic was recognised as a new source of economic and cultural opportunities for Italy.[15] More recently, the articles published in the Trieste-based review *Est-Ovest*, have pursued this – now mainly economic – mission. Rossi surveyed in his work all the Central European markers that make Trieste a dependency of Vienna. He focused generously on cafés and

The rediscovery of Central Europe in the 1980s 35

multiculturalism and on the fact that when the Triestine hinterland was attached to socialist Yugoslavia, the region's historical tradition in fostering cultural transfers came to an end. Little attention, however, was paid either to the forced Italianization of the city after 1918 at the expense of Slovenes and other regional cultures, or to the disappearance of the Jews. The literary scholar we have mentioned before, Claudio Magris, himself from Trieste, attempted to address these issues: he referred to the culture of his city as 'posthumous' in the absence of the former Jewish, German and Slavonic influences (Ara 1987: 131; Magris 1991b). Magris's work marks a substantial advance in the rediscovery of Central European plurality well beyond Italy. The Italian initiatives were gradually accompanied by meaningful Slovene contributions alongside the resumption of the Italian-Slovene dialogue around 1980 (Ara 1987: 33). The border town of Gorizia, north of Trieste, where the Italians had created in the 1960s the *l'Istituto per gli incontri culturali mitteleuropei* came to play a central role in this new context (Konstantinović 1994: 50).

The term Mitteleuropa – signifying the former Habsburg empire – became an accepted and commonly used tem all over Italy just as it subsequently did in France in the 1980s. The emergence of this interest prepared Italy for participation in various regional projects after the 1989 transition and the break-up of Yugoslavia, which facilitated the process of overcoming the legacy of conflicts with neighbours. In the regions bordering on Austria (Trentino, South Tyrol, Trieste), but also in Lombardy and Tuscany, resentment of the Habsburg Empire that had dominated mentalities since the end of World War I was gradually turning into nostalgia at the turn of the 1980s, giving rise to numerous associations and publications (Mouzon 1986: 119–20).

At the beginning of the 1990s the renewed interest in Central Europe crossed both the English Channel and the Atlantic. The work of Timothy Garton Ash had even earlier raised awareness of Poland in the middle of the 1980s, but the impact of his articles remained limited to a narrow circle of academic readers (Ash 1983). The communities of exiles from Central Europe in the United States kept making representations of their culture, but their anti-communism disqualified them in left-wing academic circles predominant in France and in Italy, at least until 1956 if not 1968. Their voice, however, grew stronger as soon as the disenchantment with the Soviet Union set in among intellectuals (who were then to turn their gaze towards the non-aligned countries and the Third World [Judt, 1991: 28]). The late American historian, Tony Judt, primarily a specialist of France, dates his change of heart to the time of the publication of *The Gulag Archipelago* by Aleksandr Solzhenitsyn and considers the years 1973–81 as the starting point for the rediscovery of Central Europe. The erosion of the former prestige of the Soviet Union, the communist parties and Marxism was matched by the increase of interest in events and personalities in Central Europe's process of evolution, which ended in 1989 (Judt 1991: 30).

For a long time the history of Central Europe was taught in Britain and to some extent also in the United States by specialists of the Soviet Union who tended to see the region as the backyard of Russia.[16] They lacked adequate

36 Catherine Horel

familiarity with the region, and looked upon it with disdain typical of the superiority complex of the great powers (Judt 1991: 46). Authors writing in English used the term Mitteleuropa less than the French and preferred Central Europe or East Central Europe. When talking about Central Europe they had in mind the five countries that were integrated into the European Union in 2004: the rest of the region being designated as Eastern or Balkan-based. By the 1980s authors writing in German had practically forgotten the term 'Zentraleuropa' and even more 'Zwischeneuropa', which had connotations to Nazi ambitions in the inter-war period. For Anglo-American authors historical memories are, of course, less traumatic, and also the rediscovery of Central Europe for them is unburdened by the European sense of nostalgia (Rupnik 1991: 234).

The collapse of the Soviet system in Central and Eastern Europe was often compared to the fall of dominoes and seemed to confirm in the West that Central Europe was being revived even as the West was winning the Cold War. The rapid Euro-Atlantic integration dispossessed Central Europeans of a cultural legacy regained in the 1980s. The 'come-back' to Europe was consequently accompanied by a slow but inexorable decline of a specific Central European sense of identity. The rediscovery of Central Europe was nevertheless a crucial moment in the evolution not only of the region but the whole of Europe which, in spite of nostalgia-induced exaggerations, played an indisputable role in the democratic transition.

Notes

1 Unless otherwise stated, translations are mine (CH).
2 Catherine Horel is Professor and Research Director at CNRS, UMR, IRICE at the University of Paris.
3 The group was created in 1991, first with three countries (Hungary, Poland, Czechoslovakia) and then with four after the separation of Czechoslovakia. See http://www.visegradgroup.eu/ The choice of Visegrád, former residence of the Anjou kings on the Danube, recalled the meeting of the Hungarian, Bohemian and Polish kings in 1335.
4 When the neutrality of Austria was proclaimed in October 1955 the exiled Czech politician Hubert Ripka advocated the adoption of a similar solution for Czechoslovakia (Kolouchová 2006: 151).
5 Croatia at the time of writing is scheduled to join in July 2013.
6 In a poll issued by the German weekly *Der Spiegel* in September 2000 ('Offen für den Osten', 2000), the question was as follows: 'Which in your opinion are the countries that should enter the European Union?'. The first was Hungary with 82 per cent (81 per cent in 1997), then the Czech Republic, 69 per cent (71 per cent in 1997), Poland, 66 per cent (57 per cent in 1997), Slovakia, 65 per cent (57 per cent in 1997), the three Baltic states, 63 per cent, and Slovenia, 61 per cent (52 per cent in 1997). The countries of Eastern Europe had weaker percentages even if Bulgaria gathered 55 per cent (39 per cent in 1997); Romania on the other hand had only 44 per cent (32 per cent in 1997) ('Offen für den Osten' 2000: 34–36).
7 See also 'Mitteleuropa, gibt es das? Im Gespräch mit Zdeněk Mlynář', *Wiener Tagebuch* 10, 1986.

The rediscovery of Central Europe in the 1980s 37

8 The Alpe-Adria organisation started in the 1970s as a regional project between Italy (Friuli–Venezia Giulia), Yugoslavia (Slovenia) and Austria (Carinthia). Hungary joined in 1980 and after the break-up of Yugoslavia, Slovenia and Croatia were recognized as member states. See: http://www.alpeadria.org/english/index.php

9 One of its founding members, Otto, was Vice-President (1957–73) and President (1973–2004) of the Pan-European Union.

10 The most remarkable book featuring this tendency is François Fejtö's *Requiem pour un empire défunt* (1993), which provoked a polemic among historians.

11 See Introduction by Alexandre Smolar (Michnik 1983: 17).

12 See also the journal *La nouvelle alternative*, no. 8, 1987. The Hungarian edition of Konrad's book, *Antipolitika. Az autonómia kísértése*, was published illegally in 1989.

13 Cf. Istvan Bibo (1993) *Misère des petits Etats d'Europe de l'Est*, Paris: Albin Michel, 1993 (2nd revised edition).

14 See an analysis of his theories of German expansion in the region in Horel 2009: 264–71.

15 See Rossi's 'Una nuova frontiera a Est', in *Itinerari* no. 176–79, Juin–Septembre 1972 ; 'L'Adriatico riscoperto a Trieste', in *Itinerari* no. 180, October 1972.

16 Some notable exceptions are historians of the late Habsburg Empire, such as Robert J. Evans in Britain an Charles W. Ingrao in the United States.

Works Cited

Ara, A. (1987) 'Das Erbe Mitteleuropas in Italien', *Europäische Rundschau* 15: 127–38.

Ash, T. G. (1983) *The Polish Revolution: Solidarity 1980–82*, London: Jonathan Cape.

——(1990) *The Uses of Adversity. Essays on the Fate of Central Europe*, Cambridge: Granta Books.

Bled, J-P. (1987)1 *François-Joseph*, Paris: Fayard.

Brechtefeld, J. (1996) *Mitteleuropa and German Politics: 1848 to the Present*, London: St Martin's Press.

Busek, E and Brix, E. (1986) *Projekt Mitteleuropa*, Wien: Überreuter.

Busek, E. and Wilflinger, G. (eds) (1986) *Aufbruch nach Mitteleuropa. Rekonstruktion eines versunkenen Kontinents*, Wien: Herold.

Busek, E. and Stourzh, G. (eds) (1990) *Nationale Vielfalt und gemeinsames Erbe in Mitteleuropa*, Wien-München: Oldenburg.

Clair, J. (ed) (1986), *L'apocalypse joyeuse: Vienne 1880-1938, Exhibition catalogue*, Paris: Éditions du Centre Georges Pompidou.

Dalos, Gy (1988) 'Gibt es heute eine mitteleuropäische Literatur?', in Gy. Meszáros (ed.), *Mitteleuropa. Traum oder Trauma? Bremen-Wien: Österreichische Gesellschaft für Außenpolitik und Internationale Beziehungen*: 154–60.

Fejtö, F. (1993) *Requiem pour un empire défunt*, Paris: Lieu Commun.

Habsburg, O., Habsburg, G. and Habsburg, K. (1997) 'Paneuropa als Weg und Ziel', *Die Presse*, 18 October: 3.

Hanák, P. (1995) *Ragaszkodás az utópiához*, Budapest: Liget Mühely Alapitvány.

Horel, C. (2009) *Cette Europe qu'on dit centrale. Des Habsbourg à l'intégration européenne*, Paris: Beauchesne.

Hobsbawm, E. J. (1989) 'Mitteleuropa, Politik und Kultur. Heimweh nach Kakanien und die vergessene Gegenwart', in *Wiener Tagebuch*, November: 17–19.

Jaworski, R. (1988) 'Die aktuelle Mitteleuropadiskussion in historischer Perspektive', *Historische Zeitschrift* 247: 529–50.

38   Catherine Horel

Judt, T. (1991) 'The Rediscovery of Central Europe', in S. R. Graubard (ed.), *Eastern Europe, Central Europe, Europe*, Boulder: Westview: 28–48.

Kende, P. (1991) 'Deux Europes, trois, ou une seule?', in G. Beauprêtre (ed.), *L'Europe centrale. Réalité, mythe, enjeu XVIIe-XXe siècles*, Warsaw: Les Cahiers de Varsovie (Centre de civilisation française de l'université de Varsovie).

——(1994) *Miért nincs rend Kelet-Közép-Európában?* Budapest: Osiris Kiadó.

Kiš, D. (1987) 'Variations sur des thèmes d'Europe centrale', *Le Messager Européen* 1: 299.

Kolouchová, Z. (2006) *Hubert Ripka, occidentophile ou soviétophile? Parcours croisés d'un homme politique et d'un pays dans la tourmente géostratégique de l'avant Guerre froide*, Master II dissertation, Centre d'histoire de l'Europe centrale contemporaine, Institut Pierre Renouvin, Université de Paris I.

Konrad, Gy. (1986), 'Der Traum von Mitteleuropa', in E. Busek and G. Wilflinger (eds), *Aufbruch nach Mitteleuropa. Rekonstruktion eines versunkenen Kontinents*, Wien: Herold: 87–98.

——(1987a) *L'antipolitique. Méditations mitteleuropéennes*, Paris: La Découverte.

——(1987b) 'L'Europe du milieu patrie intérieure', *Cadmos* 10 (39): 29–31.

——(1989) 'Mitteleuropäische Meditationen an der Bruchlinie zweier Zivilisationen', *Dialog, Beiträge zur Friedensforschung* 15: 7–28.

——(1990), *Le rendez-vous des spectres*, Paris: Gallimard.

Konstantinović, Z. (1994) 'Les Slaves du Sud et la Mitteleuropa', *Revue germanique international* 1: 48–50.

Konstantinović, Z. (1991) 'Gibt es heute mitteleuropäische Literatur?', in A. Pribersky (ed.), *Europa und Mitteleuropa*, Wien: Sonderzahl, 205–6.

Kreisky, B. (1968) 'Chance Mitteleuropa', *Neues Forum* 15 (171–72): 145.

Liehm, A. (1991) 'Anmerkungen zur mitteleuropäischen Identität', in A. Pribersky (ed.), *Europa und Mitteleuropa? Eine Umschreibung Österreichs*, Wien: Sonderzahl 125.

Löser, J. and Schilling, U. (1984) *Neutralität für Mitteleuropa. Das Ende der Blöcke*, München: Bertelsmann.

Magris, C. (1991a) *Le mythe et l'empire dans la littérature autrichienne moderne*, Paris, Gallimar.

——(1991b) *Trieste, une identité de frontière*, Paris: Seuil.

Michnik, A. (1983) *Penser la Pologne*, Paris: Maspéro.

Mlynář, Z (1988) 'Mitteleuropa im Ost-West Konflikt', in S. Päpke and W. Weidenfeld (eds), *Traumland Mitteleuropa? Beiträge zu einer aktuellen Kontroverse*, Darmstadt: Wissenschaftliche Buchgesselschaft.

Mouzon, R. De (1986), 'Schwarzgelbe Nostalgien in Grün-Weiß-Rot', in E. Busek and G. Wilflinger (eds), *Aufbruch nach Mitteleuropa. Rekonstruktion eines versunkenen Kontinents*, Wien, Herold.

Naumann, F. (1915), *Mitteleuropa*, Berlin: Reimer.

'Offen für den Osten', (2000) *Der Spiegel* 37: 34–36.

Pelinka, A. (1990) *Zur österreichischen Identität. Zwischen deutscher Vereinigung und Mitteleuropa*, Wien:Überreuter.

Reszler, A. (1991) *Rejoindre l'Europe. Destin et avenir de l'Europe centrale*, Geneva: Georg. (1975, 1976) 'Triestinità' di ritorno e le occasioni dell'Italia', *Itinerari* 22–23: 216–25.

Rovan, J. (1988) 'Mitteleuropa gegen Europa', in S. Päpke and W. Weidenfeld (eds), *Traumland Mitteleuropa? Beiträge zu einer aktuellen Kontroverse*, Darmstadt: Wissenschaftliche Buchgesselschaft: 8–11.

Rupnik, J. (1991) 'Central Europe or Mitteleuropa?', in S. R. Graubard (ed.), *Eastern Europe, Central Europe, Europe*, Boulder, San Francisco, Oxford: Westview.

Schlögel, K. (1986) *Die Mitte liegt ostwärts. Die Deutschen, der verlorene Osten und Mitteleuropa*, Berlin, W. J. Schiedler.

Willms, B and Kleinewefers, P. (1988) *Erneuerung aus der Mitte: Prag, Wien, Berlin; diesseits von Ost und West*, Herford: Busse Seewald.

4 Gulfs and gaps – Prague and Lisbon – 1989 and 2009

Wolfgang Müller-Funk[1]

> Die Wahrheit ist das, was jeder Mensch zum Leben braucht und doch von niemand bekommen oder erstehen kann. Jeder Mensch muss sie aus dem eigenen Innern immer wieder produzieren, sonst vergeht er. Leben ohne Wahrheit ist unmöglich. Die Wahrheit ist vielleicht das Leben selbst.
>
> (Franz Kafka)[2]

> Der Mensch besteht in der Wahrheit – gibt er die Wahrheit preis, so gibt er sich selbst preis.
>
> (Novalis)[3]

The French philosopher Jean François Lyotard published an essay in 1993 with an unashamedly engagé title: 'Wall, Gulf, System'. He was referring to the 'historical situation' that emerged in the wake of the fall of the Iron Curtain and the first Gulf War (Lyotard 1998: 67–69). The lecture on which the essay was based had been given earlier, probably after his two trips to the then still existing German Democratic Republic and immediately after the beginning of the first Gulf War against the Iraq of Saddam Hussein. In his text, this – at that time almost completely forgotten – French philosopher who had given postmodernism a decisive meaning in his book *The Postmodern Condition* (Lyotard 1986: 157–74), commented on the specific practices of French left-wing critics in engaging with international events. Lyotard did not fail to mention that in the 1950s and 1960s he, too, used to be a member of the leftist group *Socialisme ou Barbarie*. The point of view of East Berlin's intellectuals reminded him of his own views three decades earlier: the criticism both of Western liberalism and communist totalitarianism drew upon the work of Rosa Luxemburg and Antonio Gramsci whose understanding of socialism signified their protest against the threat of barbarism, fascism and Stalinism. This 'third position' could also be considered as a challenge to the binary opposition between capitalism and – what the Soviets liked to call – 'real Socialism'.

Lyotard argues that after 1989, the year the Iron Curtain and the Berlin Wall came down, such a 'third option' was no longer possible (Lyotard 1994). This is in keeping with Lyotard's view that 'grands recits', including leftist utopias, have no validity as they depend for their existence on a strong and emphatic

Gulfs and gaps – Prague and Lisbon   41

historical-philosophical narrative framework. According to Lyotard, such frameworks had lost credibility.[4] Events in 1989 confirmed that the political energies of the Marxist project – the last offspring of the Enlightenment and of Christianity – had been wasted. A long time earlier, Enrico Berlinguer, the leader of the reformed Italian Communist Party (PCI) had concluded that the Russian Revolution of October 1917 was no longer in a position to offer a perspective for the future (Berlinguer 1978).

Prior to becoming a postmodernist, Lyotard passed through all stages of left-wing thinking. He welcomed the revolutions of 1989. For him, the end of the socialist grand narrative did not mean that a barbaric future now awaited humanity. The logic of politics, however, had radically changed. The political struggle was no longer aggressive – it was rather defensive, entailing engagement for the rights of ethnic, sexual and social minorities, for women, for the rights of children, animals and the environment. It became evident in 1989 that the goals fought for no longer represented an alternative to existing social reality but instead they merged with the targets of the liberal system itself. Lyotard's diagnosis converges with Fukuyama's thesis about the end of history which, in turn, is based on a commentary by the French-Russian philosopher, Alexandre Kojève (Fukuyama 1992; Kojève 1973: 133–88).

The term 'revolution' is not entirely adequate to describe the events of 1989 and their consequences. The 'velvet' revolutions in Berlin, Budapest, Warsaw and Prague were counter-revolutions and revolutions at the same time. They cancelled the revolution of October 1917 yet, at the same time, they completed the democratic revolutions and transformations of 1848 and 1918. The context in which the changes of 1989 occurred was completely different though. Communism seemed nearly completely to have disappeared as a historical and political practice and capitalism seemed to have won on all levels. Today, more than twenty years later, such a straightforward diagnosis cannot be formulated. The banking crisis of 2008–9 was not the first in the history of capitalism, however, it has undermined the legitimacy of a project that may be more a destructive and greedy game than a system. There can be no doubt that the deep structures of capitalism have been affected by this crisis.

It is quite evident that people had lost faith in state socialism well before 1989 (in former Czechoslovakia in fact this happened immediately after 1968[5]) when it was overthrown. Twenty years later, however, disenchantment set in again. However, this time with a crucial difference: unlike communism, market capitalism has no limitations and limits. More a game of Monopoly than a system, capitalism cannot be got rid of. Nevertheless, it is becoming increasingly clear that the financial crisis of our days will change our perspectives on the soft and velvet revolutions in Central Europe and the former Soviet Union that paved the way to a market-based economy everywhere in Europe. The market now possesses boundless power and opportunity to generate social inequality.

What are the real and sustainable gains derived from the changes in 1989? What contribution did they make for general emancipation within the context of liberal democracy? Do they indeed owe a great debt to the small groups of

42 Wolfgang Müller-Funk

intellectuals in all the countries involved who rose to the challenge of the historical moment? It was David's victorious fight against Goliath – an enemy who seemed invincible. As the original title of Václav Havel's book has it, this struggle enacted the narrative about the 'power of the powerless' who nevertheless possessed the symbolic power of language and ethics (Havel 1980). Their credo combined ethics and aesthetics: one's life and art should be dedicated to the pursuit of truth. This maxim draws upon such predecessors in German-speaking civilization as Novalis and, later, Kafka. The 'velvet' heroes of 1989 changed the world in a manner similar to the struggle against colonialism by Mahatma Gandhi and Nelson Mandela. This was evident at writers' conferences I attended in the Slovenian 'Karst', at the University of Brno, at symposia my friends and I organized in those years on the Austro-Czech border and at conferences in Budapest in the early 1990s (*Magyar Letter* 1996). Whereas frequently hardly any German or Austrian writers were present at these events, one could meet prominent intellectuals from France, Italy or the United Kingdom, some of whom had done university level teaching arranged in private houses prior to 1989. The reasons that many leftist Austrians were not pleased about political change in the neighbourhood would have to be the topic of a different article. Suffice it to say that the unwillingness among left-wing West Germans and Austrians to show solidarity with the protagonists of 1989 had firstly to do with the anti-socialist aspect of the transformation and secondly with the 'peace partnership' between the Western Social Democrats and the Eastern European communist parties. In fact, the narrative of Austrian neutrality had been reformulated in the 1970s accordingly. This also played a certain role in the nostalgia expressed by Austrian intellectuals for Tito's Yugoslavia (Müller-Funk 2009: 341–54), for example in Peter Handke's novel, *Die Wiederholung* (The Repetition, 1918). Tito is represented here as the benevolent double of Emperor Franz Joseph, looking reproachfully from a poster at the novel's protagonist (1986: 18).

Former dissidents, like Václav Havel or Gábor Demszky, combined a touch of elitism with gentle sarcasm; these liberals, whose language remained incomprehensible, albeit very threatening, to the communists were also misfits both on the left and the right in Western Europe. They embodied the spirit of freedom of the Italian philosopher Benedetto Croce, Mussolini's liberal opponent at the beginning of the twentieth century. They were longing for the benefits gained from the popular movements of the 1960s which, of course, never took place in the countries of the Warsaw Pact. Their wish for liberty for the individual but unencumbered by the realities of market-based capitalism, was unsustainable and their triumph was temporary. Václav Havel, writer, dissident and a Rolling Stones enthusiast, heading to Prague Castle towards his presidency, with members of the visiting Pink Floyd pop group among the crowds following him, captures the spirit perhaps most tellingly (Ash 1990a: 401–50).

What legacy then have these people left behind? Such writers as the Hungarian Esterhazy, Kertesz, Konrad and Nadas opened up a new literary landscape unknown to many readers in the West. They proposed the possibility of living together peacefully and on an equal footing, no longer as latent enemies

Gulfs and gaps – Prague and Lisbon 43

(Konrad 1984). But never before did a revolution displace its proponents so swiftly as was the case, for example, in former Czechoslovakia: Jiři Dienstbier or Václav Havel became nearly forgotten in their homeland. At an underground station in Lisbon – where the 'Lisbon Treaty' was signed – a huge screen in February 2009 reported that the other Václav, Václav Klaus, had declared Brussels to be the new Moscow and the European Union the new Soviet Empire. What may people in Lisbon have made of this radical nationalistic nonsense? But then Lisbon, the symbol of a successful transition from dictatorship to liberal, postnationalistic, civilian society, is indeed a long way from Prague and Budapest.

The velvet revolutionaries were only a tiny group and it was unavoidable for professional politicians to enter the stage of politics as soon as possible. In a civilian society, this is a return to normality. But in the case of the new postcommunist democracies it implied a dramatic turn. Nearly everywhere there appeared the disagreeable grimace of a clammy, petty-bourgeois nationalist. Václav Klaus's statement is the perfect confirmation of the neonationalist frame of mind, according to which each critic of his or her own country becomes suspect, 'unreliable' and a 'traitor'. Such attitudes are not limited to Central and Eastern Europe (xenophobia is sadly far from being unknown in my own county, Austria), but the recent (re)appearance of some social trends in Hungary, Poland, Bulgaria and the Slovak Republic are bloodcurdling: the hostile treatment of sexual or ethnic minorities, the refusal to confront and analyse one's country's history, xenophobia, anti-Semitism, the hatred against the Sinti and Roma. The base of this nationalistic populism is rooted in the damage and disability experienced by the majority of the population after decades of totalitarian communist rule. The human burden of communism is relevant not only for the old, but also for today's middle-aged, generation that grew up under authoritarian structures. Postcommunist consumerism, while offering a very reduced form of freedom, is able successfully to hide these phenomena. Cynically speaking, consumerism has a great advantage. Its sole focus on the future induces forgetfulness about the past. To quote from Johann Strauss's *Die Fledermaus*: 'Glücklich ist, wer vergisst, was doch nicht zu ändern ist' (happy is the one who can forget what cannot be altered).[6]

Quite evidently, the post-Stalinist political system in Eastern Europe was so repressive and so strongly regulatory that it did not allow for ordinary people to acquire argumentative skills for conceptualising opposition to the government of the day. Critical intellectuals in Romania, such as Mircea Dinescu and Mircea Cărtărescu, believe that their 'revolution' was more or less organized and carried out by the secret service, Securitate, which became fed up with the Communist nomenclature and the 'Royal Communism' of the Ceaușescus (Dinescu 1990). If this is true, it would reveal the other, less attractive side of 1989. Seen from this angle, the communist implosion was followed by the disappearance, transformation and re-appearance of the old nomenclature. The ruling elites had lost faith in the system created by their parents. To some extent, they were responsible or co-responsible for the breakdown of 'real Socialism' and its unproductive economy. They came to occupy important jobs in the new system, especially in the economy. They left the sinking ship before it was too late. Unlike beliefs and ideas, habits change very slowly. Communism has not disappeared totally but it still exists in the attitudes and behaviour of men and women. Maybe it will take one generation more for this hidden spirit of un-freedom to leave the bodies and souls of so many. Now that totalitarian state-communism is no longer possible, nationalism with a social touch has become very attractive in many postcommunist countries. Not all new nationalist parties have been recruited by former Communists, and they had been busy distracting attention from the biographies of their leaders prior to the fall of the communist system. There are, however, numerous xenophobic, chauvinistic groupings in the former Soviet bloc with ex-Communist members and representatives both on the far left and on the far right. The new nationalism is encouraged by a perverse game of ping pong between the East and West of Europe. It has the clear purpose of neutralising or destroying the so-called 'dictatorship' of the European Union by fostering an analogy to the implosion of the Soviet Union after 1989. Nationalism is no longer a hangover from the nineteenth century. Nationalism is a trump card which enables one to do tricks within the game of politics.

There is a branch of research in political theory that deals with transformation and transition of modern societies (Fassmann *et al.* 2009). It has an implicit narrative structure and a distinct goal. It provides a roadmap from authoritarian social structures to functional civilian society. Spain, Portugal and – to a lesser extent – Greece succeeded in building a working parliamentary system of the Western European model within the space of two decades. After the end of right-wing dictatorships and some dramatic intermezzi, fully functional social democracies, capable of governing, arose in Southern Europe. With outside help, the Social Democrats marginalized their rivals, the communist parties, or forced them to reform themselves. In contrast, conservative and Christian Democratic parties emerged as the necessary democratic corrective element, ensuring the possibility of democratic change of rule. Such politicians as Felipe Gonzáles and Adolfo Suárez, and later their conservative counterparts, became well-accepted figures within Europe's political landscape. Spain, Portugal and Greece are less wealthy than the Benelux countries, Scandinavia, France and the Western part of Germany; nevertheless, in spite of high levels of unemployment, they have witnessed an enormous growth of prosperity over the past thirty years. Their political structures are remarkably stable. Spain and Portugal are well represented in the political institutions of the European Union. Suffice it to say that the Portuguese José Manuel Barroso has been the President of the European Commission for the past eight years

A comparison with the situation in the ex-Soviet bloc countries of Central Europe is striking. The political forces that guarantee the stability of most of the European democracies do not exist in these countries. Christian Democrats, Social Democrats, Green parties or leftist postcommunist groups – liberals – are either marginalized or do not exist at all. It may be understandable that the

Gulfs and gaps – Prague and Lisbon   45

democratic left had fundamental problems after 1989 in the ex-Warsaw Pact states but the reverse image in Southern Europe illustrates that it was possible for democratic right-wing parties to attain solid political legitimacy within ten years in spite of their historical complicity with erstwhile right-wing dictatorships. By contrast, we have yet to wait for the emergence of a credible and reliable democratic left in Central Europe.

The instability of the political landscapes in many Central or Eastern European countries is highly disconcerting: corruption, the rapid rise and fall of obscure political groups and 'one-man shows' have become commonplace. The velvet revolutionaries declared that human rights were to be the foundation for the post-Soviet systems; their successors, however, are preaching the gospel of nationalism, the sacro-egoism – chauvinistic isolationist policies – that they would like to implement across the whole of the European Union. This is not a very stimulating and calming interim result. Nationalism has the tendency of spreading like a large-scale fire. The appearance of one type of nationalism leads unavoidably to the next. War always begins within the violent discourse of hatred (Butler 1998). As is the case with love, hatred too always exists *á deux*. Populist nationalists have become part of political normality. Austrians, in fact, are in no position to patronize and criticize our newly democratic neighbours (Altzinger 2009). After sixty-five years of democracy and three generations since the days of national socialism, opinion polls suggest that support among the Austrian electorate for the radical right-wing party of Heinz-Christian Strache stands close to 30 per cent.[7]

But let us return to the comparison between the end of the right-wing dictatorships in the three Southern European countries in the 1970s and the velvet revolutions around that magical year, 1989. The new democracies in the south of the continent had to integrate programmatically into a social market system. Unlike the Central European countries, they had merely to modify rather than totally replace their economic systems. Besides, importantly, in the meantime, the economies of the older, established democracies in Europe shifted towards neoliberal practices under Britain's Margaret Thatcher and Tony Blair and Germany's Gerhard Schröder. Priorities moved in favour of the strong and the rich within these powerful economies to the detriment of the former system that was also conscious of the 'losers'. The new democracies ended up inheriting a different form of capitalism than the model that had prevailed in Europe prior to 1989. This is also an important reason for the disappointment in East-Central Europe twenty years after 1989 and it partially accounts for the rise and the success of right-wing populism and nationalism. The feelings of hatred it generates vis-à-vis the European Union, sexual and ethnic minorities, the Gypsies and, yet again, the Jews are intended to compensate for insecurity. There is one point, where the Chartists in Prague, Warsaw and Budapest were wrong. Like the neoliberal economists, they based their philosophy on the assumption that freedom was more important than justice and solidarity. But freedom reduced to economic freedom leads to structural injustice and is bound to fail eventually. Such freedom for the majority of people produces the experience of hopelessness and helplessness.

46   Wolfgang Müller-Funk

The comparison between the processes in Southern Europe in the 1970s and those following 1989 in the countries of the Warsaw Pact is, of course, not entirely fair. A different political, social and cultural context existed in the postfascist regimes in Southern Europe. There is no doubt that the dictatorships were guilty of crimes, especially in Spain. Nevertheless, the energy and resources in Spain, Portugal and Greece that were invested in destroying their own populations were nowhere near as disastrous as within the regime of terror that the Czech communists cynically and euphemistically called 'Normalisace' (normalization) during the two decades following 1968: in many communist countries the rule of the secret police was in place literally until the day the system collapsed (Gruša 2004: 3033). The 2009 recipient of the Nobel Prize for literature, Herta Müller, documented impressively in her literary work the consequences for human beings of the humiliation, degradation and fear that the communist system produced.

The transformations of the 1970s had a broad social and political base. The many working migrants and émigrés from Portugal, Spain and Greece in Western Europe had left their countries both for economic and political reasons. After the democratic transformation, they could play an important role in the development of modern democracy. This is, with some exceptions, also true today for the countries of former Yugoslavia, especially for Croatia and Slovenia. These two countries have meanwhile developed similar political structures and parties to the older member states of the EU. The other formerly communist countries, however, had no real opportunities in the reciprocal traffic of people, goods and ideas. Opening the labour markets in Germany and Austria, which was such an unpopular option in both countries, was extremely important because it would facilitate social, cultural and political experiences for the new democracies in the East. The new democratic elites in Southern Europe could count on their brother or sister parties in Western Europe – Social Democrats and Christian democrats – not only for substantial political but also financial support within the framework of the European Community. There is today support for the post-1989 democracies, but on a significantly smaller scale than in the 1970s. The older and richer democracies in Europe clearly bear some of the responsibility for the current instability faced by our Eastern neighbours. The new language of hatred and the triumph of a capitalist market system, solely focused on the quick enrichment of the few at the expense of the misery of the many, should not be allowed to ruin the European project that gave rise to the European Union. The 'emancipation' Lyotard had in mind when envisaging progress after the terminal failure of the grand narrative of socialism, will only be possible if the democracies that emerged following 1989 are able to internalize the principles of civilian society.

Notes

1 Unless otherwise stated, translations are mine (WMF).
2 'The truth is the entity that every human being requires in order to live but one that he cannot receive or acquire from anyone else. Everyone must keep obtaining it continuously from one's own soul or else it slips away. There is no life without truth.

Gulfs and gaps – Prague and Lisbon   47

Truth perhaps is life itself'. In Gustav Janouch (1951), *Gespräche mit Kafka. Erinnerungen und Aufzeichnungen*, Frankfurt/Main: Fischer, 224.

3 'Human beings are grounded in truth: if one betrays truth, one betrays himself'. In Novalis (1981) *Vermischte Bemerkungen, 'Blütenstaub' 1797–98*, Werke, Studienausgabe, Gerhard Schulz (ed.), München: C. H. Beck, Second and corrected edition, 331.

4 Paradoxically though, the assumption of the end of grand narratives is by necessity couched within a grand narrative.

5 The only country in the former Soviet bloc where intellectuals – to whom Lyotard refers in his speech – still believed in the possibility of a human and humane form of socialism was the German Democratic Republic (Lyotard 1998: 67–69).

6 Johann Strauss, *Die Fledermaus*, Libretto by Karl Haffner and Richard Genée. First Act (Alfred).

7 Cf. www.oe 24.at/Oesterreich/Politik/Gallup-Umfrage-Strache-fpoe-holt-auf/47613832 (27 November 2011), (accessed 10 February 2012).

Works Cited

Altzinger, W. (2009) *Macht, Verteilung und Demokratie*, Wien: Sonderzahl.

Ash, Timothy G. (1990a): *We the People. The Revolution of '89*, Cambridge: Granta Books.

Berlinguer, E. (1978) *Die internationale Politik der italienischen Kommunisten. Reden und Schriften 1975/76*, (ed.) Antonio Tato, Stuttgart: Klett-Cotta.

Butler, J. (1998) *Hass spricht. Zur Politik des Performativen*, (trans.) Kathrina Menke and Markus Krist, Berlin: Berlin-Verlag.

Dinescu, M. and Maaß, W. (eds) (1990) *Der Eiserne Vorhang bricht. Die Revolution in Osteuropa*, Hamburg: Gruner & Jahr.

Fassmann, Heinz, Müller-Funk, Wolfgang and Uhl, Heidemarie (eds) (2009) *Kulturen der Differenz – Transformationsprozesse in Zentraleuropa nach 1989*, Wien: Vienna University Press.

Fukuyama, F. (1992) *The End of History and the Last Man*, New York: Free Press.

Gruša, J. (2004) 'Als ich ein Feuilleton versprach', *Handbuch des Dissens und Präsens. Essays, Gedanken und Interviews aus den Jahren 1964-2004*, (ed.and trans.) Michael Stavaric, Wien: Czernin.

Handke, P. (1918) *Die Wiederholung*, Frankfurt/Main: Suhrkamp.

Havel, Václav (1980) *Moc Bezmocných* (The Power of the Powerless), German: *Von der Macht der Ohnmächtigen*, (trans. Gabriel Laub), Reinbek: Rowohlt.

Kojéve, Alexandre (1973) *Zusammenfassender Kommentar zu den ersten sechs Kapiteln der Phänomenologie des Geistes*, in Fulda, Hans F. and Henrich, Dieter (eds), *Materialien zu Hegels Phänomenologie des Geistes*, Frankfurt/Main: Suhrkamp, 133–88.

Konrad, G. (1984) *Antipolitics. An Essay*, (trans. Richard Allen), London: Quartet.

Lyotard, J. F. (1986) *Das postmoderne Wissen. Ein Bericht*, (trans. Otto Pfersmann), Wien: Böhlau/Edition Passagen.

——(1994) *The Postmodern Condition*, (trans. Geoff Bennington and Brian Massumi), Foreword by Frederic Jameson, Manchester: Manchester University Press.

——(1998) *Postmoderne Moralitäten*, Wien: Passagen-Verlag.

Magyar Letter (1996) Volume 20, Budapest 1996.

——(2009) *Komplex Österreich. Fragmente zu einer Geschichte der modernen österreichischen Literatur*, Wien: Sonderzahl.

5 Borders in mind or how to re-invent identities

Rüdiger Görner[1]

I

In *The Wall Jumper*, first published in 1984 and translated into English in 2005, the much acclaimed German writer Peter Schneider introduced a prophetic thought that has turned into a truism after the Berlin Wall finally came down: 'It will take us longer to tear down the Wall in our heads than any wrecking company will need for the Wall we can see'.[2] To be sure, the narrator of *The Wall Jumper* refused to get used to the Wall but could not imagine life without it either. By 1984 the GDR had long turned George Orwell's novel of the same year-title into a self-fulfilled prophecy and its fortification, which resembled the security system of an oversized concentration camp, looked – not only to Peter Schneider's narrator – like an immovable manifestation of inhumanity that was to stay for good. The characters in Peter Schneider's novel defined themselves, directly or indirectly, with reference to the Wall; even those who professed that they saw the Wall no more or for whom it had become a boring fact of life. In his lucid reflections on this novel, Ian McEwan remarks that Schneider's narrator accepted that 'if he had been raised in the East, he might well have had all those opinions himself that his friend from East Germany held' (McEwan 2005: 21). By implication, the novel accuses West German writers of having failed to address the problem of the Wall and of a leftist stance that did not allow them to be embarrassed by this Soviet-inspired evidence of brutality. 'It's remarkable', one East Berliner says in this novel, 'how some people who come to visit us talk about nothing but abuses in the West – when we'd be so happy to go over and take a look at their abuses!' (69). The publication of Peter Schneider's *The Wall Jumper* represented at the time a leap across a taboo amongst West German intellectuals. The only other writer vehemently to do likewise was Martin Walser. This very taboo was sanctioned by the majority of intellectuals who subscribed to Günter Grass's idea that the Wall was Germany's punishment for Auschwitz and, therefore, had to stay.

Paradox was one of the main features that conditioned the German and European border experience before and after 1989. As it happened, West Berlin, the thorny jewel in the crown of the West, housed the most radical Marxists, Leninists and Maoists in the Western world. It became a CIA-protected haven of extreme leftism. Calls for a communist world revolution came more frequently from student circles in West Berlin, and their adopted twin town Havana, than from Moscow or Beijng. No other part of the Western world was, in proportional terms, more heavily state-subsidized than West Berlin. Unlike in the rest of West Germany, residents of West Berlin were exempted from military service: hence the youth culture of the city enjoyed constant infusion from youngsters who moved here to avoid conscription. Reflections on the Wall, however, were left to mostly Anglophone commercial thriller writers of espionage fiction. This intellectual set-up was mainly self-indulgent, even when it propagated revolutionary action for the Third World. It was, at any rate, almost entirely oblivious to the concerns of their counterparts across the rivers Elbe and along the Danube.

True, it is rare for writers and intellectuals to set general social, let alone political, agendas. But, arguably, developments that led to the cutting through of the Iron Curtain and to large-scale transformations in Europe were, at least partially, conditioned by East European intellectual concerns with *glasnost* and *perestroika* that had served as initial conceptual indicators of the change to come.[3] Ideas about political reform began, however, with the workers' rebellion in Poland against the so-called workers' state in 1980–81. It was at that time often implied among intellectuals, particularly in the GDR, that it was still possible to reform socialism and retain the identity of the state.

This case is perhaps best exemplified by the maverick writer Ronald M. Schernikau who, after a spectacularly successful start as a novelist, was the last West German to apply for GDR citizenship. Schernikau's *Kleinstadtnovelle* caused a sensation when it was published in 1980 because of its style and subject matter – the coming out of a gay young man in a small town in West Germany. After having immigrated into the GDR during the last year of its existence Schernikau, who died of Aids soon thereafter, published *Die Tage in L.* based on his studies in the Johannes R. Becher Institute in Leipzig, and worked on *Legende*, a montage in prose, published posthumously (1999) with support from Peter Hacks and Elfriede Jelinek (Frings 2009). Schernikau saw himself as a swinger between West and East who had put up his 'divan' right on the border. He contributed a soft hardliner's point of view to the GDR writers' congress in the first days of March 1990. 'Those who are looking for the colourful Western life will instead get the West's sense of desperation'.[4] Loneliness, Schernikau predicted, will become society's number one enemy after the successful 'counter-revolution' that, according to him, had just taken place in Germany and Europe. Schernikau's example not only illustrates the self-delusions of a desperado, but it also epitomizes a state of estrangement from the ideology of the West German state that had meticulously eradicated dogmatism. By 1989, however, the disillusionment and disenchantment with the socialist utopia had gone to the very core of its proponents. Schernikau conceded that any meeting of any Eastern bloc Communist Party Central Committee looked pathetic in comparison to any meeting of the World Bank. And yet, he continued to dream of social consensus whose aesthetic expression was, according to him, the

50   *Rüdiger Görner*

ability to create 'blank verse', a mode of speech that resists infantile rhymes but retains measure and rhythm as well as some notion of inner order.

This was not a merely idiosyncratic oddity of an argument, but supported by one of Heiner Müller's post-1990 epic poems, *Ajax zum Beispiel*. In this poetic deconstruction of ideologies we encounter lines such as 'Communism … exercises self-criticism in conversation with the dead' and the following command: 'Burn the longing for pure rhymes'. The latter, however, is promptly disobeyed as the next lines offer 'pure rhymes': the conceit regarding the transformation of the world into a desert and the day into a *dream* ('Traum') is followed by the phrase 'Reime sind Witze im Einsteinschen Raum' ('Rhymes are but jokes in Einsteinian space'), which in German rhymes on 'Traum'.[5]

Berlin had become for Müller an 'unreal capital' with the 'Mercedes star rotating over the tooth gold of Auschwitz' (Müller 1998: 292). As for the interplay of collectiveness and individualism, the self-abandonment and re-invention of the self, Müller offered the formula 'KEINER ODER ALLE' (none or everyone) implying that even after the collapse of the Wall individualism was dead (Müller 1998: 293). From his point of view, the nuclear and environmental threats continued unchanged as did the Nietzschean 'age of nihilism'.[6] It was clearly a matter of ideological preference whether one considered 1989/90 as a time of revaluation or of devaluation.

The poet Reiner Kunze put this sentiment in a lyrical text, written for the day of German unification on 3 October 1990, under the title *Die Mauer*:

> When we razed it to the ground we had no idea
> just how high it was within us.
> We were used to
> Its horizon
> And the stillness of wind
> In its shadow all of us
> Did not cast any shadows
> Now we stand
> Bare of any excuse.[7]

The Wall has long been a literary object – from Christa Wolf to Peter Schneider; its graffiti have been analysed by iconographers. Frederick Taylor wrote an extraordinary narrated biography of the Wall with its dates in the subtitle (13 August 1961 to 9 November 1989), as if to suggest that the Wall was a living entity that had witnessed the death of many (Taylor 2006). The Wall narratives have emerged as a special form of literature about borders. One recent example of this sub-genre is Edgar Wolfrum's study, *Die Mauer*: this text implies that only narration can offer explanation (Wolfrum 2009). Taylor identified Walter Ulbricht as the main culprit behind the ugly reality of the Wall. He pushed the Soviets into action and, for once, made the East German tail wag the Soviet dog. Wolfrum argues that this large, armed barrier dividing the city in two had a curiously consolidating impact on international relations.

Borders in mind or how to re-invent identities   51

Paradoxically, if not perversely, the Wall speeded up the inner paralysis of the GDR; this fortification against supposed Western 'fascist' aggression ultimately strangled the system and made it implode.

The writer Julia Franck, however, has recently published a revealingly comprehensive anthology of Eastern and Western *Grenzgänger*, or 'borderliners' (Franck 2009). She reminds us of the scathing remarks in West Berlin about people in 'Berlin, Capital of the GDR', only to find that after the Wall had come down people were ecstatic and embracing each other. Which of these reactions, Franck asks twenty years later, was the more genuine and sincere? Was a day or two enough for the Germans to re-invent themselves?

The enterprise was a collective one and the currency of the word 'Volk' was rapidly regaining value. Even though the concept was hopelessly discredited by the Nazis, the idea of *Volksgemeinschaft* was nevertheless, perhaps for a few moments only, in the air. This renewed sense of community achieved by self-liberation – aided by the failing Soviet Union – from state socialism suggested the return of the differentiation between community and society. The concepts were first established by the sociologist Ferdinand Tönnies during the *Kaiserreich*, later to be exploited by ideologues both on the political Right and Left. But in 1990 it was only state socialism that was discredited, not statehood *per se*. Therefore, the West felt justified in offering the GDR its Basic Law ('*Grundgesetz*') as a new term of reference and resisted temptations to call elections for an all-German constitutional assembly. This move would no doubt have captured the political imagination but it could have meant months of instability in what was an extremely volatile situation, especially in view of developments in the Soviet Union.

Images of cutting through metal fences, barbed wire and the tearing down of the Berlin Wall have become emblems of the act of political liberation. The symbolism of opening gates and the dismantling of borders nurtured the illusion of boundless possibilities. The emblematic value of these open pathways surrounded by bewildered border guards – suddenly having become the most redundant of people – is part of the cultural make-up of the Federal Republic of Germany, together with Beethoven's *Fidelio* and pictures of the opening of Nazi concentration camps. But the non-debate on constitutional issues illustrated that the newly acquired boundlessness soon encountered hidden agendas and agreements that limited the scope of free manoeuvring in political as well as other terms.

II

Personal and interpersonal identities are often defined and re-invented against the backdrop of real or imagined borders. It is a truly defining moment in the formation, or development, of personal identities when people admit to getting used to a border imposed on them by force. For instance, from time to time one could hear in both parts of Berlin and along the Iron Curtain that people had become accustomed to this armed, physical barrier. This ability literally to get used to anything is – in anthropological terms – both a disconcerting and a

52 *Rüdiger Görner*

comforting quality of our species. It can inspire resilience but it can also inform a sense of acceptance of suffering followed by indifference.

One of the most deeply rooted legal conventions – both in civil and international law – is the recognition of borders. Human beings are fundamentally territorial and many states employ border guards with a specific brief to protect political demarcations against unlawful trespassing. Legitimate border crossings constitute a privilege of a special kind, the freedom of movement, which is denied to so-called illegal immigrants, whose identity is almost exclusively but collectively defined by their infringement of border regulations. If we think of borders nowadays, we mostly associate them with the problem of immigration as epitomized by the US-Mexican border; or indeed the wall that separates the Palestinian West Bank from Israel. Its name for the Israelis is *ha'harfrada* – Hebrew for 'separation fence'. The Palestinians call it *jidar al-fasl al-'unsun* – Arabic for 'racial segregation wall'. It is, in fact, a means of separation in the Middle East, if not segregation, that has replaced the Berlin Wall. That is to say, borders not only generate narratives or are, in themselves, results of narratives; they bear particular names that constitute a narrative of their own suggesting the way in which they are being interpreted. David Grossman, the Israeli novelist, said in a conversation with David Hare about that very border: 'I want to begin to live. I want some gates in the wall' (Hare 2009: 12).

Meanwhile, in Berlin, the Wall is being remembered by a copper stripe along the lines where it once stood, to walk along or to cross by but a small step. Yet, it is conceivable that one can develop, somewhat belatedly, a border-dog-syndrome and keep walking along that very stripe, unable to make this small easy step across the copper band, fixated on, or in some cases traumatized by, personal memories, film snippets and photographs of failed attempts to cross that border in the past that keep haunting some of us.

Borders are more than dividing lines; they signify political and ideological demarcations that rarely correspond to geographical maps. Borders redefine themselves in our consciousness and collective memory. This is why the borders of the past are often more present in us than the borders of today. But in view of the virtual abolition of borders in the Schengen Agreement within the clearly demarcated political space of most of the European Union, we have lost the hidden delights or thrills of the physical border crossing experience, as Karl-Markus Gauss once pointed out (Gauss 2005). At the same time, the Schengen-zone is perceived by some from the outside, rightly or wrongly, as a bastion of borders.

Normally we associate ugliness with political borders: we imagine them as no-man's lands full of neglect and dereliction. With the exception of the Great Wall in China, Hadrian's Wall and the Roman Limes across Germany as well as, formerly, the Berlin Wall, borders tend not to be tourist attractions. Many would consider the borders between the United States and Mexico or in the West Bank as eyesores of an appalling kind. But the vertical death stripe of the Iron Curtain was ugliness in perfection. Geographical borders can count more on our appreciation. Mountains, coastlines, rivers often enjoy the benefit of natural beauty. Borders are partly determined by particular periods in time and culture

Borders in mind or how to re-invent identities 53

and, in the Western hemisphere in particular, less by states than by ethnic identities. The cultural, social and ethnic borders within a state, or community, exercise our minds today. These borders are by no means more transparent, or fluid, than state borders; often they are tribal or clan-related with particular ethnic communities being more territorially minded than others. Immigrants often form identifiable cultural pockets within a particular district or township. Social rivalries, religious tensions, the ability of one community to expand at the expense of others, but also common interests for immigrant cultures to co-exist peacefully, or even to interact constructively, will be telling about the nature of their boundaries. An all-integration policy should regard it desirable to make such boundaries disappear. But is their disappearance the main indicator of a successful integration policy or should a community support the retention of those cultural identities and the boundaries that go with them? Is the aim of integration to enable ethnic communities to learn how to live with such boundaries yet to facilitate their transgression whenever this is desired?

The contribution of German-Turkish literature to this particular problem is, from my point of view, as impressive as that of the German *Mauerliteratur* to the genre of border literature. Often, it is the literature from within such communities that enhances our understanding of their concerns, be it Monica Ali's novel *Brick Lane* or Hanif Kureishi's *The Buddha of Suburbia*. The transgression of national borders or cultural, if not ethnic, boundaries by means of literature leads to hybrid narratives or rather to cultural hybridization through narration. It can happen, as in the case of Monica Ali's novel, that the ethnic group in question (here the Bengali community in London's Tower Hamlets) rejects such artistic hybridization simply because it regards it as a corruption of its culture, if not a betrayal of its cherished traditions, which it is striving to uphold.

If seen against the backdrop of these border and boundary-related developments it is particularly fitting that an emblematic novel on this subject was rediscovered most recently. Géza Ottlik's *The School on the Border*, was first published in 1959, three years after the Hungarian uprising. The plot takes place in the mid-1920s in the Hungarian military boarding school of Köszeg. The word 'border' refers to the geographical location of Köszeg/Güns, the historical moment in time (end of the Habsburg empire whose legacy is, however, still omnipresent) and the borderline experiences to which these pupils are exposed, or rather subjected. More importantly though, it is the pain, betrayal, hatred, and mental and physical cruelty elicited in them by the repression of their masters that drives these youngsters towards the border of what is humanly endurable. For evil, too, is boarding in this school. The two narrators demonstrate, however, that imagination, emotion and the sheer act of writing can overcome these demarcations of evil.

III

As we have seen social, cultural, political and geographical dimensions join up both in the reality and in the imagery of borders. But they are challenging and

54   Rüdiger Görner

suggestive enough to invite transgressions. Any moment of transgression, however, includes a metaphysical experience. The most poignant reminder of the new social and mental borders in Europe, those between north and south, came from Claudio Magris in his acceptance speech on receiving the *Friedenspreis des Deutschen Buchhandels* (Peace Award of the German Booksellers Association) in autumn 2009 in Frankfurt. His judgement was echoed by Karl Schlögel, one of the most eminent historians of Central and Eastern Europe, in his laudatory speech on Magris. Both Magris's and Schlögel's views derive from urban identities that were, and are still, conditioned by border experiences. For Magris's Trieste and Schlögel's Frankfurt-an-der-Oder have been conditioned by belonging to borderlands. In the case of Frankfurt this status appeared in 1945, when the river Oder turned into the borderline between East Germany and Poland. Trieste, however, has been the capital of multiculturalism on the Adriatic coast for a long time. Serbs and Slovenians, Italians and Austrians have shaped this former principal sea port of the Austro-Hungarian Empire. Serb Judaism was prominent in the city for over three centuries or so, but particularly strong in the late eighteenth and in the nineteenth centuries. Magris has frequently pointed out that Trieste consisted of a multitude of borders, often along certain roads and around particular squares. The complex history of that city represents the idea of *Mitteleuropa* in a nutshell. Once a hub of commercial and cultural activities, perhaps never more so than before the First World War when the young James Joyce fell in love with this city,[8] it suffered from conflicting claims of ethnic groups after 1918 and from virtual isolation after 1945. Trieste in the South East and Gdansk in the North East of Central Europe are comparable in their contribution to the cross-formations of ethnic border identities, accentuated by the fact that both cities offered, thanks to their geographical location, a sense of openness and worldliness that seemed to counteract narrow-minded, if not dogmatic, ethnic priorities.

Trieste with its hinterland in Slovenia and Croatia exemplifies the mutual dependency between borders, real and imagined, and the formation of cultural identities. The Balkans south of Slovenia, however, remain an area where, in present-day Europe, border conflicts determine collective and individual consciousness within and outside ethnic enclaves. The Serb poet Stevan Tontić, born in 1946 in the Western part of Serbian Bosnia – today part of the Bosnian-Croat Federation – published a poem in 1993 under the title 'Granica' (border):

> Without having moved away from the threshold
> Or from the seam of a woman's skirt, not even one inch,
> I woke up in a new state,
> An acquaintance of mine told me.
> The Border was drawn
> right through my heart.
> Reason begins to comprehend and justify,
> the mad heart though is beating and denying.

I totter:
neither rising to make but one step
nor cast down to bed myself on the soil.

(Tontic 1993: 17)

Even though this was written by a Serb belonging to one of the many diasporas scattered across the states of the Balkans, this poem could have been written by any poet belonging to any ethnic minority there.

All too often it is forgotten that through the fall of the Berlin Wall and the Iron Curtain, the Balkans experienced the building up of new borders. The Austrian poet Peter Handke who, since 1991, has become a staunch, if not blinkered, defender of Serbia and the Serbian minorities in Croatia and Bosnia, argued as late as June 2006, that Slovenia, especially, had successfully taken advantage of her proximity to affluent Western European states; this, according to Handke, had made her erect virtual and real walls against the Serbs and Macedonians, against the Muslims and Albanians (Handke 2006). The ethnic cleansing that took place in the enclave of Srebrenica, committed by the Serbian army, was arguably the cruellest reminder of the *longue durée* of historical conflicts and ethnic hatred which got out of control after the break-up of former Yugoslavia. But let us remind ourselves of the sheer complexity when it comes to assessing this almost perpetual crisis area in Europe. Between 1941 and 1945 Nazi occupation made shameless use of these ethnic rivalries, supporting nationalists on all sides to fight against each other. This occupation had tried to ignite a whole system of civil wars in the Balkans and, in doing so, perpetuate Nazi rule. When in spring 1945, Tito's partisans had succeeded in liberating most of Yugoslavia from Nazi occupation, it showed an extraordinary lack of sensitivity when the British Army extradited over 12,000 Slovenian soldiers to the Serbs. These men had tried to find refuge in Austria from Tito's troops and were later killed as traitors (Kolman 1970). Clearly, ethnic and state identity in the Balkans continues to be, for historical reasons like this one, precariously in flux.

IV

The memory of the Iron Curtain and especially the Berlin Wall – this most emblematic border of borders – insists on having the last word in this essay. It was the despicable banality of its crude architecture that made its memory undeletable for those who ever saw it. The first time that the Berlin Wall partly collapsed was on 11 January 1962 when some twenty metres of it gave way owing to deficiencies in its constructions. It was, after all, a wall without foundations and consequently soon exposed to erosion. Its upkeep required constant attention, which was time-consuming and expensive. On the Eastern side of the Wall, people were encouraged to have allotments, grow flowers and shrubs, and erect ornamental fences (Briese 2009). Here, the socialist *petit bourgeois* was encouraged to turn himself into a garden gnome – the perfect kitsch against the backdrop of

56 Rüdiger Görner

ugliness. Given the sheer depth of this entire border system there were long stretches of the Wall that people in East Germany could actually not see. The Wall was there but people were supposed to forget about it. This Wall of walls was turned by GDR propaganda into a paradoxical project of visible invisibility. By the same token, but in more aesthetic terms, one could argue that the Wall was the one-dimensional reduction of the Bauhaus principle, namely to let simple forms speak whatever they have to say.[9]

The philosophical problem of the 'border situations', or 'border experiences' (*Grenzsituationen/Grenzerfahrungen*), as developed by Karl Jaspers referred to the terminal inevitability of ageing and death (Jaspers 1971: 20). It did not include considerations of what happens to individuals, or groups of people for that matter, who are suddenly liberated from such an exposure to finality. What are the after-effects of a lifted border experience? Its existential dimension remains live in the sense that the border experience is shifted to other socio-geographical or psychological areas. Twenty years after 1989 we are still experiencing this very shift, even though the remains of the Wall have long been recycled, turned into museum pieces, and used by construction firms as gravel and sand.

Notes

1 Unless otherwise indicated, translations are mine (RG).
2 Peter Schneider (1982) *Der Mauerspringer. Erzählung*, Darmstadt und Neuwied: Luchterhand Verlag, p. 45; Engl. translation: *The Wall Jumper* (2005), trans. by Leigh Hafrey, with an Introduction by Ian McEwan, Harmondsworth: Penguin, p. 64. Astrid Köhler has shown that a great deal of Schneider's inspiration for this story came from his friend and writer Klaus Schlesinger, including the idea for the very title. Schneider's protagonist, Pommerer, is – to a certain degree – Schlesinger's *alter ego*, (Köhler 2011: 10; 192).
3 For a comprehensive discussion of the concept and significance of the 'Iron Curtain' as well as its political semantics see Wright 2007.
4 See www.schernikau.net.
5 H. Müller, *Werke 1*, ed. by F. Hörnigk, Frankfurt am Main: Suhrkamp Verlag, 1998, 292–97; quote 297.
6 Cf. the lucid comment on this particular issue in Michael Ostheimer, 'Der Stier ist geschlachtet. Heiner Müller berichtigt einen Mythos', in *Neue Zürcher Zeitung*, 10–11 August 2002: 62.
7 In Karl Otto Conrady (ed.) *Von einem Öland und vom andern. Gedichte zur deutschen Wende*, Edition Suhrkamp 1829. Frankfurt am Main 1993, quoted from Peter Horst Neumann, 'Ist das Wende-Jahr 1989 auch ein Datum der Literaturgeschichte?' in *Erlanger Forschungen*, Reihe A, Band 104, Erlangen 2003 (29–43): 36. For further discussion see Görner 2007: 59–74.
8 Joyce stayed in Trieste until 1915 with two short interruptions in 1906 (in Rome) and 1909 (Dublin).
9 Walter Gropius (1919) *Bauhaus Manifest und Programm*, Weimar.

Works Cited

Briese, O. (2009) ' Die Banalität des Bauwerks. Ästhetik der Berliner Mauer', Interview with Andreja Andrisevic, in *Frankfurter Rundschau*, 3 November (No. 255).

Franck, J. (ed.) (2009) *Grenzgänger. Autoren aus Ost und West erinnern sich*, Frankfurt am Main: S. Fischer Verlag.

Frings, M. (2009) *Der letzte Kommunist. Das traumhafte Leben des Ronald M. Schernikau*, Berlin: Aufbau Verlag.

Gauss, K. M. (2005) 'Arbeit an Europa. Von den verlorenen Freuden des Grenzübertritts', *Neue Zürcher Zeitung*, 24–25 December: 59.

Görner, R. (2007) 'Notes on the Culture of Borders' in Johan Schimanski and Stephen Wolfe (eds) *Border Poetics De-limited, Tromsøer Studien zur Kulturwissenschaft*, Vol. 9, Hannover: Wehrhan Verlag: 59–74.

Handke, P. (2006) 'Der lange Abschied von Jugoslawien', *Neue Zürcher Zeitung*, 17 June.

Hare, D. (2009) 'Wall: A Monologue', *New York Review of Books*, 30 April: 8–12.

Jaspers, K. (1971) *Einführung in die Philosophie*, München: Piper.

Köhler, A. (2011) *Klaus Schlesinger. Die Biographie*, Berlin: Aufbau Verlag.

Kolman, L. (1970) White Paper, Historian Committee of the American Slovenian Anti-Communist War Veterans Association – Tabor (1 June).

McEwan, I. (2005) 'A Tale of Two Cities' in 'Review Saturday', *The Guardian*, 22 October: 21.

Müller, H. (1998) *Werke 1*, (ed. F. Hörnigk), Frankfurt am Main: Suhrkamp Verlag.

Ottlik, G. (2009) *Die Schule an der Grenze*, (trans.) Charlotte Ujlaky, *Die Andere Bibliothek* 293, Frankfurt am Main: Eichborn-Verlag.

Taylor, F. (2006) *The Berlin Wall*, London: Bloomsbury.

Tontic, S. (1993) *Handschrift aus Sarajevo*, third edition, Belgrade: Weilerswist.

Wolfrum, E. (2009) *Die Mauer. Geschichte einer Teilung*, München: Verlag C. H. Beck.

Wright, P. (2007) *Iron Curtain. From Stage to Cold War*, Oxford: Oxford University Press.

6 The Iron Curtain, the Wall and performative *Verfremdung*

Annelis Kuhlmann[1]

Since the paradigm shift of 1989, theatre has been dealing with the problem of divided space in aesthetically different and challenging ways. Added to this, after the fall of the Twin Towers in 2001, we have seen some remarkable theatre performances that have reflected society's collapsing sense of stability. In the early 1990s journals produced special issues concerned with the agenda for the stage after the fall of the Iron Curtain (*Theatre Journal* 1993 and Schechner 1990). With the benefit of hindsight today, however, it is possible to glean a more perceptive perspective. In the theatre different laws apply from ordinary daily life. At certain historical moments though, the wall between real life and theatrical action crumbles and it is specifically this uncertain space, bridging the divide between the worlds on and off stage, that this essay will aim to discuss. Elinor Fuchs wrote of how '[t]heater becomes a kind of security zone between non-cohering realms, the threshold between the twin problematic of the playwright's imagination and the materiality of the world' (Fuchs 1996: 156). Clearly, the nature of this threshold changes when events pass the boundary between spaces and the question of how to deal aesthetically with the border arises. A performative *Verfremdungseffekt*[2] – a device of stage performance that creates a sense of estrangement for the audience – is one way of combining the matter and the form of the theatre.

The concept of *Verfremdungseffekt* will be considered here not only in consideration of the fall of the Berlin Wall – this exposed part of the Iron Curtain – and repercussions of this event for theatre, but also the fall of imaginary and illusory walls inside performative space. The notion of the wall becomes a double wall in the theatre. To illustrate this we shall assess a number of European performances affected by the impact of the fall of physical barriers dividing Western Europe from the erstwhile Communist East. We shall juxtapose the socio-political experience of theatre history with subjective experiences of performance. If the 'wall' dividing performance and audience falls, will conventional theatre crumble too, and if so, how may this be identified within the aesthetics of production? In other words, how can we consider the fall of the wall as a question of theatre?

The notion of the 'Iron Curtain' is obviously a theatre-related metaphor. It refers to a stiff, vertical border-line between the stage and the audience but it

The Iron Curtain and performative Verfremdung   59

is also a psychological phenomenon affecting performance. The physical function of the Iron Curtain is to serve as protection from fire or other emergencies on stage that could harm the spectators. This is the traditional rationale for the iron curtain in the theatre. But this device could also be viewed as a form of protection of the stage from the audience. The audience could react against the production in a powerful, unexpected or uncontrollable manner. Although today this is unlikely to happen, in the past it was known for spectators to throw tomatoes onto the stage if they were not pleased with what they saw.

Years become magical, even dates are worthy of memories like birthdays. They are orientation points for us – places where we can stop, recall, mourn or celebrate. Time becomes like a pocket that you can sneak into if you have a moment to spare. Time can be associated with symbolic numbers, linked to events and to the cultural changes that ensue. The fall of the Berlin Wall (9 November 1989) opened up the notion of space for art. But the fall of the Twin Towers of the World Trade Centre in New York on 11 September 2001 occurred in this post-Iron-Curtain order. This event triggered the collapse of the notion of space in art.

Dramaturgical perception benefits from framing history in terms of events taking place around turning points. These turning points – like the rise and fall of the Berlin Wall and like 11 September 2001 – can be seen as a kind of breakthrough in the past, or a historical change in direction. Major changes of fortune owing to human error or such natural calamities as earthquakes give rise to productive foci in the cultural history of theatre, probably because of their imbedded potential to generate conflict. These turning points – what Aristotle called *peripeteia* – produce new perspectives. Of course, more than one single frame of reference exists for grasping and responding to the consequences of the fall of the Iron Curtain. We shall take advantage of the significant parallels that may be drawn between the notion of the Berlin Wall and what in theatre is called the fourth wall.

In 2001 in the courtyard of the Kronborg Castle in Elsinore, Denmark, a production of *Hamlet* was staged by the Lithuanian theatre director Eimuntas Nekrošius.[3] The inevitable consequence of the crimes at the end of the tragedy – when most of the principal characters are murdered – was visualized with a huge ice cube hanging on a rough chain over the stage, melting slowly. Alluding to the cold war between empires destined to fall, the drips looked like a curtain of rain as they were blown in the wind and lit by the spotlight. Little by little it became evident how the frozen material contained the dagger, which Hamlet would use to kill in cold blood in order to take revenge on his father's death. The change of political systems found its metaphor in a game with the supernatural.

Since the advent of the concept of the national theatre in the nineteenth century and since the beginnings of representational, verisimilar productions on stage from the eighteenth century, theatres in Europe have experienced different forms of cultural heritage. Many of the original theatres belonged to such centres of political power as emperors' palaces or royal courts. As a result, the exterior of the theatre was in many cases physically imposing and built of materials to last

60   *Annelis Kuhlmann*

through the centuries to come. The stage met the audience at the proscenium arch where most theatres hung heavy curtains hiding performers from spectators (and vice versa) until the start of the performance. Normally, what was occurring on stage was representing reality created within dramatic fiction, often intended for performances in theatres of this kind of architectural design. And over the years, not only did actors develop particular performing styles connected to this space; the building also elicited a style of behaviour and manners of communication on the side of the audience. Thereby at least two sets of performative behaviour came to share the theatre. Furthermore, a third form of behaviour – that of the monarch when present – could have an impact on conventions both on the stage and among the spectators. These juxtaposed forms of reality affected both the comic and the tragic forms of drama.

Thus the legacy of dividing shared space within the building became the most powerful convention to underpin our contemporary forms of theatre and one to last even after many physical and metaphorical walls and curtains have been torn down within society and between countries. One of the lessons learned by theatre spectators and critics after the fall of the Berlin Wall was that history and historiography had reached a turning point. The causes and effects of what many scholars of theatre knew from history up until 1989 were no longer valid. Take the unpredictability of this event itself: nobody could have predicted the exact timing of the end of the Cold War. Only the American president Ronald Reagan – originally an actor – dared to suggest that Soviet General Secretary, Mikhail Gorbachev, should 'tear down this wall'. The theatrical convention – spectators anticipating the end of the play even as it is being performed – was never transferred to the geopolitical situation with respect to the destiny of the Berlin Wall. The fall of the wall was for many politicians the unpredictable event marking the end of the Iron Curtain. In the theatre, however, the fall of the wall could be attributed to the demand for renewed signification of the notion of presence, and as such its fall was expected.

In European theatre for decades, if not centuries, the curtain had not really been a curtain per se but a signifier of this object's aesthetic function. Throughout its entire existence it has had its opponents. Hence instability and aesthetic premise are inherent in the very notion of the curtain. The fall of the wall emphasized that our own mentality and our own conventional image of the world could change and could in fact be followed by perceptions of an unstable world. This impression has been expressed in many different ways in European theatres. The historical notion of presence on stage or in the ranks of the audience had by 1989 collapsed, or at least the perception of presence had been endowed with new meanings.

> 'Life must be represented not as it is,
> neither as it ought to be;
> but as it appears in dreams'[4]

In 1895 the Russian playwright Anton Chekhov in *The Seagull* made the character of Konstanin Treplev, a young man aspiring to become a playwright, explore

The Iron Curtain and performative Verfremdung   61

new dramatic forms in his play-within-the-play, and at a certain moment he articulates the cited words above to his beloved, also his leading actress, Nina Zarechnaya. Treplev engages here with the age-old debate about the role of how theatre should represent the world. His thoughts at the dawn of Symbolism revolve around the removal of boundaries in the creation of theatrical imagery. If Konstantin had lived in Eastern Europe in the 1980s, a theatre without curtains would doubtless have appeared in his dreams. Theatre in Europe was envisaged as a *shared event*. Teatron – one of the oldest concepts of theatre in Ancient Greece – implies the gaze of a physically present spectator: if there is no spectator, there is no theatre. It is this specific relationship between stage and audience, this double presence, that has been called a unique art of the moment and what Erika Fischer-Lichte called 'co-presence' (Fischer-Lichte 2008: 38). In her view, not only the performer has an impact on the spectator but the spectator also has an impact on the performer. The performer thus is no longer simply transformed through a kind of romantic inspiration but the spectator also becomes an active participant. This unique relationship in contemporary theatre performances recalls a less representational, but more ritualistic understanding of the theatrical event.

During performance we witness changing attitudes among the characters on stage. But an aesthetic connection also occurs between the world of the stage and the world of the spectators. The disposition of the latter towards events and characters on stage also keeps being affected by constant changes.

A dramatic narrative about changing mentalities is not exclusively based on singular and individual opinions; it is in the most plural sense a collective matter. As the years go by there are inevitably fewer and fewer people around in Germany who remember theatre' prior to the building of the Berlin Wall. Thus we need to rely on memoirs, reviews, film footage and, of course, documentary materials pertaining to the performance to grasp the moments of 'before' and 'after'. This issue informs the play *Vorher/Nachher* (2002), written by the contemporary German playwright, Roland Schimmelphennig. The play consists of more than fifty scenes, drawing upon the Brechtian technique of *Verfremdungseffekt* as a compositional form; characters exist in both first and third person ('I' and 'he', 'I' and 'she'). In this way the author creates doubles both for characters and locations (Brecht 1963: 153). Doubling captures time both in retrospect and as a vision of the future. The notion of presence appears in a 'gap' between the past and the future. Schizophrenically, the present becomes squeezed into a space between *before* and *after*.

Schimmelphennig addresses the *absence of presence*. In performance this means that the actors mainly perform their relationships with the other characters filling the zone of absence with a sense of life. Aesthetically the technique of performing absence takes place through leaning on conventions from a performative use of the *Verfremdungseffekt*. On a thematic level the *Verfremdungseffekt* is turned into a performative topic on stage, and in many of the situations the question of time and space on stage draws on the traditions of the theatre of the absurd. In *Vorher/Nachher* lives are divided within the ambient condition of

62   *Annelis Kuhlmann*

time and space, thereby characterizing the mentality of late modern subjectivity in an unforeseeably changing world. In addition to addressing the dilemma of past and presence, the play also scrutinizes the heritage of local theatre stages in Berlin, especially those with some relation to the destiny of the legendary Berliner Ensemble, founded by Bertolt Brecht and his wife, the actress Helena Weigel, in 1949, only a few months before Germany was divided into two states.

The curtain in theatre has a much longer history than the iron curtain. However, since the appearance of the geopolitical Iron Curtain across Europe after World War II, artistic attempts to manipulate the relationship between the curtain and the stage in the theatre have obtained a new set of references. Bertolt Brecht found that the curtain – like a guillotine – could cut off the stage from the audience. In order to change this situation but still hide some of the preparations on stage he suggested a 'half-size' curtain, which would add a new symbolic dimension to the spectator's visual experience. The half-size curtain would allow the spectator to see the curtain not only as an object that covers part of the stage, but also as a device for eliciting ideas about what the curtain does *not* cover (Fuegi 1987: 141). Thus ironically, like a mask, the curtain could become both a means for covering and discovering at the same time. A sophisticated realization of the half-size curtain occurred shortly before the fall of the wall – the end of communism in Easter Europe, that is – in the Russian theatre director Anatoly Vasiliev's famous staging of Luigi Pirandello's modernistic play, *Six Characters in Search of an Author*. This production also marked the opening of his theatre, the School of Dramatic Art, in 1987. The performance provided an 'in-between space', a transparent curtain passed diagonally through the entire space of the theatre, forming a dividing line that crossed both the space of the stage and the space of the audience. This use of the curtain enhanced the sense of division and the imaginative borders that the geopolitical Iron Curtain was about to leave behind. Practically all the actors came into contact with the curtain, either playing with it or using its conventional functions to cover or to uncover. Spectators were able to watch the action occurring on both sides of the curtain simultaneously. The discordant curtain managed to upset the spectator's conventional perception of 'here' and 'there'. The performances of *Six Characters in Search of an Author* elicited unexpectedly strong reactions among different audiences around the world. For several years the performance was on tour; the modernist play could clearly convey a sense of people's abused illusions and their desperate resistance against Wall and Curtain that imprisoned them. In several of Vasiliev's subsequent performances this emblematic use of the curtain would convey the sense that we would never become convinced that the Curtain would ever disappear. Of course, this was not only a piece of theatre but also a profound comment about human illusions.

The performance *Lamentations of Jeremiah*, directed by Vasiliev in 1996, was based on the Biblical myth about the destruction of the walls of the capital of Jerusalem (Borisova 2003). The scenography for this tragedy revolved around a heavy-set Holy Wall, which during the one-act performance was slowly falling towards the ground, eventually to rise again. Accompanied by lyrics sung to

The Iron Curtain and performative Verfremdung   63

music inspired by the Middle Ages, composed by Vladimir Martynov, the play dealt with the theme of falling and rising. This powerful staged metaphor, together with the numerous allusions to the history of a divided society, turned out to be a monumental statement about the mental wall that remained after the fall of the Iron Curtain. While *Six Characters in Search of an Author* addressed the absence of faith on a metatheatrical level, the *Lamentations of Jeremiah* embodied the mystery of lamentation as a basic requirement in contemporary tragedy.

The second connotation of the 'Iron Curtain' concerns the so called *fourth wall*, an expression which is traditionally used about the imaginary 'wall' at the front of the stage in the proscenium. Historically, the notion of the fourth wall was used by Jean-Baptiste de Molière in the metatheatrical play *L'Impromptu de Versailles*, but it has mostly been associated with Denis Diderot's *De la poésie dramatique* (1758), and later *Le Paradoxe sur le comédien* (1773). The latter explores the paradox of the transitory space of the actor situated between the stage and the audience (Pavis 2002: 7). During the nineteenth century this 'invisible' illusory wall gained prominence in the increasingly popular theatre of realism and of naturalism. The stage between the 1870s and the 1890s often represented the inside of a bourgeois house, perhaps the dining or living room. These spaces were enclosed except for one wall – the side facing the audience – which was physically missing, enabling the spectators to see what was happening within.

During the twentieth century different ways of organizing theatrical space were explored but, surprisingly, realist practices of the late nineteenth century still prevail in the majority of theatres in the first decade of the twenty-first century. This leaves the spectators open to manipulation by the potential fourth wall. The represented life on stage is thus viewed from a particular angle as if it were a living tableau. This set-up also has a strong affect on the actors on stage. From the mid-nineteenth century, the use of gas and, later, electric lamps made it possible for the lights in the stalls, circles and boxes to go out before the act commenced. Simultaneously, the spotlight points in the direction of the stage and the actors can physically sense but no longer see the spectators: they are 'blinded' by the light coming from the direction of the audience. The actors can only see the reality of their own fictional world from the inside. In this situation the actors mostly act as if there were no spectators watching and witnessing what happens on stage. The actors play within the convention of this 'fourth wall' that marks the boundary between the fictional reality of the world on stage and the non-fictional, real world of the spectators. The 'fourth wall' begs the question though: which one of the two worlds is more illusory?

The discursive context of the fall of the wall configures allegories for life in divided European society. In January and February of 2010, within a double bill at Aarhus Teater, the municipal theatre in Denmark's second largest city, the German director Milan Peschel staged a shortened version of Henrik Ibsen's *A Doll's House*. The stage design was created by the Norwegian director Rolf Alme. He was also the author of the second play, *Nora's Sons*. The two performances took place within the same set where the floor of the stage looked

64 *Annelis Kuhlmann*

like a skateboard ramp. Moving about, the actors kept falling at regular intervals, conjuring up the image of a crumbling wall. The characters played with Lego bricks placed on the stage to represent the remnants of a deconstructed doll's house. The political symbol had become a pedagogical toy and the ramp supplied the physical barrier between the stage and the audience. While watching the performance many spectators had the impression that the whole set might collapse and fall on the audience. This, of course, did not happen. The possibility, however, that the stage – alongside the traditions it represents – could crumble and fall created a context for contemplating the human dimensions of the physical disappearance of barbed wired fences and walls keeping people apart. That in the meantime the dialogue in Ibsen's *A Doll's House* was addressing the problem of whether or not Nora should leave her husband obviously enriched the allegory further still. The construction of new identities on the basis of the heritage left behind by the Berlin Wall and the Iron Curtain would always be a reminder of an inescapable recent past.

As the Iron Curtain became a reality shortly after the end of World War II in 1948, ironically one of the most celebrated international drama festivals, the Festival d'Avignon, founded by Jean Vilar (1912–71), also emerged that year. From the beginning it was clear that the festival intended to make a statement: the aggressions of war were over and, at least in the theatre, people should be able to come together regardless of the emerging geographical and political boundaries in Europe. The purpose was to heal Europe, to overcome the wounds and to learn to live with the wandering ghosts of the past. Yet Eastern Europeans could not attend freely because of the often insurmountable restrictions on travel to the West. Only carefully vetted 'delegations' comprised of 'loyal' citizens of their communist states would be authorized to travel to Avignon. The records of the Avignon Festival chronicle events in both European 'theatres' (the stage) and the potential zone of conflict along both sides of the Iron Curtain. They also trace the fate of the so-called off-repertoire – both in theatre and in society – which was, little by little, reaching mainstream status.

Another important theatre festival in Europe is the Berliner Festspiele – Theatertreffen, which since 1964 – the year of its foundation in the Western part of the city, shortly after the building of the Berlin Wall – has become an important forum for experimental theatre. After almost half a century, it still fulfils an important role. After the end of communism in Europe, many other festivals have developed. Since the 1990s practically all European countries have been running international theatre workshops and festivals. The notion of the theatre festival has become the gateway to international relationships and markets. Not only do audiences come from different places to see performances from different countries, but these events emphasise the need for forums for professional exchange and provide the platform for presenting cultural products and works of art. These micro-units of globalization within the world of theatre have always encouraged artists to break down walls within their craft. When considered from the vantage point of these festivals, it would seem that walls in theatre had begun to fall long before political and economic walls.

The Iron Curtain and performative Verfremdung   65

Prevailing attitudes among Western European playwrights and directors were changing in the 1950s. John Osborne's play, *Look Back in Anger*, first performed in 1956, was one of the first successful British plays to reflect the post-war frustration. The psychological issues in the play emphasised that the new society in peacetime might simply revert to the ways of the old regime. Europeans had seemingly longed for the healing process in drama after the war. A few years earlier Samuel Beckett's first plays had seen the light of day, with the emblematic *En attendant Godot*, 1948/49 (*Waiting for Godot*, 1955), which often was interpreted as an existential abyss of hopelessness, taking the audience into the territory of the theatre of the absurd. This term was coined by Martin Esslin in *The Theatre of the Absurd* (Esslin 1961), perhaps subconsciously reflecting the Berlin Wall that was built the same year. By the early 1960s, the notion of *dramatic perspective* was changing and a new negotiation of presence in the theatre was taking place. The characters on stage had become means for voicing contemplation of minds locked within their own separated individual worlds. Dialogue ceased to move the play forward. The conceptualisation of these solitary worlds had become reality on the stage, as it was in Europe, thanks to the Iron Curtain, whose deadly symbolism was later reinforced by the Berlin Wall.

When Georgio Strehler at his Piccolo Teatro in Milan staged Chekhov's *The Cherry Orchard* in 1955 and then again in 1974, he signified the nostalgic view from the land of lost childhood by confronting the spectators with a pure white stage set. The toys belonging to the children formed a wall before the audience in the shape of the city's skyline. This way of considering border-lines – registered within children's acculturation into society and formative within their identities – was a strong metatheatrical statement about walls. Chekhov's classic was recreated for its potential to tell stories about our life and the nostalgic gaze of a lost innocence and the subsequent vision of alienation in metropolitan space yet again drew upon the symbolic potential of the wall.

The classical Aristotelian normative perception of character was challenged by Bertolt Brecht through his *Verfremdungstechnik*. Brecht's purpose in depriving characters of their sense of situation and context was to re-educate the spectator in an attempt to tear down walls demarcating bourgeois life. By the postmodern 1960s, however, the *Verfremdungstechnik* was being used to different ends in addressing the audience. The disruption of the unity of the character became a question of subjectivity in a broad sense. Roland Barthes's famous text, 'The Death of the Author' (Barthes 1977 [1967]), offered new theatrical perspectives on the notion of the authorial subject, while Wolfgang Iser stressed the 'gap' that spectators would need to fill in for themselves to create meaning in the play enacted on stage. The idea of the 'death of the character' (Fuchs 1996: 169 ff) shifted the emphasis from Pirandello's modernist search of an author towards the search for the lost content of the subject.

In the 1960s the actor's body became regarded as basic material for creating a performance. Jerzy Grotowski's experimental Laboratory Theatre in Wroclaw, Poland, comprised thirteen rows in his search for new ways of letting the

66 Annelis Kuhlmann

actor's expressivity perform the trauma of humanity. This topos had previously been discussed in Antonin Artaud's first and second manifesto on the theatre of cruelty in 1938 (Artaud 2010: 89–101; 122–33). What Grotowski called '*via negativa*' rejected the 'satisfied' attitude and the 'novelty for novelty's sake' theatre (Grotowski 1984: 101). The Laboratory Theatre's performance in 1967 of *The Constant Prince* in Juliusz Slowacki's free Polish adaptation from Calderón evoked memories of living under conditions similar to those in a concentration camp. Post-traumatic stress came across in representations of punishment, the sounds of humiliation, the music of capturing pain (Osinski and Burzynski 1979: 37 ff). It was as if the classical Greek notion of catharsis, normally considered a concern for the spectators or the witnesses of the tragic event, had now entered the stage and taken exile inside the actors' bodies. This new orientation had the greatest impact on the work of Peter Brook and Eugenio Barba.

The years of the Berlin Wall, 1961–89, were a time both for *isolation* and *revolution*. This is a key to understanding the consequences of the construction of the wall because, in the theatre at least, the response was self-conscious performance whose main concern was with itself – performance. The action no longer had either a beginning or an end. Peter Brook's concept of *empty space* stood for the passing of characters, stories and dramatists (Brook 1968). The empty space annihilated both the curtain and the 'fourth wall'. Emptiness needed neither limits nor borders: these had been relegated to the spectator's imagination. With the benefit of hindsight it is astonishing that it took twenty years for the imbedded paradox implied in the concept of empty space to be understood as a metaphor for the political geography of European society. Peter Brook used empty space when directing the intercultural production of *Mahabharata* (1985) based on the ancient Indian epic and presented for the first time at the Festival d'Avignon that we have discussed earlier.

In 1967, as Grotowski's Polish experiments were taking place, new methods of theatrical production were being developed by the French director, Ariane Mnouchkine. Her troupe, Le Théâtre du Soleil, produced the '*création collective*' (Williams 1999), noted for its collaborative performances which replaced the more conventional hierarchical approach in which all decisions came from the director while the rest of the employees followed instructions. The collective initiated a new sort of group dynamism for producing theatre, which had a distinct socio-political impact. In 1970, Le Théâtre du Soleil created a production with a memorable title: *1789*. It dealt with the collective memory of one of the fundamental events of not only French but also European history, the French Revolution. The production's aesthetic narrative strategy enabled the spectators to participate in the creation of the performance. The play had a spatial composition in which there was no single centre providing space for the major narrative and action; instead, multiple spaces of action spread over several smaller stages within the the huge space in La Cartoucherie on the outskirts of Paris. During simultaneous performances, spectators could choose the stage they wanted to watch and they could leave and walk over to another stage. Not only did the large space accommodate multiple action on different stages but

The Iron Curtain and performative Verfremdung 67

the voices of the actors also resonated around La Cartoucherie. The example of *1789* shows how – within a particular aesthetic and political gaze – a topic from European history concerning human rights and freedom of expression could be transformed into a piece of theatre in which the members of the audience could experience the theme of the unhindered circulation of ideas through their own physical freedom of movement about the large venue, free from barriers, curtains and walls – real or imaginary.

The male-dominated political administration of society was for many people perceived as synonymous with the wall. German theatre director Peter Stein, along with his company Schaubühne an der Halleschen Ufer challenged this view with some impressive theatrical work, including two productions of the Greek classical trilogy, Aeschylus's *The Oresteia*. The first of these opened in German in West Berlin (1980), the second was performed in Russian (1994). In their symbolic ways the two versions framed the Fall of the Wall: the 1984 production was prophetic, while the Moscow production acted as a reflection upon the history of this event. *The Oresteia* marked the culmination of two artistic projects. The *Antiken Projekt I* resulted in producing Euripides' *The Bacchae* (1974), directed by Klaus-Michael Grüber, and it configured new methods of dramaturgy. *The Oresteia* (1980) was the product of the *Antiken Projekt II*, directed by Peter Stein. Both projects focused on the essence of theatre, and especially Dionysus, in order to gain a new understanding of the place of the actor. How could an actor express the ritualistic birth of a character? What rights could be conferred upon an actor uttering the words: 'I am Orestes'? What level of 'identification' is required of an actor, and how does this affect the spectators in the audience? For what reason should the public decide to go to see such a theatrical production? In short, actions and relationships in theatre were to be investigated from the bottom up. It was as if the founding principle of simply calling something *theatre* were being questioned at a time when the most fundamental issues about European identity were also coming under close scrutiny. The interpretation by Stein and Grüber of *The Oresteia*, relating the mythical story of the birth of democracy, was theatre's response to the need for a (re)birth of democracy in an undivided Europe. In the 1980 production of *Agamemnon,* the first part of the trilogy, the choir – comprised of men – was staged to resemble the clique of senior figures in the GDR *politburo.* Stumbling about, leaning on sticks, these political dinosaurs were reciting words of exhausted anxiety regarding the future and their own vulnerability in the face of the birth of democracy. The second performance in Moscow in 1994, shortly after the collapse of the Soviet Union, was staged in the gigantic Theatre of the Soviet Army. Framing the judge's announcement about the arrival of a fair society in the final tragedy of the trilogy, *The Eumenides*, the vast venue – redolent of reminders of communism and Soviet power – highlighted the fragility and vulnerability of this promise.

Identity used to be cultural and culture was to a large extent national. This formula has reached its date of expiry. Multicultural society in European democracies at the turn of the century posed a challenge to the theatre.

68 *Annelis Kuhlmann*

Although the gaze of the other has entered productions, it still has not, however, obtained equal rights with the gaze of the self in theatrical expressivity. Changing mentalities are reflected not only in contemporary political themes taken from page to stage – it is the changing of formal conventions in the space of theatre that can offer new gazes to spectators to acquaint them with global perspectives. Ariane Mnouchkine's filmed performance of *1789* about democratization of theatrical space incorporated the spectators' bodily participation as a compositional principle. Almost four decades on, Mnouchkine's experiment still remains a very convincing model for theatre to engage with alienated, oppressed mentalities. Cultural events like theatre performances literally bring people together and provide alternatives to the political hegemony of strategies of isolation. Theatre's organizational models have a great deal to teach political establishments. Cultural intolerance still often competes with curiosity to watch performances not only with, and about, others, but also through the gaze of otherness. Identification with the stage still demands the fall of the walls in minds.

Notes

1 Unless otherwise stated, translations are mine.
2 Bertolt Brecht's notion of *Verfremdungseffekt* is often translated as a distancing effect or alienation effect. There are ongoing discussions on the origin of the *Verfremdungseffekt*, which some scholars argue Brecht did not invent himself, but merely copied from the Russian formalist tradition or from the Chinese tradition.
3 Eimuntas Nekrošius's production of *Hamlet* was created in 1997.
4 Anton Chekhov, *The Seagull*, Act I.

Bibliography

Andreasen, J. and Kuhlmann, A. (2000) *Odin 2000*, Aarhus: Aarhus University Press.
Artaud, A. (2010) *The Theatre and its Double*, (trans. Victor Corti), Richmond: Oneworld Classics.
Barnett, D. and Skelton, A. (eds) (2008) *Theatre and Performance in Eastern Europe*, Lanham: The Scarecrow Press.
Barthes, R. (1977) *Image Music Text*, London: Fontana Press.
Bauer, G. (2002) 'Ost/West: Zur aktuellen Theatersituation Berlin', *Maske und Kothurn*, 47 (3–4): 133–38.
Borisova, N. (2003) *A Journal in Theatrical Space. Anatoly Vasiliev and Igor Popov: Scenography and Theatre*, Part I, Moscow: Novosti.
Brecht, B. (1963) *Schriften zum Theater 3. 1933–1947*, Frankfurt am Main: Suhrkamp Verlag.
Brook, P. (1968) *The Empty Space*. London: MacGibbon & Kee.
Delgado, M. and Rebellato, D. (eds) (2010) *Contemporary European Theatre Directors*, London and New York: Routledge.
Esslin, M. (1961) *The Theatre of the Absurd*, Baltimore: Penguin Books.
Fischer-Lichte, E. (2004) *Ästetik des Performativen*, Frankfurt am Main: Surhkamp Verlag.
——(2008) *The Transformative Power of Performance*, London and New York: Routledge.

The Iron Curtain and performative Verfremdung 69

Fuegi, J. (1987) *Bertolt Brecht: Chaos According to Plan. (Directors in Perspective)*, Cambridge: Cambridge University Press.

Fuchs, E. (1996) *The Death of Character. Perspectives on Theater after Modernism*, Bloomington: Indiana University Press.

Grotowski, J. (1984) *Towards a Poor Theatre*, (ed. Eugenio Barba), Preface by Peter Brook, Holstebro: Odin Teatrets Forlag/Methuen and Co [1968].

Lehmann, H. (1999) *Postdramatisches Theater*, Frankfurt am Main: Verlag der Autoren.

——(2006) *Postdramatic Theatre*. London and New York: Routledge.

McAuley, G. (ed.) (2006) *Unstable Ground. Performance and the Politics of Place*, Dramaturgies no. 20, Brussels: Peter Lang.

McCullough, C. (1996) 'Around the Fall of the Berlin Wall and the Changing Map of Europe: 1986–95', *Theatre and Europe: 1957–1992*, Bristol: Intellect Books, 79–90.

Osinski, Z. and Burzynski, T. (1979) *Grotowski's Laboratory*, Warsaw: Interpress Publishers.

Pavis, P. (2002). *Dictionnaire du Théâtre*, Paris: Armand Colin.

Rose, R. (2009) *Understanding Post-Communist Transformation. A Bottom up Approach*, London and New York: Routledge.

Schechner, R. (1990) 'After the Fall of the Wall', *The Drama Review*, 34 (3): 7–9.

Stefanova, K. (2000) *Eastern European Theater After the Iron Curtain*, Amsterdam: Harwood Academic Publishers.

Theatre Journal (1996) Special Issue (March): *The Fall of the Wall*, Washington D. C.

Verheyen, D. (2008) *United City, Divided Memories? Cold War Legacies in Contemporary Berlin*, Plymouth: Lexington Books.

Williams, D. (1999) *Collaborative Theatre: The Théâtre du Soleil Sourcebook*, London: Routledge.

Yarrow, R. (1992) *European Theatre 1960–1990. Cross-cultural Perspectives*, London and NewYork: Routledge.

7 The re-emergence of national cultures following independence in the Baltic states

Charles de Chassiron[1]

In Eastern Europe history, culture and national identity have always been even more intimately bound up with politics than in other parts of the continent. The Baltic states are no exception. In two noticeable ways though, their post-communist history differs from the region's other countries. First, communist rule was not finally removed until the middle of 1991, even though by 1989 it was already in retreat: the nationalist popular fronts in each Baltic country and their nascent parliaments were gathering strength, encouraged by what had happened in Prague and Budapest. The central authorities in Moscow under Gorbachev were struggling to regain the initiative, concerned about the knock-on effects on the rest of the Soviet Union of letting the Balts loose. This brings me to my second point. The three Baltic countries were, of course, part of the Soviet Union, not merely situated alongside it as unwilling allies, and that made their struggle for freedom all the more difficult. The famous image by the Estonian painter Jüri Arrak of St George and the dragon: the spectator suddenly realises why the artist has depicted St George not as attacking the monster but as struggling inside it to burst out of its red skin.

The difficult history of the Baltic area is common knowledge. Their small populations have inhabited areas between Germany and Russia and, in addition, at times they were dominated by other once-powerful neighbours like Sweden. Judging by comments made in conversation, it would still appear to be the case that Balts consider Sweden to have been the least worst colonizer: the Swedes at least abolished serfdom in Livonia, opened schools for peasants and had the Bible translated in the 1640s. Besides, the Swedish king, Gustavus Adolphus, founded the University of Dorpat, now Tartu, in 1632.

The three states are not homogeneous in language, religious tradition or culture, though their modern history has been as similar as their geography. The nationalist movements of the late nineteenth century asserted their cultures at a time of strong Russification in an outpouring of literary, philological and musical enthusiasm. This was a 'national awakening', inspired in its early stages in Estonia and Latvia by Baltic German intellectuals. It was also driven by pride in local languages and the area's rich folklore, as well as by recollections of past grandeur. Notably, Lithuania was part of the Polish-Lithuanian Grand Duchy, stretching right across Europe in the fourteenth century. Lithuania in

Re-emerging national cultures in the Baltic states   71

this respect differs from the other two countries, just as the extent of the Catholic influence on its national identity was substantially greater than in Latvia or Estonia. The size of the ethnically Russian minority in Lithuania is less than 10 per cent, compared to 33 per cent and 50 per cent in the other two states at the time of independence.

The three did share, however, one crucial experience, not unique in Central Europe but culturally critical: over twenty years of increasingly precarious independence in the interwar years from 1918 up to 1940 preceded their incorporation by force into the Soviet Union. Far too many post-communist Russians have been unwilling to admit this fact. All three states date their legal personality from 1918, treating the half-century of occupation as an alien interruption. The ninetieth birthday celebrations held in 2008 puzzled British friends who know so little of Eastern and Central European history. The Balts may have been inside the beast, but as the historian Ernest Gellner once said, their somewhat romanticised memories of independence and the fact that they had to endure fifty rather than seventy years of communism did make a difference.[2] In 1945 the Baltic states were the only former members of the League of Nations not to be restored to full sovereignty, at least in theory. They were in effect written off by the West, though most countries refused formally to recognize the occupation. The Soviet state was determined that they would never regain independence and drafted in large numbers of settlers – Russian industrial workers – as required by the central planning system. This was a shock for small, homogeneous and well-educated populations, though, as we said before, Lithuania escaped the worst of it. The Russian economic model also meant the heedless development of oil-shale based power in Estonia, involving discharges of toxic waste into rivers and the sea, and the use of phosphates as fertilisers in all three states, spurring the environmental protests in 1987–88, which in part underlay the nationalist movements.

To take Estonia again as an example, it is striking how liberal innovations in cultural policy were made early in the 1990s, just as radical free-market economic changes were taking effect as well. Censorship finished officially in 1990, and a free press was guaranteed in the Constitution of 1992. The state monopoly on broadcasting was ended, though the state broadcaster ETV was required to carry Russian-language news and cultural programmes aimed at the population of ethnic Russian extraction. The Ministry of Culture and Education was set up in 1990. The early years of independence were characterised by the privatization of many previously state-run cultural institutions such as book publishing, film and broadcasting. 'Cultural heritage', the protection of which had been another rallying point for the nationalist movement in the late 1980s, remained under governmental control. This coincided with the return of property to private ownership and a policy strongly emphasizing economic liberalism and privatization. Private organizations took charge of the management of theatres and concerts. Money-strapped as it was, the state-run opera in Tallinn remained nevertheless ambitious and imaginative. But at the same time new state-owned cultural foundations were created, such as Kultuurkapital – the

72   *Charles de Chassiron*

Cultural Endowment Fund – in 1994, consciously copying a similar body which had existed between 1925 and 1940. A new law on cultural autonomy for ethnic minorities was passed in 1993, on the model of the one passed in 1925. Film production began to expand in the mid 1990s, and book publishers expanded, too. But the lack of money was painful, and I often noticed a certain resentment among the cultural elite that the fast-expanding young entrepreneurial class in Tallinn seemingly preferred to put its money into Western luxury cars and property rather than into sponsoring culture. Some of the gap was bridged by the Open Estonia Foundation, funded by George Soros, replicated in the two other Baltic countries as indeed elsewhere across the former Eastern bloc. Buildings were carefully restored as resources permitted, starting with the Musical Academy in Estonia.

There were various strands in the cultural reawakening of Estonia in the early 1990s, which drew on earlier experience. Estonians have always taken literature very seriously, and near-universal literacy underlay the flowering of writing in Estonian in the late nineteenth century. This took the form of the recording of folklore, the recreation of the national epic *Kalevipoeg* and the first newspapers in Estonian. Developments in Latvia had been very similar: the equivalent of *Kalevipoeg* was the epic about the bear-slayer Lacplesis. In the 1990s, the greatest name in Estonian literature was Jaan Kross, the only Soviet-era novelist favoured with translation into English early in that decade, though he had already been well-known in Germany. Of his well-researched and gripping novels, the best-known still is *The Czar's Madman* written in 1978 and depicting what happened to a Baltic German nobleman who talked frankly to his former childhood friend Czar Alexander I about the need for democracy. Ostensibly the book's theme – set in the past – was how to cope with life in a country under oppressive foreign rule. The manuscript got past the (fairly mild) local censors – just as Solzhenitsyn had been allowed a few years earlier to write most of the *The Gulag Archipelago* in the farmhouse of an Estonian friend, Arnold Susi, whom he had met in prison. The subtext of Kross's novel was not lost on Estonian readers in the 1980s. The plot engages with the reaction of an authoritarian regime against a brave but obstinate man calling for democracy, and with the hero's refusal to accept an offer that would enable him to go into exile. Kross himself made the choice to stay in his homeland. In this and other books, he attacked oppression with irony and with historical allusion. The Estonians in my time there had high but unrealised hopes that Kross would win the Nobel Prize, and he remains their greatest recent writer. His other novels also draw on history and on his gruelling experiences first of Nazi prison and then of Soviet internment for eight years in Siberia. Kross was allowed to go into print thanks to his ability to outwit Soviet control with irony, with historical knowledge and with his skilful use of language.

Tõnu Õnnepalu, whose novel *Borderland* reflected on the complex relationship between Western and Eastern Europe, attracted equally great interest at the time. He won acclaim abroad, as did the poet Jaan Kaplinski, who drew in his work on folklore and minority languages. Like Kross in 1992, Kaplinski was

Re-emerging national cultures in the Baltic states 73

also elected to the Parliament together with another poet, Paul-Erik Rummo. A journalist commented that whatever its failings (such as weak party structures and name-calling about members' alleged KGB links) the Riigikogu was the only legislature in the world to contain three potential Nobel laureates.

But the great calling card of the Baltic states was music. Orchestral music and opera were one part of this, and in Latvia the opera house in Riga was one of the first major buildings to be refurbished in the early 1990s. The Riga opera had a fine reputation, and the Tallinn one was not far behind. Arvo Pärt is of significant international renown; although he had left Estonia in the 1980s for Germany, he returned frequently in the next decade, and continues to do so. The music of Veljo Tormis and Sven-Erik Tüür also became known outside the region at that time. However, the most impressive aspect of the Baltic musical scene was the profile of choral music. The tradition of song festivals, which began in the swell of the nationalist movement in the 1860s, took on a profound political and nationalist colouring in the 1980s as a way of bringing together tens of thousands of participants and hundreds of thousands of listeners – really astonishing percentages of these small populations. It was at the Baltika festival in 1988 that the three national flags, hitherto banned under Soviet rule, were first raised together. This is why the Baltic independence movement acquired the title of 'the Singing Revolution': in this case it definitely meant a great deal more than a lazy journalistic label.

The presence at these events of groups of Baltic exiles from Canada or Sweden also served to illustrate their 'coming home' despite the forced exile of their families forty years earlier, and showed how their culture had been preserved during that exile in small communities in Ottawa, Malmö and Leicester. The sound of huge choirs in harmony symbolized national pride and renewal in an unusually impressive way. The Estonian Philharmonic Chamber Choir was also a prominent standard-bearer of the cultural tradition, led by its star conductor Tõnu Kaljuste, touring repeatedly with its superb singing of European classical choral music and showcasing Arvo Pärt in particular. The revival of such half-forgotten masterpieces as the oratorio 'Jonah's Mission' by Rudolf Tobias, first performed in 1909, rediscovered in the late 1980s by the musicologist Vardo Rumessen, and promoted in Estonia and more widely in Europe in the 1990s by the conductor Neeme Järvi with the Estonian National Symphony Orchestra and Kaljuste's choir, contributed substantially to the impact of the process of cultural rebirth. Järvi even enlisted my help as ambassador in trying – unsuccessfully – to persuade the BBC to insert it at a late stage into the programme of the Henry Wood Promenade Concerts – the 'Proms' – in London's Albert Hall in the summer of 1996. This oratorio with its late romantic Mahlerian themes helped to put Estonia on the musical map again.

Culture's fusion with political trends was inevitable as illustrated by a prominent musician and politician, Professor Vytautas Landsbergis, the leader of the Lithuanian reform movement Sajūdis. His family has deep roots in the Lithuanian literary and theatrical tradition and his own musicological expertise was put to use to promote the work of Lithuania's great composer Mikalojus Čiurlionis,

74 *Charles de Chassiron*

who died in 1911. Landsbergis more than anyone else kept knowledge of Čiurlionis alive in Soviet times. This was nothing short of an act of cultural resistance. He was also instrumental in taking the Lithuanian Union of Composers out of the Soviet organization, paving the way for writers to follow them shortly thereafter. This was a powerful tool of cultural politics, and though Landsbergis's political star quickly waned, he gave a mighty push to Lithuania's aspirations to independence in 1989–90, when it led the Baltic group. I found him to be an engaging speaker when I heard him talk in Tallinn a few years later.

Undoubtedly, however, the Baltic politician-cum-cultural polymath *par excellence*, and certainly the one I knew best and most admired, was Estonia's president from 1992 to 2000, Lennart Meri. He was a man of enormous moral and intellectual stature who did more than anyone to relaunch his country. His father had been a senior diplomat in 1940, and as a result the family had been deported to Siberia in 1941, from where he returned years later. Incredibly, he returned a decade later of his own free will to make anthropological films about small Finno-Ugric ethnic groups. He produced many books and films in the 1970s and, like his father, became a literary translator. Meri senior had tackled Shakespeare and his son chose Graham Greene. In 1988 he founded the Estonian Institute, which was intended to promote cultural contacts with the West, and which became the nucleus of the new country's network of embassies in 1991. Meri set up the Foreign Ministry, and represented Estonia at the CSCE and in Finland, before being elected president. Sadly he died in 2006. The journalist Edward Lucas said of him that he was 'by far the most impressive figure [he] met in 20 years of reporting on Central Europe. Only Vaclav Havel comes near in moral stature, cultural depth and achievement and even he seems a half-hearted and provincial figure by comparison' (Lucas and Meri 2009: 11). The conversations that I held with him in Tallinn always ranged over history to literature to geography before we got to the point of whatever we were supposed to be discussing officially – usually something to do with Russia or Estonia's wish to join NATO. He would lace his talk with entertaining tales of his marathon, and often tempestuous, negotiating sessions with Yeltsin over final Russian troop withdrawals in 1993–94. Meri had a very clear sense of Estonia's vocation as a member of NATO and the EU and he contributed greatly to the achievement of both objectives. He had an impressive historical range, telling me about Baltic links with Britain of which I was completely unaware: King Canute's help to the Danes in the defence of Narva against Novgorod in 1030, or Hanseatic Tallinn's links with the Steelyard in London in the sixteenth century (I remember him pointing out to me where the Steelyard's crest had once stood on the facade of the medieval House of Blackheads in Tallinn's Old Town). The new Estonia was fortunate to have him as its first leader.

Meri was enthusiastic about Estonia's vocation as a full-scale investor in information tchnology as an economic and educational priority from the mid 1990s onwards. He called it the 'tiger leap', sensing how to make a small country large, and the result has been Estonia's well-known prominence in this field, from advanced e-banking to parking payments by mobile phone, through

Re-emerging national cultures in the Baltic states   75

paperless Cabinet government, to connecting all schools to the internet ahead of any other country in the Central and Eastern European region. This has exposed potential vulnerability, as was shown when the Russians mounted a cyber-attack against Estonian IT structures after controversy over a Russian war memorial in 2007. On the whole, however, the country has gained immensely from this strategic choice. Famously, Skype was invented and developed there and Estonia now hosts NATO's cyber-warfare centre. I can remember Meri telling Western diplomats that the most important person he would be seeing during his 1996 State Visit to the United States was not Bill Clinton but Bill Gates. I had never heard of Gates and had to ask the others who he was: only my American colleague knew. But Meri was right. In a sense this was an echo of the voice of Jakob Hurt, a Lutheran pastor, who had studied at Tartu well over a century earlier. His belief that a small nation could be made great through culture rather than size or military might provided an early form of advocating what came to be known as soft power.

I have concentrated on Estonia. The experience of the other two countries has been broadly similar. Resentment elsewhere of Estonian smugness, and even a certain conceit, as well as of its economic success, was evident in the mid 1990s, but the natural inter-Baltic rivalries and jealousies have been subsumed in their common success in achieving together EU and (to their relief and even surprise) NATO membership, just as they cooperated in forcing their way out of the Soviet Union in 1991. This was symbolised by the Baltic Way demonstration of August 1989, when over 1 million people joined hands to form a human chain, 600 kilometres long, to mark the fiftieth anniversary of the Molotov-Ribbentrop Pact and its secret protocol dividing up Central Europe into spheres of German and Soviet influence. Baltic representatives in the Congress of Peoples' Deputies had demanded that this should be published, and this was backed by the Baltic Way protest organised by the three national movements. Shortly afterwards the Pact and its protocol were declared null and void. Even then, the power of new technology had been recognized and used by the Balts. One of their leaders, the scientist and politician Endel Lippmaa, told me that thanks to a then rare fax machine he had got the hitherto secret text out of the Soviet Union to be published immediately abroad. The Baltic Way documents preserved in the three national archives have been put by UNESCO into its Memory of the World Register. On the whole, Baltic sibling love has eclipsed sibling rivalry, as former Latvian president Viara Vīķe-Freiberga has put it.

The self-confidence of the three Baltic states and their image of economic success have been badly dented by the impact of the recent economic recession, especially in Latvia, where property prices have tumbled and civil servants have taken large pay cuts. But their position in the EU and NATO is secure, and their cultures are part of the European mainstream again. This was exemplified by the choice of Vilnius as European Capital of Culture in 2009 and of Tallinn in 2011. The Estonians have recently inaugurated an impressive new building as the National Art Museum, KUMU for short. The Lithuanians did likewise this summer, and there are ambitious urbanisation plans for Riga involving the

76   Charles de Chassiron

Dutch architect, Rem Koolhaas. The three countries emerged twenty years ago from the ruins of empire, and the Soviet legacy is still visible in the landscape, in the form of urban towerblocks and environmental damage from Soviet military activity and agriculture. Not everything is perfect in cultural terms either. The Lithuanian dissident poet, Tomas Venclova, expelled in 1977 for his involvement in the Lithuanian branch of the Helsinki monitoring process, has been fiercely critical of the narrow chauvinism of Lithuanian nationalist politicians. The Estonian poet-politician Jaan Kaplinski has criticised his fellow citizens for their heedless consumerism and what he called the 'Barbiefication' of society – a phenomenon that he considers to be more dangerous even than Bolshevism.

But all things considered, what has happened in this part of the continent in the last twenty years is one of the great success stories of post-1989 Europe. I am very conscious of my good fortune in having been a witness to it at a critical time, and to have lived among people who showed such a passion to defend their culture, such courage in facing down a tyranny and such determination in rebuilding their societies.

Notes

1 Charles de Chassiron was British Ambassador to Estonia between 1994 and 1997. At the present time he is retired and lives in London.
2 Verbal communication at the Anglo-Italian Pontignano Conference in Siena, Italy, in September 1994.

Work Cited

Lucas, E. and Meri, M. (eds) (2009) *Lennart Meri. A European Mind*, Tallinn: Meri European Foundation.

8 Explosions, shifts and backtracking in post-Soviet fiction

Hélène Mélat[1]

Do new borders mean new imaginary worlds? This is a legitimate question to ask about the culture of the ex-communist countries, from Germany to Russia, following the geopolitical upheavals triggered by the fall of the Iron Curtain and subsequently the official disappearance of the USSR in 1991. At the age of twenty a human being is still young yet already stepping into adulthood. Thus, twenty years after the social and political reshaping of the landmass that was known as the Soviet Union, we can now assess the changes that shook post-imperial Russian literature and jolted it into contact with other, especially European, cultures. The profound shake-up of Russian society at the end of the twentieth century led to extensive shifts in its relations of power. Intellectual authority – the object of our study – slipped away from Russia's writers and poets during this period. Soviet society used to be heavily literature-centred, but in the post-Soviet era the importance of books crumbled and the status of intellectuals changed dramatically. Post-Soviet writers, having mostly become outcasts and deprived of their erstwhile prestige and good income, were confronted with a number of challenges such as 'remaining relevant', as Andrew Baruch Wachtel put it.[2] They had to assert their identities and manage the heavy inheritance of the past while assimilating to a no less problematic present.

Russia's cultural legacy is two-fold. It is well-known that the central tenet of Russian literature was to offer answers to social, moral and existential questions. Soviet high culture was coupled with socialist realism and it had been firmly imposed by the 'literary authorities'. This method of representation, although avoided or circumnavigated by the most creative and courageous authors, remained the yardstick by which all writers in the USSR were measured. Moreover, the theory contained a *contradictio in adjecto*: it postulated 'a true representation of reality in its revolutionary development' (First All-Union Conrgress of Soviet Writers 1934: 176). This theory had 50 per cent to do with literature and 50 per cent with politics; it blended present and future and orientated representation according to an ideological scheme that can only deform reality and lead away from it. Let us recall the dull pieces produced through the socialist realist machine, which beautified the real and cloned the stereotypical tale of socialist success. Reality is nowhere to be seen in those idyllic pictures of a romanticised world of fantasy. Imitating the style of representational

78 Hélène Mélat

realism, they offer a utopian model of a perfect world that cannot be improved upon. Régine Robin dismantled the socialist realist formula to the letter and concluded that the very premise of social realism is predicated upon a dead end (Robin 1986).

The combination of these two legacies undepinned literature after the break-up of the USSR. The so-called 'civic' literature reached its pinnacle in the late 1980s. The 'three Ps', *Pozhar* (The Fire) by Valentin Rasputin, *Pechalnyi detektiv* (The Sad Detective) by Viktor Astaf'ev, and *Plakha* (The Scaffold) by Chingiz Aitmatov – all published in 1986 and 1987 – denounced the faults of the Soviet system. Aleksander Solzhenitsyn's *The Gulag Archipelago*, his most seditious work, was published in the Soviet Union at exactly the same time as the Berlin Wall came down; this novel is the most telling symbol of the geographical and cultural reunion of territories that had been artificially kept apart. These novels represent the violent yet final appearance of literature as powerful social criticism. Indeed, this triumphant era for Russian prose is also its swan song.[3] With the sharp decline of writers' authority as the true chroniclers and analysts of Russian life, critics predicted nothing less than an inevitable death of literature. Viktor Erofeev sounded the death toll of Soviet literature in a vitriolic article (Erofeev 1990), but did not propose any alternative successor to take its place.

The Stalinist buildings that adorn Moscow's skyline offer an analogy for visualizing 'monumental' literature that was intended to stand for Soviet society. The sycophantic writers of the regime, the civil servants of the Union of Writers as well as the great and the good of the party nomenclature occupied the most luxurious apartments in the skyscrapers.[4] In the more modest dwellings – on the fringe – lived published writers who carefully avoided any ideological involvement, for example Iurii Trifonov, Iurii Kazakov and Vladimir Makanin. Finally, in the basements, cellars, or boiler rooms resided the internal dissidents, who did not emigrate and who wrote for the 'long drawer'. Initially, this well-organized vertical hierarchy of the totalitarian world was replaced by post-totalitarian 'rhizomatic horizontality'.[5] It is no coincidence that many critics used this metaphor in likening literature to a confused landscape with no signposts (Berg *et al.* 1994: 222–38). The quick-paced publication of previously forbidden authors, appearing often in the same issues as the work of contemporary authors, filled in the gaps within the mosaic of twentieth-century Russian literature. Such a simultaneous emergence of literary texts from different historical periods is unique. It blurred the literary landscape, making it increasingly difficult to find one's way in it.

This landscape has over time been modified with great frequency. After the demise of the Soviet empire, new geopolitical territories emerged, empowered to establish contacts with other cultures, not least because of the rise of the Internet. All of a sudden writing was becoming deterritorialized and the author virtualized. Émigrés could rejoin the literary process of the country they had left: Mikhail Shishkin who had emigrated to Switzerland and Dina Rubina, living in Israel, both received prestigious Russian literary prizes. Barriers between genres also became more permeable. During the first years following

Shifts in post-Soviet fiction 79

the Soviet era, the conventional forms of literature dissolved and diversified: pehaps the most striking phenomenon was the sudden emergence of popular culture on a very large scale. Hitherto banned, or severely restricted, literary experimentation flourished.

Sally Dalton-Brown remarked:

> [I]t is rather obvious that Russian culture today is in crisis … The precise nature of the crisis is less easy to define, but one may argue that it derives from the problem of dealing with freedom; the new responsibility in the new Russia for literature, always so conscious of its civic responsibility, is one using freedom well. As literature emerges from the long years of its self-appointed duty as the custodian of truth during the Stalin years and their stagnant aftermath, it finds that it has landed up in the dole queue. How have writers responded? This is the fascinating aspect of the current cultural scene in Russia, as responses can be broadly collated under three headings: shock therapy, shop therapy, and retrotherapy.
>
> (Dalton-Brown 2000: 7)

This 'triad' depicts post-Soviet prose in the 1990s quite perceptively. We shall nevertheless propose three different categories to describe literature's reaction to socio-economic upheaval: shock, escape and reaction. And with the fall of the Iron Curtain and the USSR, it is shock that sets the tone in the first years of post-Soviet prose.

Shock: a disenchanted world

The implosion of the communist regime led to a verbal explosion and it shed light on what had been hidden by censorship. After a seemingly calm period of stagnation, time accelerated and events followed one another in quick succession. *Zhyoltaia strela* (The Yellow Arrow), Viktor Pelevin's short novel in 1991, epitomizes the contemporary Russian writer's sensitivity to current issues. The first chapter, presenting characters who live in a train that constitutes their entire world, is centred around a lack of action. The regular pounding of the wheels on the rails only emphasises the a-historicity of a world where nothing evolves. Then the mentor of the hero, followed by the hero himself, goes onto the roof and off the train altogether and the train finally comes to a halt. This metaphor of a train bound for nowhere illustrates gnawing existential anxiety intensified by entropy.

This entropy, which characterizes the period of stagnation whose end no one could predict, evaporated within a few short years. Shock with a sense of freedom added to it produced transgression. In its 'supermodernity' Russia closed in on Western European culture. Marc Augé characterized the motif of the first years of the post-Soviet era as 'excess' – the excess of events, of space and of ego (Augé 1992: 40–56). Authors felt literature no longer possessed an overtly ideological function. There were some notable exceptions to which we shall

80   *Hélène Mélat*

return later. Initially texts focused on the individual experience. Writers explored conventional reality in such an obsessively dark way that the term describing this trend was derived from the adjective 'black' (the 'chernukha' movement).

The preferred area of the Degree Zero of post-Soviet writing is daily life, the banal contingency of which emerges in particular in works that take place in such zones of female confinement as the house or the hospital.[6] Thanks to the refined narrative nuance of Ludmila Petrushevskaia, the recognized leader of this trend, the viewpoint of cruel or intelectually limited characters frequently comes to the fore, highlighting all the more acutely the breakdown of human relations. The male microcosm, too, is marked by recurring topoi of confinement, violence, camps, war (in Afghanistan in Oleg Ermakov's early prose and Chechnya in works by Zakhar Prilepin, Arkadiï Babchenko and German Sadulaev), and military service (cf. Oleg Pavlov's texts). This comes as no surprise in a country still at war. Representations of marginality produced a highly unflattering portrait of society. The gravediggers and squaddies described by Sergei Kaledin towards the end of the period of 'perestroika' in behaviourist and hyperrealist prose comprised mainly dialogues. Vladimir Kozlov's novel *Gopniki* (The Idlers) about minor criminals, published in 2002, foregrounds society through the filter of teenage psychology. The eschatological disposition of the late twentieth century in Russia feeds into the description of a decaying society: we could consider for example the patients from a psychiatric ward as in Vladimir Sharov's works or the crippled homeless people in Iuri Mamleev's *Bluzhdaiushchee vremia* (Wandering Time, 2001) sheltering in a basement and victimized by bandits. The recurring presence of physically or mentally handicapped people is a metaphor for monstrosity. Thus the world described by Ludmila Petrushevskaia is often childless. Alternatively, children are severely retarded or ill-formed, like the girl suffering from Downs Syndrome in Mikhail Shishkin's *The Vziatie Izmaila* (The Seizure of Ismail). This novel, published in 1999, problematizes the 'justification' of infanticide in a society in deadlock.

Themes of the 'double', the rear view and marginality already appeared in the grey descriptions of daily life and the non-heroic style of the so-called prose of 'everyday morality' that the Soviet 'cultural authorities' used so much to vilify in the 1970s. Iurii Trifonov, for example, who presented the moral dilemmas of his characters beyond the difficulties of daily life remained relevant during perestroika. But this kind of concern about morality disappeared in post-Soviet prose, letting raw facts speak for themselves. Eliot Borenstein has suggested that

> chernukha is no longer the implicitly moral crusade to expose. Instead, in a world in which the private has been made public for the first time, and in which the publicly owned has been privatized, the rhetoric of neo-chernukha is, if anything, that of overexposure: let us see once again what horrifies us every day.

> (Borenstein 2007: 17–18)

Shifts in post-Soviet fiction   81

The predominance of the individual's private life in literary representation exposed the intimate, the unsaid, the hidden and the taboo. The release of previously repressed discourse often led to obscenity. Understatement, the 'Aesopian' style – the trademark of Soviet writers – was replaced with overstatement, with all its associated techniques: enumeration, exaggeration, demetaphorization and crude language.

The body was the great absentee of Russian literature and was only allowed into high culture very gradually. It invaded late twentieth-century prose though in its more physiological and least aesthetic form – a far cry from the neo-classical statuary of socialist realism. In texts written by women, the destruction of the sleek image of the female body typical of Russian literature happens from the inside. The grotesque vision of the body leaking blood, urine and saliva goes in the face of literary conventions (the Gogolian grotesque, for instance, restricted itself to the surface of the body, venturing at the most to the nose) while nevertheless protesting against the traditional portrayal of women. Furthermore, the theme of abortion in the works of feminist writer Mariia Arbatova links suffering to sterility. The hospital where women were allowed to speak about their physical sufferings was the favourite setting for the tales of women's lives that multiplied in the post-Soviet era, countering trends in a literary tradition historically dominated entirely by men. The female body is never a source of pleasure but rather of suffering: it is a matter of sad sex in a sad body. Sex gives no joy to Nina Sadur's heroines in the 1990s but, instead, they feel disgusted. Instead of eroticism in post-Soviet writing, an authorised form of pornography finds accommodation within texts that attracted attention because of their focus on transgressions of all kinds, including incest, zoophilia and violence.

In the dystopic story 'Laz' (Escape Hatch, 1992) by Vladimir Makanin, the space of futuristic Moscow is divided in two: the higher space, which is that of the street occupied by a dangerous and savage crowd, and the lower space, the underground world, where the intelligentsia, the cultured part of the population, took refuge. This division does not only refer to historical events and the structure of intellectual space. It also exposes the clandestine underground world of unconscious impulses and the shadows cast at the dawn of the 1990s when the barriers of the Soviet regime collapsed. The figure of inversion in Makanin best characterizes the representation of the raw material of reality in the literature of this period.

Soviet society was technocratic in the sense that it glamorized engineers and technicians and relied on practical skills. The inflation of the rational relegated the irrational to the backyard of the collective unconscious. The Soviet population was aware of the closed towns, secret military factories with armies of nameless workers and, finally, of underground movements and dissidence. A schizophrenic dichotomy prevailed between official public life and private life. Soviet citizens were thus simultaneously in two places and two dimensions. These two separate dimensions were to collide after the fall of the regime. Furthermore, the principle of social equality initiated promptly after the October Revolution in a country where 85 per cent of the population was rural and

82 Hélène Mélat

patriarchal, entailed some deep modifications in the social fabric, particularly in terms of the family. The relationship between men and women was transformed, leading to the 'masculinisation' of women and a 'crisis' of manhood. Men and women alike suppressed their sexuality. After the end of censorship, Jung's archetype of the Great Mother recurs across different genres, confirming fear of the cruel and castrating woman even in works produced by women writers. Set in post-nuclear Moscow, the dystopian novel *Kys* (The Slynx) by Tatyana Tolstaya (2000), revolves around a female creature, a bird or a cat, who generates fear for the entire community.[7] The hero's wife and mother-in-law are decked out with bird's claws that allude to the evil bird of Russian legend and to a mythical animal that symbolizes humankind fallen back into savagery. The burst of irrational thought also comes across in Dmitrii Lipskerov's novels through the use of animality, which reveals existential anxieties mostly linked to the image of women. Hence the female rat, the protagonist of *Oseni ne budet* (Autumn will never come) (2004) illustrates a fear of being devoured. The frequent use by Pelevin of fantasy, time lapses, and the theme of reincarnation – embodied in a vampirical vixen – highlights the sense of fragility in the post-Soviet individual.[8]

Destruction, however, features not only on a thematic level, inside misogynistic plots. Vladimir Sorokin, the 'enfant terrible' of Muscovite conceptualism, goes to battle with the norms of speech and literature themselves in the mid-1980s. His unconventional narrative technique destroys the smooth surface of the text from inside, representing yet again the main mission of post-Soviet literature: drag out whatever was hidden from sight to the surface. His stories begin as pastiches of texts that an informed reader would immediately recognize, but then they spiral out of control so that the text gets stuck and pure physicality invades the narration. However, while Sorokin sanctions disarray and the destruction of all clichés (be they ideological, cultural, stylistic or thematic), he nevertheless embalms them in his writings in the same manner as a collector pins down multicoloured butterflies. Like other conceptualist authors and artists, Sorokin curates Soviet antiques. In turn, the autotelic and self-creative narrative style of Valeriia Narbikova typifies ultimately sterile and closed 'metatextual and palimpsestic' one-way texts (Chernetsky 2007: 134), intent on ridiculing, destroying and reusing the past in order to subvert it.[9] The conspicuously eccentric storytelling voice of Nina Sadur and Baian Shirianov represents 'anti-eros',[10] autism and withdrawal from the world, suggesting in another way that literature has run its course.

Literature about violence and destruction broke taboos. It has been argued that '[v]iolence released from the connection with the societal sacred appeared as the sole signifier of the (Lacanian) real in the hyper-reality of postmodern simulacra' (Brodsky *et al.* 2006: 9). The excess of violence in the first years of the post-Soviet era – and still present in mass culture (Borenstein 2007) – proved to be another way of anchoring oneself in reality. The cathartic literature that resulted provided an outlet for suffering and trauma: 'scriptotherapy' – the healing power of writing – for the writer (Henke 1998; Schiwy 1994) and 'lectotherapy' for the reader.

Escape: travelling in space and time

Focusing on the unconscious reveals the fragility of reality and the realm of fantasy offers escape from the everyday world. The early Viktor Pelevin's characters find themselves between two existential dimensions, constantly questioning their ontological status. (Are they human beings or chickens, insects, pawns in a game of chess, heroes of a video game? And so on.) Fantasy even creeps into stories, seemingly written in the manner of representational realism. The hero in Aleksei Slapovskii's 1997 novel, *Ia ne ia* (I'm not I), transforms into various other people and animals; the hero of Boris Evseev's 2009 short story 'Lavka nishchikh' (The shop for beggers') buys a homeless boy who gradually puts him out of his own home.

The haunting and frightening uncertainty of the present forced writers to look back and anchor themselves in bygone days.[11] Some authors through stylization and pastiche appealed to the literature of the past or to foreign literature; others turned to forgotten genres, or genres that had never existed in Russia. Popular culture skilfully exploited this niche and took off spectacularly in the mid-1990s in a dramatic departure from the drab and predictable products of this genre in Soviet times. Set in the present, Aleksandra Marinina's crime fiction follows the adventures of the female protagonist, detective Dar'ia Dontsova, with whom many female readers can identify. She considers herself a doctor of the soul, and her tales, beyond the piles of dead bodies, revive the genre of the sentimental novel that did not survive the Bolshevik revolution of 1917. Fantasy fiction, borrowed from the West and adapted to Slavonic tastes, became highly popular thanks to the series Volkodav (The Wolfhound), comprised of five novels and published between 1995 and 2003 by Maria Semionova. Boris Akunin, the Russian creator of the intellectual detective novel sprinkled with literary allusions, attempted to rehabilite the historical novel by adopting the style of late Victorian crime fiction and applying it to his plots set in nineteenth-century Russia. But unlike Vladimir Sorokin's pieces, these works disguise the fact that they replicate nineteenth-century classic realist narrative techniques. No meta-literary reflections burden the easy flow of the plot, which functions like trompe-l'œil.

In the wake of extensive literary experimentation with the discourse of literary fiction in the 1990s, it was not only popular culture that returned to rigorous conventionality. The novel *Khorovod* (The Circular Dance, 1998) by Anton Utkin, is an obvious tribute to the great Russian classics of the nineteenth century. The historical subject matter could provide a means of demystifying the past and an opportunity to smile at what used to be sources of trauma. Such is the case in *Khoziaika istorii* (The Mistress of History, 1999) by Sergei Nosov, in which the heroine, who has the gift of telling the future when she has an orgasm, is used by the KGB as a strategic weapon. The Gogolian style, based on several unreliable narrators, entails a comic distortion of Soviet foreign policy in the 1970s as well as the counter-espionage service – the ultimate centre of totalitarian terror. Through pseudo-history the past is reinvented, and fanciful accounts are put forward as foundations for anecdotes rather than reflection.

84 *Hélène Mélat*

Thus Vladimir Sharov's novels fictionalize past events, transforming these into a carnival-like dance of endless reincarnations, predictably without any sense of progress.

This way of reinventing the past happens also on an individual scale and this phenomenon is well demonstarted by the increasing popularity of auto-biographical writing. Apart from prose in which narrators are identical with the actual authors (e.g. Mark Kharitonov, Nikolai Klimontovich, Boris Evseev and many others), such texts were also produced by academics (Mikhail Gasparov, Mikhail Bezrodnyi), unofficial 'underground' poets (Sergei Gandlevskii, Bakhyt Kenzheev), translators (Andrei Sergeev), painters (Grisha Bruskin, Viktor Pivo-varov) and literary critics (Viacheslav Kuritsyn, Aleksandr Genis and Andrei Nemzer, who wrote several volumes of a diary blending the exegeses of books with more general and personal remarks).

Biographical works also allow us to look back to the 1970s and 1980s. Books written in prose became memorials to the past and commemorated the dead. Archives proliferated at the end of the twentieth century in response to the desire to preserve the past (Nora 1997: 31). Many publications recorded phenomena that disappeared after the Soviet regime collapsed. Aleksandr Etkind describes post-Soviet society as 'melancholy', never having completed the process of grieving, and he considers literature alone to be capable of accomplishing this task (Etkind and Lipovetski 2008).[12] Often life writing is fragmentary, signifying the loss of unity. Detailed description becomes an empowering and exhilarating activity: the narrator of Aleksandr Kabalov's *Vsyo popravimo* (All will be well, 2004) clearly derives pleasure from undertaking detailed examination of the ingredients comprising the 'New Russian'. The degree of precision in the representation of the physical world also allows for the scrupulous re-creation of the past with clear instances of nostalgia. This is to do with emotions rather than analysis: the past is mythologized even as the writer's ego is being constructed.[13] The danger of distortive representations of the past is that retrospective beautification easily turns into kitsch. These texts tend to eliminate trauma by justifying past actions and by mystifying the context in which one lived in order to produce a sense of one final rapprochement with friends in former times.

Reaction and reconstruction: the quest for meaning(s)

Some literary attempts to understand the past take their point of departure in considering 'timeless' and existential questions. The trend for sagas is very telling of the interest of Russian writers and readers in well-structured epic accounts of the Soviet Union. This approach analyses historical events in a new light, untainted by the official pictures of that period.[14] Vasilii Aksionov's *Moskovskaia saga* (The Moscow Saga)[15] evokes the varied and mostly tragic destinies of families of the intelligentsia. The novel was popular enough in Russia to be serialised on television in the 2000s. The same was the case with *Kazus Kukotskogo* (Kukotskii's Case, 2000) by Liudmila Ulitskaia, which relates the story of a gynaecologist. A change in historical perspective is apparent in the novel that won the Russian Booker Prize in 1995. Written by the former dissident, Georgii Vladimov, *General i ego armiia* (The general and his army, 1994) is an extensive piece of writing in the style of psychological realism.[16] It depicts the time of World War II through details of daily life. The changing points of view allow for different perspectives to arise on the same character, avoiding a Manichean view of the world. Vladimov even goes as far as to present a German general in addition to a traitor of the Soviet homeland, General Vlasov, as rather appealing characters. The changing attitude apparent in the book scandalized many veterans: World War II is still a highly sensitive topic. In his weighty tome, *Andergraund, ili geroï nashego vremeni* (The Underground, or the hero of our time, 1998), Vladimir Makanin assesses the first years of the post-Soviet era while recalling the 1960s and KGB repression. Owing to its intertextual nature, the novel bridges the gap between the past and the present and pinpoints obsolete and anachronistic models of conduct inherited from Romanticism at the grimly materialistic end of the twentieth century. Ironically though, the very existence of this novel, which derives its meaning from persistent engagement with the masterpieces of classical Russian literature, casts doubt on the author's postulate that literature no longer matters.

Some fragmentary sagas, centring on one or two characters, have also appeared. A number of works about the 1930s focus on the idea of legacy and respect for previous generations. They rehabilitate ordinary people who were neither heroes nor outcasts. No camps, no arrests, no historical trauma feature in this type of fiction. Andrei Dmitriev's novel, *Zakrytaia kniga* (Closed Book), published in 2000, relates the story of three generations: the grandfather is a geography teacher, knowledgeable about the outside world; Seraphin, his metaphorically named son, gives talks in the planetarium and is a stargazer; and finally the grandson, Jonas, ends up as a cheesemonger: the social circumstances of contemporary Russia have forced him to break with the intellectual tradition of his family. Jonas resembles the NEP man in Iurii Olesha's novel *Zavist* (Envy, 1927) – the jovial Andrei Babichev – who is as pink as the sausages he sells (Nivat 2006: 139). The weakest link in the chain, angelic Seraphin of the mid-generation, gets murdered by the Russian Mafia, symbolising in his death the defeat of the intelligentsia.

Traditionally considered to epitomize dullness in Russian literature, the provinces in Soviet times were an ideal hiding place for the intellectuals who felt like potential victims of the regime. It is remarkable how many post-Soviet books take place in the provinces. They testify to the revolt of the periphery against the centre, the abandonment of a predominantly vertical ideology whose summit is the capital. Thus the stories and novels by Alexei Slapovskii, Oleg Zaionchkovskii, Aleksandr Ikonnikov and Dmitrii Bavilskii treat ordinary individuals akin to Gogol's 'little people'. The viewpoint is narrow and images of a tranquil, uneventful life, along with anecdotes (which characterize this form of storytelling) and sometimes features of the literature of the absurd, illustrate the paradigm of smallness at work here. These texts can also harbour

86 *Hélène Mélat*

discreetly satirical views about contemporary society. Thus the three drunken heroes of Slapovskii's *Den deneg* (The Day of Money, 2000), upon finding a huge amount of cash, try to get rid of it, demonstrating the contempt that the Soviet intelligentsia had for money – the ultimate sign of success in post-Soviet Russia.

Few texts portray contemporary reality and its new 'heroes' favourably: businessmen, the world of the new, wealthy bourgeoisie and white collar staff of newly created firms. The successful and lightweight novels of Oksana Robski, the well-known owner of a trendy gallery, have glamorous heroines – determined, superficial and snobbish young women – occupying an affluent milieu whose fascination for ordinary people lies in its inaccessibility. The 'Grishkovets phenomenon', named after Evgeniï Grishkovets, an actor, playwright, and prose writer, functions as a microscope enlarging images of society. He produces monologues for the stage – 'monodramas' – and texts in prose. Written in the first person, in a distinctly conversational style, they address the public, the reader or an imaginary interlocutor. Grishkovets's character have an average level of education and are unexceptional white collar members of post-Soviet society. Cultural references are limited to mainstream cinema and the lack of precise information about time, place or the characters leaves the spectator/reader in a general haze. Rather than examining the national, racial or social origins of his characters, Grishkovets traces the narcissistic nuances inside his heroes' minds.

Criticism of the current state of society articulates in dystopian fiction, one of the most active genres in post-Soviet Russia. It peaked at the end of the 1980s and then again at the beginning of the 2000s. Post-Chernobyl worries carried on well after the explosion of the reactor, and social disillusionment rekindled the genre. In *Den oprichnika* (The oprichnik's day, 2006), Vladimir Sorokin's Russia regresses into violence. *ZhD* (JD, 2006), by Dmitri Bykov, recounts an eternal war between Varegs and Khazars waged on Russian soil, occupied by harmless and passive natives. It introduces a new opposition in Russia between North and South. *The Slynx* by Tatyana Tolstaya, which we discussed earlier, refers to Russian society as distressingly primitive. These anti-utopian works convey the sense that Russia is regressing into a wilderness. In the face of this overwhelming sense of hopelessness, a number of literary works shy away from overtly ideological themes, often withdrawing into the self instead.

The 2000s proved in Russia to be years of an obvious backlash by intolerant ideologies. The conflict between neo-slavophiles and neo-westernizers is still alive.[17] Religious and nationalistic values in which characters act as symbols of Russian purity and simplicity have surfaced in 'red-brown'[18] fiction. We cannot fail to mention Aleksandr Prokhanov, not because of his literary qualities but rather because of his dubious reputation. *Gospodin Geksogen* (Mr Hexagon, 2002), was at the heart of a polemic that demonstrates how 'red' and 'brown' ideologies became blurred in Russia in the first decade of the twenty-first century.[19] The primitive and crude qualities of the novel, a cross between a thriller and a story about spies, cannot alone explain its success. This disappointment

Shifts in post-Soviet fiction 87

has more to do with the novel's vitriolic satire of the Yeltsin era, when many hopes were raised only to lead to disappointment. The latter was the result of the obvious corruption of the highest echelons of power left over from the Soviet period. Prokhanov portrays the two oligarchs of the time, Boris Berezovskii and Vladimir Gusinskii, easily recognizable behind fictitious names, and of course Boris Yeltsin himself, who appears in a particularly grotesque light. This period is thus represented with brutal animosity, which might explain how the book was able to rally those who lost out during the first phase of post-Soviet democracy and capitalism.

Explicitly ideological discourse is now appearing in texts whose construction markedly differs from the novels and stories published in the ultra-conservative *Nash Sovremennik* (Our Contemporary) or *Molodaia Gvardiia* (The Young Guard). A new generation of writers – born at the beginning of the 1980s – has emerged, with few or no memories of the Soviet Union; they in fact constitute the first post-Soviet generation. It is interesting to compare the works of two young authors, both born in 1981 – *Dai mne! Song for Lovers* (Give me! Songs for Lovers, 2002) by Irina Denezhkina, and the novel *Rossiia obshchii vagon* (Russia Steerage, 2006), written in 2004, and *SOS!* (2009) by Natal'ia Kliuchariova. Both writers depict Russia as poor and a place inhabited by misfits. But whereas Denezhkina's portrait of stranded teenagers does not come with propagandistic pathos, Kliucharyova's heroes are hoping for a revolution. More didactic and one-dimensional than her first book, the novel *SOS!* tells of a young artist, addicted to drugs and alcohol, who tries to revert to normal life. The same can be said about the novel *Sankia* (2006) by Zakhar Prilepin, which recounts the life of a group of young extremists. Claiming to follow the lead of Eduard Limonov, at least in terms of ideology and the wish to remasculinize the writer's figure, Zakhar Prilepin became a real fashion icon at the end of the first decade of the new millenium. Contrary to Prokhanov, Limonov was never compromised by Soviet power, which in fact forced him to emigrate in 1973 as an alternative to becoming an informer for the KGB. He always declared himself to be in agreement with the communist ideology and never failed to say so both in exile and, following his return, in Russia. As he puts it himself: 'I was never a dissident ... I never protested against either the politics or the ideology of the USSR. The only thing I fought for was to bring more freedom into the arts' (Limonov 1996: 22). A former army volunteer in Chechnya, Zakhar Prilepin cultivates the image of a strongman ready to defend himself if attacked. In Prilepin's view, the figures of the refined intellectual or of the activist-dissident are not only not relevant any longer but downright anachronistic in a country that he considers to be at war. The admiration that he expressed repeatedly for Prokhanov only confirms the triumph of cynicism. Prokhanov's boasting about his work for the KGB has clearly resulted in his becoming a source of fascination for the new generation.

The crisis of Soviet values and the subsequent emergence of cynicism in post-Soviet society, most strongly felt perhaps in the early 1990s, could not fail to entail a search for the rise of new forms of spirituality. Some remains of

88   Hélène Mélat

mysticism, notwithstanding all efforts by Soviet civilization to eliminate them, did survive. Furthermore, the theme of religious conversion has become commonplace in literature since the fall of the USSR. Religious feelings are, of course, mainly connected with Orthodoxy, which came back into the mainstream of Russian society after seventy years of enforced atheism (which never really managed to take hold). In the novel *Rozhdenie* (The Birth, 1995) by Alekseĭ Varlamov the allegorical action takes place in a hospital and the main characters are a couple whose names and previous history are never mentioned. Going through a late and difficult pregnancy, the couple, whose feelings for each other are fading, discover that they have been given a second chance. The woman finds faith, which is clearly the significant 'message' in this novel written in imitation of the most conventional kind of classic realism.

The theme of religion though occasionally receives more detached – at times even humorous – treatment. Olesia Nikolaeva in her novel *Invalid detstva* (A Cripple From Childhood, 1990) relates the story of the conflict between an artist, a socialite, and her son joining a seminary. The representation of the contrast between the two worlds comes across as highly amusing. Almost twenty years later, the novel *Bog dozhdia* (Rain God, 2008) by Mariia Kucherskaia is a coming-of-age story, whose original perspective fuses religious and sentimental values. Throughout the novel the viewpoint is that of the heroine – a young student – Ania, who becomes increasingly alienated from the usual distractions of her fellow students: parties of drinking, smoking and sex. Her meeting with a pious young man, who gives her the Gospel, leads to her conversion and her getting baptised. The plot takes a sharp turn: the girl's falling in love with her spiritual mentor unleashes unhappiness. The book's title harks back to pagan, pre-Christian beliefs alluding to the instability of the 'born-again' consciousness.

The quest for identity has also rekindled interest in travel literature: the genre of the travelogue is back in vogue in early twenty-first century Russia. However, the former exoticism associated with Europe is now lost on travel writers. Nevertheless some texts still locate the cradle of Russian culture for their target audience around architectural sites representing former historical periods. Steeped in urban mythology is Iurii Buida's novel *Ermo* (Yermo, 1996) about Venice. In *Travel Agnets* (Travelling Agnus Dei, 2001) Anastasiia Gosteva reduces India into a hotel room in humid Delhi – a far cry from the traditional literary topoi associated with the East. Although post-Empire Russia has shrunk in size, nevertheless, owing to its proportions and the inaccessibility of some its remote regions, it still remains an intriguing topic with mythopoetic potential. With *Svirel' vselennoi* (The Flute of the Universe, 2001), Oleg Ermakov left behind the traumatic accounts of Afghanistan that got him into literature in the first place. In this novel he develops further his lyrical descriptions that were already present in his war stories. Danila, a young man with a Biblical name, wanders through Siberian forests to find inspiration and freedom in nature for his moral resistance. Vasili Golovanov's geopoetic piece, *Ostrov, ili opravdanie bessmyslennykh puteshestvii* (The Island, or Justification to Undertake Pointless Trips, 2002), recounts his expeditions to the northern region of Kolguev Island.

Shifts in post-Soviet fiction   89

This heterogeneous piece, which alternates between autobiographical accounts of actual expeditions and various notes about history, ethnography, literature and metaphysical reflexions, relates a journey of initiation and rebirth for the narrator-author. Marking the highest poins of contemplation and union with nature, the author refers to Matsuo Basho (1644–94), the well-known master of haiku, which expresses meaning through immanent being. The author finds harmony in his association with the Nenets tribes and the remains of their nomadic lifestyle.

In conclusion, the post-Soviet writer who best conveys a sense of universality and who bridges the gap between Russia and other European cultures is without doubt Liudmila Ulitskaia. Whether she engages with minor issues about minor people, as she did when she started writing, with Soviet history and its vagaries as in *Sonechka* and *Kukotsky's Case*, with religion or with the theme of intolerance, her fiction is best equipped to accommodate difference, 'the other'. More recently, this theme appeared at the heart of a reflexion about the Jewish and Christian faiths in her novel *Daniel Shtain, perevodchik* (Daniel Stein, Translator, 2006). This semi-documentary epistolary novel offers a model for seeing the world with an open mind instead of being dangerously self-obsessed.

Post-Soviet fiction then is propelled by varied and contradictory movements. Mark Lipovetsky borrows James Joyce's term, 'chaosmos', from *Finnegans Wake* to describe Russian post-modernism (Lipovetsky and Borenstein 1999). Chaosmos refers to the coexistence of heterogeneous worlds and it therefore applies closely to the condition of post-Soviet literature. Inspired by Soviet dissident or semi-dissident writers, works by Venedikt Erofeev, Vasilii Aksionov or Iuz Aleshkovsii ridiculed the neutral and grey language of triumphant socialist realism, as well as the outlandish styles of the likes of Vasilii Belov and Fyodor Abramov. Following the disappearance of censorship and the gradual opening up of the country, these tendencies have become a central part of today's Russian literary scene, even though the success of what critics call 'neorealism', which in fact is classical realism reborn, demonstrates that old traditions die hard. The appearance of historically non-literary subject matter, unconventional genres and writing styles, the themes of violence and sexuality plus the shattering of old taboos over the last two decades offered some kind of accommodation within Russian culture to the wide array of artistic and intellectual movements in the West across the whole of the twentieth century. Thanks to its 'literature of changing times' (Chitnis 2005), Russia has lost its status of being 'exceptional' and has grudgingly, for better or worse, joined the rest of us in the globalization of culture.

Notes

1 The chapter was translated into English from French by Anne-Sophie Olive.
2 Wachtel has studied the strategies that the writers of the ex-Soviet Union adopted to remain relevant, from journalism (the most frequent and least 'degrading' activity) to military activity – in the case of Eduard Limonov – as well as writing airport novels (Wachtel 2006).

90   *Hélène Mélat*

3 The words often cited at the time by Russian intellectuals, 'reading is more interesting than living', supposedly came from the satirist Mikhail Zhvanetskii in the late 1980s. Unless otherwise noted, translations from French or Russian sources into English are by Anne-Sophie Olive.

4 To illustrate the close link between power and official culture, suffice it to remember that Leonid Brezhnev himself was responsible for a few tomes of fiction: *Malaya zemlya* (A small land), *Vozrozhdenie* (Rebirth) and *Tselina* (Virgin soil), *Novyi mir*, 1978 (issues 2, 5 and 11).

5 It is around this time that Russian social scientists discovered the work of Gilles Deleuze; this term became very fashionable at the beginning of the 1990s because of its applicability to the cultural reality of the period.

6 See Benjamin Sutcliffe's comprehensive study on everyday prose (Sutcliffe 2009).

7 The 'threat' posed by women features already in her stories from the mid-1980s: for example in 'Okhota na mamonta' (Hunting the Wooly Mammoth) the heroine kills the man she could not keep.

8 Cf. the hero of Pelevin's novel *Sviashchennaia kniga oborotnia* (The Sacred Book of the Werewolf), published in 2004.

9 Sally Dalton-Brown refers to it as 'metafictional self-strangulation' (Dalton-Brown 2000: 7).

10 As is common knowledge, Eros – in the Freudian and in the Jungian sense – stands for the life instinct and the link with others respectively.

11 See Rosalind Marsh's study on the representation of history in post-Soviet literature (Marsh 2007).

12 This feeling of loss is the subject of Dmitrii Galkovskii's scholarly monograph *Beskonechnyi tupik* (The Infinite Deadlock, 1997), which focuses specifically on Vassilii Rozanov; to Mikhail Bezrodnyi's *Konets tsitaty* (End of Quote, 1997) which engages with the 'Petersburg text' of Russian literature in Germany, where he lived but never ceased to feel like a foreigner; to Mikhail Gasparov's *Zapisi i vypiski* (Notes and Excerpts, 2000).

13 See also Robin 2003: 19–20.

14 Cf. Vasili Grossman's two-volume *Za pravoe delo* (For a just cause, 1952) and *Zhizn'i sudba* (Life and Fate, 1960); Anatolii Rybakov's *Deti Arbata* (The Children of the Arbat, 1966 – published only in 1987).

15 This novel was published in the USA in English translation – Vasilii Aksionov (1994) *Generations of Winter*, (trans. John Glad and Christopher Morris), New York: Random House.

16 This distinguishes it from other pieces since there were very few *romans-fleuves* at that time. The 2000s witnessed the renewed popularity of long books, such as Dmitri Bykov's novels.

17 For a discussion relating to this topic see: http://magazines.russ.ru:81/znamia/ant2/liberalizm.html

18 This term is widely use in Russia, referring to neo-Nazis and neo-Stalinists.

19 The novel *Gospodin Geksogen* (Mr Hexagon) was published by Ad Marginem, a publishing house that initially arose from the democratic movement, and that built its reputation on being one of the pillars of editorial progress in the first years of the post-Soviet period. It was therefore highly surprising when this publishing house issued the works of an author who, during the Soviet era, was conspicuously compromised by his close ties with the regime (Prokhanov was a well-known informer and opportunist), and whose nationalistic and chauvinistic tendencies are no secret all the more that, as the chief redactor of the newspaper *Zavtra* (Tomorrow), he misses no opportunity to exhibit them. Another intriguing factor is that in 2002 this piece was awarded the National Bestseller Prize, only just created at the time, which did not fail to cause a scandal and generate a great deal of debate.

Works Cited

Augé, M. (1992) *Non-lieux: Introduction à une anthropologie de la surmodernité*, Paris: Seuil.

Berg, M., Genis, A. and Shenker M. (1994) 'Granitsy v sovremennoi literature', *Vestnik novoj literatury*, 7: 222–38.

Borenstein, E. (2007) *Overkill. Sex and Violence in Contemporary Russian Popular Culture*, Ithaca and London: Cornell University Press.

Brodsky, A., Lipovetsky, M. and Spieker, S. (eds) (2006) *The Imprints of Terror. The Rhetoric of Violence and the Violence of Rhetoric in Modern Russian Culture*, Sonderband 64, Vienna: Slawistischer Almanach.

Chernetsky V. (2007) *Mapping Postcommunist Cultures: Russia and Ukraine in the Context of Globalization*, Montreal: McGill-Queen's University Press.

Chitnis, R. A. (2005) *Literature in Post-Communist Russia and Eastern Europe. The Russian, Czech and Slovak Fiction of the Changes, 1988–98*, London/New York: Routledge-Curzon.

Dalton-Brown, S. (2000) *Voices from the Void. The Genres of Liudmila Petrushevskaia*, New York/Oxford: Berghan Books.

Erofeev, V. (1990) 'Pominki po sovetskoj literature', in *Aprel'*, 2.

Etkind, A. and Lipovetski, M. (2008) 'Vozvrashchenie tritona: Sovetskaia katastrofa i postsovetskii roman', *Novoe Literaturnoe obozrenie*, 94. Available at http://magazines.russ.ru/nlo/2008/94/li17-pr.html

Henke, S. A. (1998) *Shattered Subjects. Trauma and Testimony in Women's Life-Writing*, New York: St Martin's Press.

Limonov, E. (1996) Interview, *Trud*, 23 March.

Lipovetsky, M. and Borenstein E. (eds) (1999) *Russian Postmodernist Fiction. Dialogue with the Chaos*, Armonk, New York, London: M. E. Sharpe.

Marsh, R. (2007) *Literature, History and Identity in Post-Soviet Russia, 1991–2006*, Oxford, Frankfurt, Bern, Berlin: Peter Lang.

Nivat, G. (2006) '"La ruse de dieu" ou la reductio narrative dans la prose russe d'aujourd'hui', in Mélat, H. (ed.), *Le premier Quinquennat de la prose postsoviétique*, Paris: Institut d'Études Slaves, 137–38.

Nora, P. (ed.) (1997) *Les lieux de mémoire* [Realms of memory], Paris: Gallimard.

Robin, R. (1986) *Le Réalisme socialiste: une esthétique impossible* [Socialist Realism: An Impossible Aesthetic], Paris: Payot.

Robin, R. (2003) *La mémoire saturée*, Paris: Stock/Un ordre d'idées.

Schiwy, M. A. (1994) *Voice of Her Own: Women and the Journal Writing Journey*, New York: Fireside.

First All-Union Congress of Soviet Writers (1934) *Stenogram of the First All-Union Congress of Soviet Writers*. Moscow.

Sutcliffe, B. (2009) *The Prose of Life. Russian Women Writers from Khrushchev to Putin*, Madison: University of Wisconsin Press.

Wachtel, A. B. (2006) *Remaining Relevant after Communism: The Role of the Writer in Eastern Europe*, Chicago: University of Chicago Press.

9 Neither East nor West

Polyphony and deterritorialization in contemporary European fiction

Maria Rubins[1]

Relying on [the] unity among the civilized people, countless men and women have exchanged their native home for a foreign one, and made their existence dependent on the intercommunication between friendly nations. Moreover anyone who was not by stress of circumstance confined to one spot could create for himself out of all the advantages and attractions of these civilized countries a new and wider fatherland, in which he would move about without hindrance or suspicion. In this way he enjoyed the blue sea and the grey; the beauty of snow-covered mountains and of green meadow lands; the magic of northern forests and the splendour of southern vegetation; the mood evoked by landscapes that recall great historical events, and the silence of untouched nature. This new fatherland was a museum for him, too, filled with all the treasures which the artists of civilized humanity had in the successive centuries created and left behind. As he wandered from one gallery to another in this museum, he could recognize with impartial appreciation what varied types of perfection a mixture of blood, the course of history, and the special quality of their mother-earth had produced among his compatriots in this wider sense. Here he would find cool, inflexible energy developed to the highest point; there, the graceful art of beautifying existence; elsewhere, the feeling for orderliness and law, or others among the qualities which have made mankind the lords of the earth.

(Sigmund Freud, 'Thoughts for the Times of War and Death')

Cultural diversity is the great European value.[2]

(Milan Kundera, 'Die Weltliteratur': 28)

The re-mapping of geographical and political boundaries between East and West in the wake of the fall of the Iron Curtain, the collapse of the Soviet Union and the disintegration of the Eastern bloc created a new reality and as a result the conventional terminology used to describe cultural patterns and models has gradually become inadequate. In particular, there seems to be an urgent need to revise and to re-define such concepts as 'exile', 'émigré', 'refugee', 'diaspora', 'host country', 'homeland', 'nostalgia', 'mother tongue', 'adopted tongue', 'insider', 'outsider', 'foreign', 'native', 'national literature' and even 'East' and 'West'.

Contemporary European fiction 93

In the first instance, I propose to discuss the evolution of the ideological and social parameters outlined above, focusing on Russia. Between the October Revolution and the late 1980s, there existed a powerful Russian culture beyond Soviet borders. For most of the communist period, the relationship between literature created in Russia and in emigration was characterized by hostility and mutual exclusion. There was a stark contrast between the topics and discourses used by Soviet writers and by émigré authors. With a few exceptions,[3] texts published abroad had a very slim chance of being released in the USSR. The underlying paradigm described the country of origin as the centre and the diaspora as the periphery. Russian verbal artists living in exile, cut off from millions of readers in the Soviet Union and having access only to a very limited audience abroad, were forced by and large to admit their marginal status.[4]

At the same time, there also existed a discourse that challenged this relationship, only to invert it and to replace it with its direct opposite: the diaspora was regarded as a true locus of Russian culture, literature and spirituality, whereas Soviet fiction was seen as peripheral and insignificant or was dismissed altogether as non-existent and 'non-Russian'. Thus many die-hard anti-Bolsheviks among the 'first wave' of Russian emigration (1920–30s) promoted the rhetoric of the diaspora's 'mission' to preserve the memory of their phantom homeland through, first and foremost, the conservation of classical Russian culture (as émigrés often labelled both Golden and Silver age culture, lumped together), which had been brutally eradicated by the Bolsheviks. A formula expressing the gist of this mission was promptly coined, most likely by Nina Berberova, although frequently attributed to Zinaida Gippius: 'my ne v izgnan'i, my v poslan'ii' (we are not in exile, we are on a mission).[5] Ivan Bunin's speech 'Missiia russkoi emigratsii' (The Mission of Russian Emigration, delivered in Paris on 16 February 1924) was an important step in the initial articulation of this idea. In her article 'Nashe priamoe delo' (Our Immediate Task),[6] Gippius evaluates Russian emigration as a unique and unprecedented historical event, a thought dear to many of her fellow exiles. According to Gippius, the Russian diaspora is not only all of Russia in miniature; more than that, it encompasses everything valuable in Russia's culture. What logically follows from this premise is that émigrés are destined to preserve the national cultural heritage and to develop it further. In another article, 'Polyot v Evropu' (The Flight to Europe, 2002), Gippius declares: 'contemporary Russian literature (as represented by its leading authors) has been dumped into Europe. And this is where one should look for it' (Gippius 2002: 60). Further, she charts additional aspects of the émigrés' 'mission': to 'rejuvenate' Europe (and here the 'mission' appears in the guise of traditional Russian messianism), and to enrich Russian culture with the best artistic and intellectual achievements of the West:

> From this point of view, our catastrophe may turn out to be beneficial. After all, Russian literature possesses a certain spirit, and if it saturates Europe, it will be to Europe's advantage, rather than disadvantage: Europe will be rejuvenated. Our writers will not be harmed by this rapprochement

94 *Maria Rubins*

either. There is something to learn from the old West. Literature was thrown out the window, and the window was closed. That's just fine. One day the doors to Russia will open, and literature will return there, God willing, with a greater consciousness of worldliness than before.[7]

Because of this ideological divide, which persisted for many decades, the relationship between the Soviet Union and Russia Abroad can best be described as mutually exclusive; consequently, émigré authors occupied a space that could never have been filled by their Soviet peers, and vice versa.

During the last two decades, however, most of the binary oppositions that characterized the previous period have collapsed. It is no longer appropriate to define Russian authors residing abroad as exiles. Today, voluntary migration has replaced forced emigration, and there is no longer any centrally sanctioned ban on the publication in Russia of literary works of any political, ideological or aesthetic import. Many former émigré writers returned to Russia (Irina Odoevtseva, Alexander Solzhenitsyn and Eduard Limonov, to name just a few well-publicized cases), or split their time between two countries (for example, practically until his death in 2009 this was the case with Vasilii Aksionov, who had exchanged his American exile for an alternating residence in the south of France and in Moscow). Most importantly, Russian writers abroad have the opportunity to publish their texts in Russian periodicals before releasing them in book form, both in Russia and abroad. In this post-exilic context, the relations between Russia and various diasporic centres have become complementary.

Writers who have some experience living in other countries introduce original, perhaps slightly exotic, voices into the polyphony of contemporary Russian writing, and occupy their own niche in the Russian book market. In other words, in the early twenty-first century, literature is becoming more and more deterritorialized, or dissociated from a definite, fixed geographical location, acquiring a truly international identity.

This new condition was articulated in the collective manifesto-style introduction to an anthology entitled *Simvol 'My': Evreiskaia khrestomatiia novoi russkoi literatury* (Vrubel'-Golubkina 2003, Symbol 'We': Jewish Anthology of New Russian Literature), which contains prose, poetry and interviews from a score of Russian Jewish authors living in different countries, from Israel and the United States to Italy and Germany. They conceptualize the contemporary situation in Russian-language literature abroad as one marked by a transition from 'emigration', with its possibly obsolete political connotations, to 'diaspora' – a transition marked by the breakdown of hierarchical relations with Russia and a significant degree of emancipation: for diaspora writers from the Soviet and Russian past, mentality, thematic repertoire, cultural tradition and conventional forms of expression

> literary emigration as a legitimate phenomenon, laying a claim to a particular cultural-historical mission, ... has ceased to exist. ... The international character of contemporary Russian literature is unquestionable—a major

transition from emigration to diaspora has taken place. … Russian literature as it has emerged by the beginning of the XXI century appears not only free from the confrontational division into Russian and foreign, which was typical of the previous period … but also from the hierarchy of 'dominance and subordination,' determined by the geographical location of the text and the author. To be in the diaspora means for us to develop the aspects of the Russian word which … cannot be developed in the country of origin. Consequently, the relationship between the metropolis and the diaspora is defined by complementarity, which is as indispensible as it is mutually beneficial. … [T]he geography of our speech has expanded to fit the proportions of the entire world.[8]

Moreover, this introduction rather paradoxically urges authors residing in the diaspora to distance themselves linguistically as far as possible from their country of origin, and to cultivate their 'foreignness'.[9] This illustrates a clear and radical break with the 'mission' of conservation of the Russian tradition and the Russian language in emigration in its purest form, articulated repeatedly by the leaders of the cultural community of Russian exiles in the twentieth century.

The Russian cultural diaspora in Israel, by far the most compact, well-equipped and organized among all the centres of Russian dispersion, has been in the forefront of the process of gradual emancipation from Russia. Russian-Israeli writers, united into the Israeli Union of Russian Writers (founded in 1971), assimilate a range of traditions, with Russian influences competing against the Jewish intellectual and religious tradition, Israeli culture and the modern context of the Middle East. Meanwhile, postmodernism in its Western and Russian expression is superimposed onto a powerful post-Zionist trend. It is unsurprising that the language of contemporary Russian literature in Israel[10] displays signs of creolization, due to cross-pollination with Hebrew (including words and concepts such as olim, moshav, Sokhnut, tsevet, vatic, motek, written in Cyrillic and left without any explanation, which routinely crop up in the texts of Russian-Israeli authors). This specific 'middle-eastern' intonation and vocabulary often results in word play, with Hebrew words filtered through the prism of Russian phonetics, saturating these texts with an absurdist, experimental and often non-sensical quality.[11] This provokes a split in linguistic consciousness, whereas the superimposition of Russian and Hebrew creates new meanings, underscoring the carnivalesque character of textual reality.[12] At the same time, the popularity in Russia (and across the entire international Russian reading audience) of such authors as Dina Rubina, David Markish, Svetlana Schönbrunn, Mikhail Gendelev and Anna Gorenko, among others, who interpolate into their texts Hebrew words and concepts that would be incomprehensible to someone unfamiliar with life in Israel, is a sign of a new openness of post-Soviet Russian readers, the Russian book market and, most importantly, the Russian language itself, to a range of international influences. (This process also finds powerful expression in an avalanche of borrowings from English and other foreign tongues into Russian over the last twenty years).

96   *Maria Rubins*

Symptomatic of the new cultural reality, distinguished by a higher level of diversity, is the Mark Aldanov Prize, introduced in 2006 by the primary literary journal of the Russian diaspora, *The New Review*, based in New York. The prize is awarded annually to a prose writer living outside the Russian Federation and writing in Russian. The main objective of this initiative is conceptualized as 'the preservation and development of the traditions of Russian literature *in the context of world culture*'[13] (emphasis mine). Since its inception, award-winning and short-listed authors have included writers from dozens of countries, in particular from post-Soviet republics. This geographical area, defined as the 'new Russian diaspora', adds to the complexity of the mosaic pattern of Russian culture today. Voices of Ukrainian, Kazakh, Georgian and Byelorussian authors join in the polyphonic chorus of international Russian literature. They are quite distinct from the voices of writers living in Russia and of those who reside in the West. The majority of these authors never left their homeland, not all of them are ethnically Russian and their main point of reference is not Russia proper but their own immediate reality. The importance of this category of Russian-language writers, living in the post-Soviet space, was also emphasized by the establishment in 2005 of another literary competition, 'the Russian Award' (Russkaia premiia). In 2009, this Russian Award was transformed to include Russian-language authors living all over the globe outside the Russian Federation.[14] In addition to the awards in three categories (poetry, short prose and long prose),[15] a special prize is given for the 'contribution to the conservation and development of the traditions of Russian culture beyond the borders of the Russian Federation'.[16]

Obviously, the decentralization of literature is not a uniquely Russian phenomenon. In fact, it goes hand in hand with analogous processes in literatures in other languages affected by the globalization of culture. For example, in the contemporary French context, the traditional Gallocentrism of the literary establishment has been gradually replaced by a new willingness to include markedly foreign elements. Foreign-born authors were occasionally awarded literary prizes for their contribution to French letters before, but they were as a rule completely assimilated and positioned themselves as French writers. For instance, the Russian immigrant Lev Tarasov was advised to choose a French-sounding pen-name if he wished to achieve recognition in his adopted country. Heeding this advice, he reinvented himself as Henri Troyat, and in 1938 received the most prestigious literary prize for contributions to French literature, the Prix Goncourt. Irène Némirovsky, a popular writer of the inter-war period, presents a more extreme case: her dream of complete assimilation led her not only to deny her Russian/Jewish/Ukrainian background in a number of interviews in the French press, but also her ability to write or even speak her mother tongue. At the same time, under her original name – Irina Nemirovskaya – she was publishing book reviews in perfect Russian in émigré journals such as *Chisla*.[17] The writing of immigrants who did not wish to undergo such mimicry was eventually marginalized by way of isolation from the dominant French literary canon and by being labelled as 'francophonie'. This literature became known as 'minor literature' (literature mineure), to use the definition popularised by Gilles Deleuze and Felix Guattari;[18] it encompassed primarily authors from former French colonies.

However, since the 1990s, French literature has been defined by the influx of writers with overtly foreign-sounding Arab, African, Vietnamese, Greek, Chinese, English, Russian or Czech names. Major literary prizes, including the Prix Goncourt, Prix de Médicis, le Grand Prix de l'Académie française and Femina, have been awarded to authors who were not born and brought up in France and whose mother tongue frequently was not French, but who chose French as the linguistic medium for their creative self-expression. Among these writers are Daj Siji, Vassilis Alexakis, Tahar Ben Jelloun, Andreï Makine, Nancy Huston, Alain Mabanckou, Calikst Beyala, Assia Djebar (an Algerian writer who in 2005 became the first non-French member of the Académie française), not to mention Julia Kristeva and the winners of the Prix Goncourt in recent years: New York-born Jonathan Littell (2006, for the novel *Les Bienveillantes*) and Kabul-born Atiq Rahimi (2008, for *Syngué sabour. Pierre de patience*). Although the winner of 2009 Prix Goncourt, Marie NDiaye, of Senegalese descent, was born and educated in France, her African-sounding name is another reminder of the conscious effort of the Goncourt committee to promote multiculturalism and to encourage polyphony in contemporary French fiction.

This policy of the establishment was reinforced by a 'grassroots' initiative. On 16 March 2007, a multinational group of authors who write in French published a manifesto, entitled 'Pour une "littérature-monde" en français' (For a 'world literature' in French; Barbery *et al.*).[19] In this manifesto, the authors proclaim an end to French 'cultural imperialism' and assert the de facto deterritorialization of French literature no longer circumscribed by traditional geographical and national boundaries. The signatories of this manifesto take issue with the term 'francophonie', which they characterize as 'virtual reality' (because 'no one speaks or writes in francophone'). They proclaim that the French language has now been liberated from its 'exclusive pact with the nation', and as a consequence demand that the notion of francophonie be replaced by 'literatures in French language' or 'French international literature'.[20] These writers, who compose directly in French, an adopted tongue for most of them, claim equal status in French letters alongside 'native' authors. But on the other hand, their manifesto is an interesting attempt to revisit, in a new and emphatically different context, the concept of *Weltliteratur* advanced by Goethe in the nineteenth century.[21] With increasing frequency, contemporary writers choose their language of artistic expression based on a combination of aesthetic and commercial considerations (book markets, target readership, the ambition to write themselves into a particular linguistic, cultural and literary tradition or to reproduce fashionable models of fiction writing), thereby dramatically obscuring and even cancelling the conventional notion of 'national literature'.

For many 'translingual' authors who adopted a new language, this shift became a sign of liberation from the constraints of a previous identity. As Irina Prokhorova observes, in the contemporary 'globalized and multicultural' world,

98   *Maria Rubins*

'the (self)identification of a writer through a mono-cultural or linguistic affiliation is no longer mandatory or sufficient'.[22] Furthermore, the 'affirmation of the
dual identity as a norm entails a drastic revision of the attitude to emigration.
Departure from "the soil and destiny" is no longer a curse, a life catastrophe,
but instead an act of free choice and therefore a positive strategy'.[23]

Among the numerous (formerly) Eastern/Central European writers who have
reinvented themselves in the Western European literary context, Milan Kundera
is particularly noteworthy for a militant campaign he waged for many years
against the persistent attempts to conceptualize him as a dissident celebrity
from the Eastern bloc. His lack of engagement with Czechoslovakia after his
emigration to France, withdrawal into a strictly literary domain, shedding of
any 'exotic' features of Czech identity and positioning himself as a European
(rather than specifically Czech) author, eventually resulted in his switching to
French, first in his essays, and later in his fiction.[24] After 1989, Kundera fru-
strated the expectations of his countrymen by rejecting the idea of a 'grand
return' both on a personal and fictional level.[25] As Petr Bílek observed, in 'the
early 1990s situation … the Czech cultural context just wanted to fill out the
idea of "eternal return" and bring back Kundera to the same position he had
had in the late 1960s. Kundera's refusal to return physically as well as to play
the role of a Czech cultural icon was then perceived as a gesture of betrayal'.[26]
Predictably, his offended compatriots accused him of hubris, of writing for fame
and money, producing superficial bestsellers, pursuing the goal of entertainment
above all, and even catering to Western demands for pornography (thus reinvi-
gourating the pathos of Milan Jungmann's controversial 1985 article, 'Kunder-
ian Paradoxes', in which Jungmann attacked Kundera on similar grounds[27]).
Meanwhile, having rejected any public role in the Czech context (and moreover,
not authorizing until quite recently the publication of some of his key texts in
Czech[28]), Kundera has remained 'unrepentant' in his view that exile was an
escape for his art from potential parochialism, and that, in exile, the French
language has improved his art.[29]

Kundera has also attempted to deconstruct the 'grand return' myth through
the medium of fiction. His novel *Ignorance* narrates the story of two Czech
émigrés who, persuaded against their will by their Western friends to return
'home', visit the post-communist Czech Republic after twenty years in the
West, only to realize that they no longer have very much in common with their
homeland or the people there. This polyphonic text incorporates different types of
discourse, genres and registers, including essays (the story of Arnold Schönberg
and other prominent exiles), quasi-scholarly musings on the etymology of the
word 'nostalgia' and even an ironic rewriting of *The Odyssey*. Challenging the
archetypal interpretation of the Homeric epic, characterized as the 'foundation
epic of nostalgia', Kundera states provocatively that Odysseus' best years were
spent outside Ithaca. Upon his return home after twenty years of wandering,
Odysseus, much like the contemporary Czech protagonists of *Ignorance*, feels
like a stranger. The author proceeds to subvert such 'sacred' notions as
'homeland', 'return', 'mother tongue' and 'nostalgia' (the latter, according to

Kundera's etymological musings, no longer signifies 'pain induced by one's separation from one's country of origin', but rather 'pain induced by ignorance' about the place of the émigré's birth).[30]

In his recent essay, 'L'exil libérateur selon Vera Linhartová (The liberating exile according to Vera Linhartová), Kundera identifies with a fellow Czech émigré, the poet and writer Vera Linhartová, who after emigration (like Kundera himself) switched to writing in French. After the fall of communism, Linhartová accepted the invitation of the French Institute in Prague to deliver a speech on the topic of exile. In that speech, Linhartová responded to the dominant post-communist Czech discourse addressed to émigrés – aimed at luring them back home – by stating that an individual should not be considered to be the property of any nation. Moreover, the writer, according to Linhartová, is not obliged to serve as guardian of his mother tongue, because '[l]'écrivain n'est pas prisonnier d'une seule langue' (a writer is not a prisoner of any one language). In fact, only the natural limitations of the human life span prevent the author from taking full advantage of this freedom by adopting ever new languages and inhabiting ever new cultural spaces. Kundera enthusiastically develops the theory of his compatriot's cultural nomadism, and challenges the conventional formulae of a writer's identity: 'Quand Linhartová écrit en français, est-elle encore un écrivain tchèque? Non. Devient-elle un écrivain français? Non plus. Elle est ailleurs'.[31] (When Linhartová writes in French, is she still a Czech writer? No. Has she become a French writer? Not that, either. She is somewhere else.)

A slightly different but no less eloquent example of a former Eastern European with multiple cultural identities who has successfully made a place for himself in the cultural processes of a Western country is the bestselling writer and pop culture personality Wladimir Kaminer. Kaminer emigrated from Russia to eastern Germany in 1990 without speaking a word of German, but just ten years later he published a collection of vignettes on Russian émigré life in Berlin, entitled *Russendisko*, and became an instant celebrity. He has since produced a dozen more books in German, and each landed on the *Der Spiegel* bestseller list. Kaminer releases books in audio format, writes regular columns for several leading German newspapers and magazines, for some time produced a show on the radio station Multikulti, and hosts a 'Russen Disko' night in one of Berlin's nightclubs. He is a regular guest on TV and radio and frequently goes abroad as an emissary of German culture, giving talks in the framework of the Goethe Institute and other networks in various countries, including Russia. Although Kaminer writes exclusively in German (in what Adrian Wanner calls 'a demotic … idiom, a rather earthy, no-frills language characterized by a simple syntax replete with colloquialisms and occasional four-letter words'[32]), he speaks the language with a thick Russian accent and occasionally makes grammatical mistakes; this does not seem to bother his fans, nor German cultural policy makers, who continue to send him on cultural missions around the world. Indeed, as Kathleen Condray suggests, Kaminer's 'multimedia success is due largely to the charm of his foreign identity'.[33] In fact, his image also fits the needs of the partisans of 'political correctness': 'Kaminer's foreignness is part of

100 *Maria Rubins*

his allure and intrinsic to his artistic and public persona. The fact that ZDF employs him as a correspondent despite his heavily accented German implies some degree of increasing tolerance for foreigners among the German viewing public.'[34]

In his books, Kaminer contributes to the popularity in Germany of Gastarbeiterliteratur (even though he hardly belongs to this category himself) as he skilfully capitalizes on German clichés about Russians, as well as Russian stereotypes about Germany, ironically conflating the perspectives of insider and outsider. In his typical tongue-in-cheek interviews, he insists on his hybrid identity: 'Meine Heimat is die Sowjetunion. Meine Muttersprache ist Russisch, privat bin ich ein Russe, beruflich ein deutscher Schriftsteller und mein über alles geliebter Wohnort ist Berlin'.[35] ('My homeland is the Soviet Union. My mother tongue is Russian. Privately, I'm Russian. By profession I am a German writer. And my most beloved place of residence is Berlin.')

At the very beginning of World War I, Sigmund Freud wrote an essay entitled 'Zeitgemässe über Krieg und Tod' (Thoughts for the Times of War and Death, 1915), a passage from which serves as an epigraph for this article. In this essay, Freud conjured up an idealistic vision of an individual migrating freely between various friendly countries (i.e. an individual who does not need to be, to use Kundera's words, the 'property' of any single nation). For most people at the time, this vision was not only unrealizable but even inconceivable. The Great War, the Russian Revolution, World War II, the Cold War and many other calamities that shook the twentieth century, made the Freudian dream appear ever more utopian. However, with the fall of the Iron Curtain, the enlargement of the European Union, the liberalization of border controls between its member states and the rapidly developing process of globalization, this dream has partially turned into reality – at least within the European cultural space, as testified by the unprecedented polyphony of 'languages' and 'accents' in today's literary landscape and the plurality of writers' national, cultural, linguistic and aesthetic identities.

Notes

1 Maria Rubins is Senior Lecturer at the School of Slavonic and East European Studies at University College London.

2 Unless otherwise indicated, all translations are mine (MR).

3 The most notable exception was the phenomenon of 'Russian Berlin' of the early 1920s, where émigré and Soviet writers mingled freely in literary clubs and artistic cafes. Moreover, for several years Berlin-based Russian publishers received steady commissions from the Bolshevik government and supplied the Soviet book market. On Russian Berlin see, for instance, L. Fleishman, R. Hughes and O. Rayevskaya-Hughes (1983) *Russkii Berlin 1921–23*, Paris: YMCA Press.

4 In a peculiar *mise-en-abime* twist, this pattern of dominance and marginality was duplicated within the émigré community itself. For instance, during the inter-war period, Paris was considered the 'cultural capital' of Russia Abroad, and it was rather difficult for Russian writers living in other, 'peripheral' locations (Harbin, Belgrade, Sophia etc.) to get their works published in prestigious Paris-based Russian literary journals.

Contemporary European fiction   101

5 In her long narrative poem 'Liricheskaia poema' (A Lyric Poem), in which the post-revolutionary emigration from Russia is projected upon the story of creation and the exile of Adam from paradise, Nina Berberova used several variants of this phrase: 'I esli zdes' ia sred' drugikh, –/Ia ne v izgnan'i, ia v poslan'i/ I vovse ne bylo izgnan'ia, /Padenii ne bylo moikh!' (227) ; and 'Ia govoriu: ia ne v izgnan'i, ia ne ishchu zemnykh putei. /Ia ne v izgnan'i – ia v poslan'i,/Legko mne zhit' sredi liudei'(230); (Sovremennye zapiski, 30 (1927): 221-30).

6 Z. N. Gippius and I. I. Bunakov (1930) *Chto delat' russkoi emigratsii?*, Paris: Rodnik.

7 Cited from O. A. Korostelev and N. G. Mel'nikov (eds) (2002) *Kritika russkogo zarubezh'ia*, Vol. 1, Moscow: Olimp: 60.

8 *Simvol 'My': Evreiskaia khrestomatiia novoi russkoi literatury* (2003) Moscow: NLO: 5–8.

9 Ibid.: 7.

10 Ironically but pointedly characterized by Mikhail Gendelev as a 'non-Russian literature' ('nerusskaia literatura').

11 Dina Rubina, a best-selling Russian Israeli writer, is particularly prone to such word play and her prose contains countless witty meta-remarks on 'double-coded' Hebrew words. See, for example, her novel *Poslednii kaban iz lesov Pontevedra*.

12 For a more detailed discussion of the peculiarities of Russian Israeli literature, see Maria Rubins, 'La prose israélienne d'expression russe', in Hélène Mélat (ed.) (2006) *Le premier quinquennat de la prose russe du XXIe siècle*, Paris: Institut d'Etudes Slaves, 74–86.

13 'Laureaty literaturnoi premii imeni Marka Aldanova', *The New Review*, 246 (2007): 5–7.

14 A chief partner and sponsor of the 'Russian Award' is the Foundation 'B.N. Yeltsin's Presidential Centre'.

15 The list of the winners of the 2010 competition demonstrates the geographical diversity and the wide range of ethnic and cultural identities in contemporary Russian-language writing. The award in the category 'Poetry' went to Maria Timatkova (USA); in the category 'Short Prose' to Aleksei Tork (Kyrgyzstan); and the winner in the category 'Long Prose' was Mariam Petrosyan (Armenia).

16 In 2009, this prize was awarded to Dr Olesia Rudiagina, poet and professor of the Slavic University in Chisinau (Moldova).

17 For details see my articles 'Irène Némirovsky. Strategii integratsii' (*The New Review*, 253, 2008: 228–58) and 'Figures de l'émigré russe dans les écrits d'Irène Némirovsky', Tatiana Viktoroff and Charlotte Kraus (eds) (2012) *Figures de l'émigré russe en France au XIXe-XXe: fiction et réalité*, Amsterdam: Rodopi: 377–92.

18 Cf. Gilles Deleuze and Felix Guattari, *Kafka. Pour une littérature mineure*, Paris: Minuit, 1975.

19 'Pour une "littérature-monde" en français', *Le Monde littéraire*, 16 mars 2007.

20 The pathos of this manifesto, informed by a globalized (rather than Gallo- or even Euro-centric) vision of contemporary cultural identities, is at odds with the main thesis of Tijana Miletic's study, according to which the adoption of French is a way for foreign authors to validate their European identity, subsequently leading to the intensification of their adherence to European cultural values (cf. Tijana Miletic [2008] *European Literary Immigration into the French Language. Readings of Gary, Kristof, Kundera and Semprun*, Amsterdam: Rodopi).

21 The ideas of the manifesto found further elaboration in a collective volume under the same title, *Pour une literature-monde en français*, edited by Michel Le Bris and Jean Rouaud. For a contextualized commentary of both the manifesto and the volume, see Jacqueline Dutton, 'Littérature-monde or Francophonie? From the manifesto to the great debate', *Essays in French Literature and Culture*, Number 49, November 2008: 43–67.

22 Irina Prokhorova, 'Iskusstvo pamiati i zabveniia. Sovremennaia rossiiskaia literatura v poiskakh identichnosti' (unpublished).

102   *Maria Rubins*

23 Ibid. Cf. an earlier attempt to debunk the archetypal notion that exile equates to death (first articulated by Ovid), and to proclaim the positive creative potential resulting from one's separation from the native land (Ewa Thompson, 'Writers in Exile: the Good Years', *Slavic and East European Journal*, 33(4), 1989: 499).

24 Today, Kundera's French-language books include several collections of essays: *L'Art du roman* (The Art of the Novel, 1986), *Les Testaments trahis* (Betrayed Testaments, 1993), *Le Rideau* (The Curtain, 2005), *Une Rencontre* (A Meeting, 2009), and three brief novels: *La Lenteur* (Slowness, 1995), *L'Identité* (Identity, 1997), and *L'Ignorance* (Ignorance, 2003; first appeared in Spanish translation in 2000).

25 The mythologeme of the 'grand return' and the reluctance of Kundera and another contemporary Francophone author from Eastern Europe, Andreï Makine, to assume an identity based on their country of birth, constitute a focus in Maria Rubins, 'In fremden Zungen: Milan Kunderas and Andreï Makines französische Prosa', in B. Menzel and U. Schmid (eds) *Der Osten im Westen. Importe der Populärkultur*, Special issue of *Osteuropa*, 57, Jg. 5, 2007: 169–88. This issue of *Osteuropa* contains a number of other case studies, which demonstrate various creative strategies of inhabiting Western culture developed by some formerly Eastern European artists. Ironically, the content of this special issue suggests that the very title of the journal may be obsolete.

26 Petr Bílek, 'A Journey of a Name from the Realm of Reference to the Realm of Meaning: The Reception of Milan Kundera within the Czech Cultural Context', *Kosmas: Czechoslovak and Central European Journal*, Fall 17 (1), 2003: 22.

27 Cf. Milan Jungmann, 'Kunderovské paradoxy', *Obsah* 5, September–December, 1985.

28 The ban included even his masterpiece, *The Unbearable Lightness of Being*, which for a long time was only available in the authorized French version or in translation into other languages. In 2006 Kundera finally agreed to the publication of the novel in the Czech Republic and in the original tongue. Ironically, he gave the rights to the publishing house Host, whose name means 'guest' in Czech.

29 Michelle Wood (2006) *Translating Milan Kundera*, Clevedon: Multilingual Matters Ltd: 22.

30 For a detailed discussion of the problems outlined above see Maria Rubins, 'L'Odyssée à la tchèque: le roman de Milan Kundera *L'Ignorance*', in Anne-Marie Gresser et Boris Czerny (eds), *L'hôte étranger: stratégies de l'hospitalité*, Caen: Presses universitaire de Caen, 2010: 213–20.

31 Milan Kundera, *Une rencontre*, Paris: Gallimard, 2009: 124.

32 Adrian Wanner, *Out of Russia. Fictions of a New Translingual Diaspora*, Evanston: Northwestern University Press, 2011: 52.

33 Kathleen Condray, 'The Colonization of Germany: Migrant and German Identity in Wladimir Kaminer's Mein deutsches Dschungelbuch', *A Journal of Germanic Studies*, 42 (3), September 2006: 321–36, 332.

34 Ibid.: 332.

35 Wladimir Kaminer, 'Feurige Tänzer!' Interview with Jan Boris Wintzenburg, *Stern*, 17 October 2003.

Works Cited

Barbery, M., Jelloun, T. B., Borer, A. *et al.*, 'Pour une "littérature-monde" en français'. (2007) Le Monde des livres, 16 mars.

Berberova, N. (1927) 'Liricheskaia poema', *Sovremennye zapiski*, 30: 221–30.

Bílek, P. (2003) 'A Journey of a Name from the Realm of Reference to the Realm of Meaning: The Reception of Milan Kundera within the Czech Cultural Context', *Kosmas: Czechoslovak and Central European Journal*, Fall 17 (1): 15–27.

Contemporary European fiction 103

Condray, K. (2006) 'The Colonization of Germany: Migrant and German Identity in Wladimir Kaminer's Mein deutsches Dschungelbuch', *A Journal of Germanic Studies*, 42 (3): 321–36.

Deleuze, G. and Guattari, F. (1975) *Kafka. Pour une littérature mineure*, Paris: Minuit.

Dutton, J. (2008) 'Littérature-monde or Francophonie? From the manifesto to the great debate', *Essays in French Literature and Culture*, 45: 43–63.

Fleishman, L., Hughes, R. and Rayevskya-Hughes, O. (1983) *Russkii Berlin 1921–23*, Paris: YMCA Press.

Freud, S. (1915) Thoughts for the Times of War and Death. Available at: http://fr.scribd.com/doc/41341163/Sigmund-Freud-Thoughts-for-the-Times-of-War-and-Death

Gippius, Z. and Bunakov, I. (1930) *Chto delat' russkoi emigratsii?*, Paris: Rodnik.

Gippius, Z. (2002) 'Polet v Evropu', in O. A. Korostelev and N. G. Melnikov (eds), *Kritika russkogo zarubezh'ia*, vol. 1, Moscow: Olimp.

Jungmann, M. (1985) 'Kunderovské paradoxy', *Obsah 5*.

Kaminer, W. (2009) '"Feurige Tänzer!" Interview with Jan Boris Wintzenburg', *Stern*, 17 October.

Kundera, M. (2007) 'Die Weltliteratur', *The New Yorker*, 8 January, 2007.

——(2009) *Une rencontre*, Paris: Gallimard.

'Laureaty literaturnoi premii imeni Marka Aldanova' *The New Review*, 246: 5–7.

Miletic, T. (2008) *European Literary Immigration into the French Language. Readings of Gary, Kristof, Kundera and Semprun*, Amsterdam: Rodopi.

Rubins, M. (2007) 'In fremden Zungen: Milan Kunderas and Andreï Makines französische Prosa', in B. Menzel and U. Schmid (eds), *Der Osten im Westen. Importe der Populärkultur, Osteuropa*, 57 (5): 169–88.

——(2008) 'Irène Némirovsky. Strategii integratsii', *The New Review*, 253: 228–58.

——(2012) 'Figures de l'émigré russe dans les écrits d'Irène Némirovsky', in T. Viktoroff and C. Kraus (eds) *Figures de l'émigré russe en France au XIXe-XXe: fiction et réalité*, Amsterdam: Rodopi, 377–92.

Vrubel'-Golubkina, I. (ed.) (2003) *Simvol 'My': Evreiskaia khrestomatiia novoi russkoi literatury*, Moscow: NLO.

Wanner, A. (2011) *Out of Russia. Fictions of a New Translingual Diaspora*, Evanston: Northwestern University Press.

Wood, M. (2006) *Translating Milan Kundera*, Clevedon: Multilingual Matters Ltd.

10 The fall of the Iron Curtain and the new linguistic landscape of East-Central Europe

Michael Moser[1]

Since 1989, a number of books and articles on recent developments of the Slavonic languages have been published, but it has rarely been asked what unites these changes across the languages at stake and what separates them from each other. This essay intends to give an overview with a focus on the rise of new languages out of former 'variants' or 'dialects', the new relations between related languages, some questions of political correctness, the penetration of colloquialisms and nonstandard elements into the public space and different attitudes towards recent loans from English.

1. The fall of the Iron Curtain and the recent history of the Slavonic languages

The fall of the Iron Curtain was not only an event – or rather process – with wide-ranging political consequences; it also had a profound impact on cultures mediated in the languages of East-Central Europe. While languages are in general more dynamic entities than everyday speakers usually assume (Keller 1994), because of various external factors they seem to change at certain historical stages more abruptly than otherwise (Language Change 2002). These changes are particularly conspicuous and, at times, exceed even the level of isolated new lexical items. Quite obviously, the years after 1989 mark a highly dynamic period in the history of the languages of East-Central Europe. And not only did the languages as such undergo rather substantial changes during the past two decades; the same applies to the relations between them. Moreover, even the sample of recognized languages has again proven not to be entirely stable. As might be expected, the Slavonic countries were particularly strongly affected by these events.[2]

Shortly prior to the break-up of the Eastern Bloc it seemed incontrovertible that there existed twelve standard Slavonic languages. There were the so-called Eastern Slavonic languages (Russian, Ukrainian and Byelorussian – as it was usually called at that time in accordance with the Russian name of Byelorussia), the so-called Western Slavonic languages (Polish, Czech, Slovak, Lower Sorbian and Upper Sorbian), and finally the so-called Southern Slavonic languages (Slovenian, Serbo-Croatian, Macedonian and Bulgarian).[3] Even in those days, however, not everybody agreed with this widely acknowledged position: František Václav Mareš, a renowned professor of Slavonic linguistics who was working in Vienna after immigrating from Czechoslovakia in 1968, used to teach his students that there was indeed a thirteenth standard Slavonic language, namely the Rusyn language in the then-Yugoslavia region of Vojvodina with a tiny number of speakers, but with a high degree of standardization and functionality in virtually all walks of life, including radio and television.[4] To be sure, this information was more like a random insider's tip, a curiosity. Only a handful of students regarded it as anything other than a minor footnote that one could safely forget about even prior to the exams.

In the years to come, the period of glasnost and perestroika was to lead to the fall of the Iron Curtain, the break-up of the Soviet Union, the civil wars in Yugoslavia, the division of Czechoslovakia and, most recently, to the EU membership of most of the states of the former 'Eastern bloc'. And not only has the political landscape changed considerably since 1989; linguistic developments have kept pace as well. Even those who had not studied the history of the formation of the standard Slavonic languages and had regarded them as quasi-primordial entities were forced to think again.

2. The splitting of languages

The most obvious development of seemingly new, independent, Slavonic languages resulted from the historical events in former Yugoslavia, namely the still well-remembered traumatic wars that shocked the world between 1991 and 1995. Communist Yugoslavia itself had been a country of active language-engineering from the very beginning inasmuch as its formation had brought about the creation of the then youngest, widely acknowledged standard Slavonic language, Macedonian. Earlier, the Slavonic varieties spoken in that area had usually been regarded as Bulgarian or, less often, as Serbian dialects.

Wide-ranging linguistic consequences followed the break-up of Yugoslavia, too. These entailed not only the ongoing emancipation of Slovenian and Macedonian (Stabej 2007) from the formerly privileged language that was usually labeled 'Serbo-Croatian'; the notion of one 'Serbo-Croatian' language itself came to be challenged (Greenberg 2004).

When the ultimate dissolution of 'Serbo-Croatian' became evident in the first half of the 1990s, primarily thanks to Croatian efforts to revive the image of an independent Croatian language, a significant number of individuals both from the academic world and society at large tended to bemoan the 'artificial' and 'politically motivated' split of the 'Serbo-Croatian' language. What they often neglected, however, was the very fact that 'Serbo-Croatian' had itself been an artificial and politically motivated construct from the beginning, and its status as one standard language was questioned throughout its history (Vince 1978; Katičić 1992). Moreover, no entirely unified 'Serbo-Croatian' language has ever existed. It has always been clear that the language consisted of at least the Serbian and the Croatian variants, which were different on all linguistic levels. Finally,

106 *Michael Moser*

many of those who bemoaned the end of 'Serbo-Croatian' overlooked that the so-called Croatian variant tended to be oppressed by the so-called Serbian variant. Croatians had opposed the very notion of 'Serbo-Croatian' even in Communist Yugoslavia at least since the late 1960s.

In the meantime,[5] it is widely accepted that Croatian and Serbian should be regarded as two distinct, though very closely related, languages because the absolute majority of Croatians and Serbians today understand the current language situation in these terms (Tošović 2008).

Many scholars believe that Bosnian efforts to provide Bosnian with the status of a language of its own have to be treated seriously (BHS 2003, Zabarah 2008). Consequently, scholars now tend to speak separately about 'the Croatian language', 'the Serbian language', and 'the Bosnian language', or they use the collective term 'Bosnian-Croatian-Serbian' if they want to refer to all related varieties spoken in that area. The developments in former Yugoslavia also served as a reminder of how closely the status of a language and the statehood of its speech communities could be intertwined. Since the 1990s, calls for a separate Montenegrin identity have argued in favor of establishing the notion of a Montenegrin language too (cf. Ostojić 2006). Now, after Montenegro gained sovereignty in June 2006, it is very unlikely that this demand can be downplayed any longer as a merely 'artificial' measure of language politics.

Needless to say that as soon as the freshly established independent languages came into being, new efforts of codification appeared, too. The direction of these was clear from the outset. Whereas in former times common linguistic elements of the Croats, the Serbs, the Bosnians and the Montenegrenians were emphasized, after the historical changes those who wished to emancipate themselves from ongoing linguistic 'oppression' focused on differences. Initially, the Croatians were most active in reshaping their separate language. They were particularly eager to replace Serbian loans with elements they deemed more acceptable, and had to ask themselves the typical questions: Which elements in particular were to be regarded as non-native? What traditional elements could be revived? To what degree should new elements be forged?

3. New relations between existing languages and the question of political correctness

The leading Communist superpower, the Soviet Empire, officially promoted the 'friendship of peoples' among its numerous nationalities. Following the creation of the Soviet Union, the Bolshevik leaders, after they had waged particularly cruel, so-called 'civil', wars against anti-Bolshevik forces throughout their empire, decided initially to go for an 'affirmative action' policy with regard to the aspirations of all Soviet nationalities (Martin 2001). In the early 1930s, however, Stalinist terror backtracked and Soviet nationality politics switched to the promotion of one, Russian-speaking 'Soviet people' (Kirkwood 2000: 710–14). With effect from October 1988, during the late 'perestroika' period and even before the superpower split into fifteen sovereign states, the new republics began endowing the languages of the titular nations with new rights (Kirkwood 2000: 214).

In the Baltic states, without regard to the situation of the particularly strong Russian ethnic minorities, the Baltic languages – Lithuanian and Latvian – as well as the Finno-Ugric Estonian were soon established as the sole official languages of the newly independent states of Lithuania, Latvia and Estonia (Rannut *et al.* 2008). All three countries entered the European Union in 2004, and the Russian Federation has only limited influence on their political developments.

Ukrainian, the mother tongue of millions of former Soviet citizens and, theoretically, the second largest Slavonic language with close to 50 million speakers, immediately upon independence became the only official language of independent Ukraine. This situation has remained unchanged to date, but it has constantly been threatened by the efforts of the large community of Russian-speakers in the country, especially those who are concentrated in the east and south of Ukraine (cf. Besters-Dilger 2009). Importantly, long before gaining independence, advocates of an independent Ukrainian identity both in Ukraine and among the émigré communities abroad had been claiming that their country should be referred to as 'Ukraine' and not 'the Ukraine' in English. Likewise, they requested that local adverbials should be formulated in Ukrainian (and in Russian) as 'v Ukrajini' ('v Ukraine') and not 'na Ukrajini' ('na Ukraine'), because in their opinion this was the usual way to refer to countries as opposed to regions of a country. After 1991 the practice of choosing the formulations proposed by the Ukrainian side was increasingly accepted across the countries of the world,[6] so that nowadays the linguistic shape of references to Ukrainian matters can be revealing about the speaker's attitude towards the country (cf. Moser 2009).

Matters of political correctness also apply to Belarusian (formerly B[y]elorussian). Initially it became the only official language of the country of Belarus'. After a referendum in 1995, however, the status of the Belarusian language changed dramatically because Russian was then accepted as the second official language in the country, and the impressive revival of the Belarusian language lost momentum (BM 1998; Moser 2000; BM 2003).

The new standing of some languages and the resulting effects of political correctness do have consequences for the study of the linguistic chronology as well as to glottonymic practice. It has become problematic to call a Croatian monument such as the 'Baška tablet' ('Bašćanska ploča' in Croatian) of 1100 a 'Serbo-Croatian' monument, and it is no less problematic to call the language of charters from fourteenth-century Galicia, or even texts from eleventh century Kyiv, 'Old Russian', despite the fact that these terms were commonly used in the twentieth century. Today it is clearer than ever that the Baška tablet should be called a monument of the Croatian language, which may be contextualized in the Croatian-Bosnian-Serbian-Montenegrin and even broader Slavonic dialect continuum. Similarly, medieval texts from today's Ukraine should be called either 'Old Rusian' inasmuch as they belong to the culture of medieval Rus (and not medieval Russia) or 'Old Ukrainian', but not 'Old Russian'. To be sure, quite a few historical linguists refute or try to downplay such questions by

108   *Michael Moser*

labelling them 'political'. Most often, however, they do so because they want to adhere to the traditional terminologies because of their own ideological affiliation.

The linguistic landscape of East-Central Europe has changed significantly, including the successor states of the Soviet Union in the west. As a consequence, in all the above-mentioned states, people in charge of language planning face a much livelier challenge to meet the demands of ongoing modernization and globalization than in Soviet times. From the early 1930s basically only Russian was the major object of truly serious language planning. All the other terminologies (and functional styles) of the languages of the Soviet Union had to come as close to the model of Russian as possible.

One should also take into account that outside the Russian Federation the Russian language itself is now used in a heavily changed linguistic environment. It has maintained a strong position in Belarus' both officially and in practical terms; in fact, quite obviously Belarusian and not Russian is the endangered language in Belarus'. As we said before, Russian maintained a comparatively strong position in Ukraine, where especially the east and the south of the country are still predominantly Russian-speaking. As regards the Baltic states, however, Russian was in former times the language of privileged minorities that were not expected to learn the language of the titular nations and in fact rarely did so. Nowadays the linguistic rights of the Russian minorities in these countries are sometimes rather 'harsh' (Kirkwood 2000: 722), especially in Latvia and Estonia (cf. Rannut *et al.* 2008 and Verschik 2008 particularly about Estonia).

This changed situation of the Russian language is, however, not only important with regard to questions of language politics, where one will have to face the challenge and deal with the inevitable frictions among the Russian-speaking minorities and the native speakers of the languages of the host countries. But, in addition, substantially new relations materialized between the languages at stake. Lithuanian, Latvian and Estonian as well – to a certain degree – as Ukrainian and – to a modest degree – Belarusian are now much more broadly used in official discourse in their countries and, thus, have a considerably stronger position vis-à-vis Russian than two or more decades ago. As a consequence, these languages are not pushed by language planners and ordinary speakers towards the Russian model as before. On the contrary, Russian minority populations in the newly independent states are nowadays increasingly likely to adopt loans from the official languages of their countries of residence.

To be sure, this new situation is also interesting with regard to the mixed languages in Belarus and Ukraine known respectively as 'Trasjanka' and 'Surzhyk'. In the current situation it is very likely that among these two non-standard varieties, which have recently attracted particular attention and turned into one of the truly 'fashionable' topics of Slavonic linguistics (Bilaniuk 2005, Hentschel and Tesch 2006, Del Gaudio 2010), Ukrainian-Russian 'Surzhyk', but perhaps also Belarusian-Russian 'Trasjanka' will continually increase their non-Russian share. If the Ukrainian language will persist as the only official language of the country, 'Surzhyk' will be likely to take on considerably more elements from Ukrainian in future. Especially, the number of lexical items referring to semantic spheres linked with education, politics, and society, which used to be borrowed from Russian, will now come to Surzhyk from Ukrainian.

Finally, it is quite obvious that the status of the Russian language has changed significantly, far beyond the borders of the Soviet Union. During the Cold War Russian had become one of the most widely-used languages of the world, and this status had been actively fostered by Soviet politicians who ensured that study of the Russian language was compulsory in all schools in the Warsaw Pact states. The intention was for as many East-Central European citizens as possible to know the language of 'Big Brother'. Although the role of Russian as an international language has certainly not entirely vanished since 1989, it has undoubtedly decreased significantly. On the one hand, this process took place in a quasi 'natural' way inasmuch as many people of the former Eastern bloc strongly associated the Russian language with oppressive Soviet and Communist politics and thus did not want to use Russian at all. On the other hand, simply for pragmatic reasons, the acquisition of Western languages instead of Russian became much more attractive from the economic point of view after the break-up of the Communist system. Besides, in the 1990s thousands of teachers of Russian were quickly retrained as teachers of English or, to a much lesser degree, German, whilst Russian became a subject on a considerably smaller scale (for the Czech Republic, for example, cf. ČJa 1998: 112–13). Consequently, the command of Russian today is much less widely distributed than twenty years ago, and the Russian language does not serve as a particularly important source of loans for the languages of East-Central Europe any more. Therefore, the Russian language of today is by far not as 'large' as it was two or more decades ago or, in other words, not only is it spoken by fewer people but its influence on 'small' languages has diminished (on the notion of 'small' and 'large' languages cf. Marti and Nekvapil 2007). Passersby on the streets of East-Central Europe are much less likely today to know Russian than two decades – or one generation – before. The extent of the study of Russian has in general decreased in many countries of the West, too. But the picture is more complicated than it might seem at first glance. The Institute for Slavonic Studies at the University of Vienna, for example, has now more than 1,500 students, the overwhelming majority of whom are students of Russian (cf. Institutsberichte 2004–8 2010). Even the recent closure of a number of departments of Slavonic studies in Germany has not necessarily entailed a decrease of interest in the Slavonic world and particularly in Russian. On the contrary, new economic relations with Slavonic countries, including Russia, guarantee that Slavonic languages will certainly not cease to be studied in the future.

4. Bottom-up 1: New languages out of dialects?

At first glance it might seem that only slight changes have occurred in the linguistic landscapes of those countries of East-Central Europe which had not been part of the former multinational states of the Soviet Union or Yugoslavia. This dubious impression partly results from the fact that political borders

110   *Michael Moser*

remained comparatively stable after 1989. Only Upper and Lower Sorbian were directly affected by the reunification of Germany (the Sorbians did indeed feel the effect of losing their formerly privileged status as the only autochthonous Slavonic minority in the only German-speaking country of the Eastern bloc) and the Republic of Czechoslovakia had split into the Czech and the Slovak Republics by January 1993 without any turmoil (SJa 1998: 22). Moreover, the sample of widely acknowledged Western Slavonic standard languages has not changed since 1989 either.

A closer look, however, reveals quite significant changes in the Western Slavonic area. Not only have the Czech and the Slovak communication spaces divided increasingly since the 1990s so that Czech and Slovak can no longer be described as two easily intercomprehensible languages (Nábělková 2007), but just like other regions of Europe, the Western Slavonic area has also witnessed the rise of new – or only seemingly new – regional and minority languages; languages that had formerly been and still are alternatively described as dialects of established standard languages. Clearly, these developments should be viewed not only against the background of the new political circumstances in the states of East-Central Europe themselves, but also within the broader context of European language politics. This particularly applies to the framework of the European charter of regional and minority languages, which was issued by the Council of Europe in 1992 and which symbolizes recent European policy; regional and minority issues have been put on top of the political agenda, and a 'Europe of the regions' is benefiting from generous subsidies (Rautz 2003: 265).

After the breakthrough of such new attitudes towards linguistic diversity in the general European framework it certainly came as no big surprise that for example in Poland Cassubian (or Kashubian) has gradually been gaining in status much more than ever before. This last remnant of the Pomeranian group of the Slavonic languages (a variety of dialects are spoken to the west of Gdynia along the Polish Pomeranian coast) has during the past decades been described by Polish linguists as a Polish dialect group primarily, whereas others have clearly tended to regard it as a language group of its own (Porębska 2006).

Not many observers would, however, have expected the results of the last Polish census of 2002, according to which a group of 173,153 'Silesians' figure as the largest 'national' minority of the country, and 56,643 among them declared that they spoke a distinct 'Silesian' language at home (Kamusella 2002, Czesak 2008). Since then the achievements of the Silesian national and linguistic movement have been less impressive, especially with a view to the initial enthusiasm. Publications in the Silesian language, not to speak of the codification in that language, certainly failed to live up to expectations. Nevertheless, the movement persists, and only the future will show its true impact.

As opposed to the 'Silesians', the 'Górals' ('mountaineers') of the Carpathian region in the south of Poland have not been so eager to declare a separate 'Góral' nation or language. Some of them, however, have produced impressive publications, such as the works of Józef Tischner, or a fine translation of

The new linguistic landscape   111

the New Testament in the 'Góral' language or rather the 'Góral' variety of the Polish language (Moser 2008).

It is not only the 'Silesians' who have created considerable interest recently by their attempts to renegotiate the mapping of nations and national languages through the revival of regional identities seemingly absorbed by nineteenth- and twentieth-century nationalism. Another new national movement of particular interest is that of the Rusyns (or Rusnaks), who had usually been regarded, at least since 1945, as a western branch of the Ukrainians but who have tried to establish – or rather re-establish – a separate Rusyn local identity during the past two decades. The Rusyn problem is further complicated by the fact that in former times all Ukrainians (and other Eastern Slavs, particularly the Belarusians) called themselves Rusyns. This applies in particular to Galician Ukrainians of the nineteenth century, who made a major contribution to the Ukrainian national and linguistic movement, but still called themselves Rusyns and adopted the new ethnonym and glottonym Ukraine/Ukrainian only at the turn of the twentieth century. At this point, the Rusyns are already recognized as a national minority in several countries of East-Central Europe (Magocsi 2004), and people of the same stock are referred to either as Ukrainians or as Rusyns in accordance with their own preference. The representatives of Rusyns from Slovakia, Poland, Hungary, Ukraine, Croatia and Serbia collaborate quite actively and meet regularly on an international scale, but, interestingly, with regard to language planning these groups of Rusyn activists have not yet overcome the categories of state boundaries. The contemporary Rusyn language, which Rusyn people usually tend to present to the public as a single new standard language, consists of at least five variants: the Slovak, the Polish, the Hungarian, the Subcarpathian (Ukrainian) and, finally, the Vojvodina variants. Moreover, a (North-)American variant and a Romanian variant also tend to be mentioned in Rusyn publications, but their status is still unclear. All these variants are alternatively regarded as more or less cultivated dialects of Ukrainian by those who do not accept a separate Rusyn national and linguistic identity and as variants of a separate Rusyn language by others. These variants are quite distinct from one another and their division is clearly not primarily based on linguistic matters, as particularly witnessed by the fact that the Hungarian variant virtually coincides with the language of Komloska, the one and only Hungarian village that has remained Rusyn-speaking to date (Moser forthcoming). Interestingly, the norms of the Vojvodina variant seem to be accepted across the state boundaries of contemporary Croatia and Serbia in spite of the break-up of Yugoslavia, although the wars of the 1990s strongly affected the region.

But not only peripheral movements have challenged seemingly well-established national and linguistic spaces during the past two decades. Suffice it to mention the fact that the latest Czech censuses of 1991 and 2001 not only revealed a small group of people who considered themselves to be of the Silesian nationality (44,445 and 10,878 respectively; these Czech Silesians do not cooperate with the Polish Silesians though). Furthermore, 380,474 people or roughly 3.7 per cent of the population considered themselves to be of a distinct Moravian nationality in

112 Michael Moser

the last Czech census of 2001 (as compared to 1,362,313 people in 1991 or roughly 13.2 per cent of the Czech population, still within the state of Czechoslovakia) (ČSU 2009). Predictably, there is a Moravian linguistic movement, too (Šustek 1998), even though it is to date very weak.[7]

5. Bottom-up 2: Non-standard linguistic material penetrating into the standard languages

Official communication and, in general, communication in public spaces in the totalitarian regimes of the former Eastern bloc used to be kept within the boundaries of quite strictly standardized languages. Official discourse was often characterized by an abundance of empty propagandistic formulae, which reached such a high degree that many observers unanimously spoke of the widespread official 'newspeak' of the Eastern bloc (Sarnov 2005). After the fall of the Iron Curtain the situation, of course, changed radically.

Colloquialisms and even 'vulgar' elements increasingly surfaced in the public sphere, not only in various formerly well-known genres disseminated by the mass media or in political speeches (Gajda 2001: 213), but also in such essentially new forms of communication as advertisements, chat shows and the like (cf. ČJa 1998). In fact, a massive pluralization of the linguistic public space has taken root in virtually all countries of the former Eastern bloc, including Russia. It comes as no surprise that such developments have been characterized by purists as processes of degradation (cf. Duličenko 1994). Alternatively, they could also be viewed as expressions of linguistic vitality and diversity, which were sooner or later to erupt after decades of political oppression and hegemonic imposition of outdated norms. Altogether, the fact that nonstandard elements turn into standard ones and vice versa (especially, but not only in the lexical sphere) is of course a widespread phenomenon. At times of abrupt societal changes, however, these processes take a particularly conspicuous shape.

Leaving aside details of the rise of nonstandard elements in various languages of the former Eastern bloc, at least two of the so-called 'colloquial languages' in the Slavonic world deserve particular attention. On the one hand, the Czech 'obecná čeština' is a variety widespread in Bohemia, but not in Moravia and Silesia (ČJa 1998), and one that differs considerably from the Modern Standard Czech language for many reasons. In particular, this situation persists because Modern Standard Czech was codified in the nineteenth century based on older varieties of Czech and not on the colloquial language of the time. On the other hand, the Russian colloquial language ('russkaya razgovornaya rech') differs considerably from Modern Standard Russian although it seems to have developed primarily from the standard language itself (Kitajgorodskaja *et al.* 1981). Both colloquial languages constitute linguistic systems of their own, which vary from the standard languages in many respects. They are used by so many speakers that in future they might become even more important sources of linguistic changes reaching far beyond the level of vocabulary. In the Czech case, however, the limited geographical diffusion of the 'obecná čeština' might hamper its impact on the standard language.

The new linguistic landscape 113

6. 'Small' and 'large' languages – English and the rest

If penetration by nonstandard elements into the public sphere was one of the central concerns of the purists in the former Eastern bloc, since 1989 the massive influx of foreign elements has become another source of anxiety for them. As in the rest of the world, there is one source language of new loans with which no other can compete: English. As the international language of our days, it has reached all walks of life both for standard and nonstandard varieties of all East-Central European languages. As in the 'West', where a massive wave of Americanization commenced after World War II, language planners in East-Central Europe approach these recent loans from English in various ways. If, for instance, Czech language planners seem to have accepted loans such as management, snackbar, broker, joint-venture, know-how, marketingové strategie (marketing strategies); grant, summit, billboard and draft in their original English spelling, yet brífing ('briefing') only in adapted spelling (ČJa 1998: 192–93),[8] Slovak language planners have accepted not only brífing, but also softvér (Czech software) and samit ('summit') only with a heavily Slovakized spelling. But in an authoritative volume on Slovak linguistics such words as 'billboard', 'boss', and also the graphically Slovakized 'biznis' (business) are written only in quotation marks and are subsequently labeled 'substandard' or 'slang'.[9] Some Slovak equivalents or explanations for these English loans such as the particularly clumsy expression podnikanie v oblasti zábavy (business in the sphere of entertainment) for the allegedly 'substandard' 'šoubiznis' (SJa 1998: 45) demonstrate the difficult position of contemporary purists: many English loans are simply irresistible.

As in the 'West', the impact of English on the languages of East-Central Europe is not limited to new loan words or even such complex terms as 'fair play' or such new phraseologisms as 'keep smiling!' (both SJa 1998: 49).[10] In some disciplines as, for example, in natural sciences,[11] English is about to replace well-established national languages altogether. As a result, these languages are gradually losing functions for which they have been carefully adapted over decades, if not centuries. Furthermore they not only fail to acquire new, updated terminology; they are simply being abandoned in certain subjects and the outcome is unknown.

Even as many linguists of the largest national languages of Europe seem to be truly concerned about the increasing impact of English, those in charge of language policy for the 'smaller' languages of Europe often pay considerably less attention to English. The reason is that they are still more concerned about those 'larger' languages in their immediate neighbourhood that have traditionally been regarded as 'the greater threat'. A comparison of the Polish volume of the series *Najnowsze dzieje języków słowiańskich* (The most recent history of the Slavonic languages)[12] and its Sorbian and Ukrainian counterparts might serve as an enlightening illustration. The authors of the Polish volume frequently point critically to the growing influx of English elements (Gajda 2001: 55–56, 97, 310).[13] The Sorbian and Ukrainian authors also mention the strong impact of English (SJa 1998: 190, 241, 244; UM 1999: 87–88 etc.), but they seem more concerned about the impact of German and Russian.

114 *Michael Moser*

As in the 'West', measures for the protection of national languages differ. The most obvious East-Central European counterpart to France – with its well-known rigorous language regulations – is Poland, where 'The Act on the Polish Language' was issued by the Polish Parliament on 7 October 1999 (Polish Government 1999). This Act says, inter alia (all quotations are taken from the official English version of the Act):

> Taking into consideration that the Polish language is a constituting element of the Polish national identity and national culture, having considered the Polish historical experience that foreign rulers and occupants repressed the Polish language and endeavoured to denationalise the Polish nation, having realised that it is inevitable to safeguard national identity in today's global environment, having understood that the Polish culture helps create a unified and culturally varied Europe and that it can be preserved and developed only if the Polish language is preserved, the protection of the language is the responsibility of all Polish bodies and public institutions, as well as all Polish citizens.
>
> (Act 1999)

Article 3 of the Act lists the principles for the 'protection of the Polish language'. Users should 'apply and use the Polish language in its codified standard' and even 'make effort to improve their language proficiency, and endeavour to establish conditions for the optimum development of the language as a tool of human communication'. They should also contribute to the 'spread of knowledge about language and its role in culture'.

One of the principles of the Act expresses the respect for 'regional expressions and dialects, and their preservation'. This, however, of course does not refer to new regional languages, but the dialects of Polish, which are endangered like other regional dialects in the modern world. The Act puts emphasis on the 'fight against the vulgarization of the language' and foresees amendments to former laws which emphasize that citizens are encouraged to 'try to use the language correctly and avoid use of vulgarisms' (Article 16), and that journalists are 'obliged to care for correct use of the language in all press materials and avoid language vulgarisation' (all quotations from Act 1999). The main focus, however, is the protection of the Polish language in Poland against other languages, in particular, against the influx of English.

The fall of the Iron Curtain and the massive social transformations after 1989 have exerted significant influence on the languages of East-Central Europe. Many general developments have been characteristic for virtually all Slavonic languages, whilst others have been more specific for only one language or group of languages. Processes of pluralization, regionalization and globalization[14] have left their marked impact on the region and have taken shape in linguistic changes.

Notes

1 Unless otherwise noted, translations are mine (MM).
2 This contribution is intended to inform discussion in an interdisciplinary context and not as an exhaustive description of the topic.

The new linguistic landscape 115

3 On the non-absolute nature of the sample of Slavonic languages cf. Kamusella 2005. Cf. also the Slavonic languages discussed in Rehder 2009 as compared with the first editions.
4 At that time Mareš had in mind only this Vojvodina branch of Rusyn, cf. chapter section 4.
5 Cf. the highly interesting intermediary assessment from virtually all perspectives in BHS 2003.
6 British English has to date been slower to change usage than American English. I am grateful to Roman Senkus from the Canadian Institute of Ukrainian Studies at the University of Toronto for pointing this out to me).
7 Regarding the so-called Slavonic 'microliterary languages' see Duličenko 1981.
8 Forms cited before the semicolon are common in German too.
9 Out of these English loans in Slovak billboard is the only word not widely used in German.
10 Both 'fair play' and 'keep smiling!' are widespread in German. 'Fair play' is called a phraseologism in SJa 1998: 49.
11 80 per cent of the texts dealing with natural sciences and 45 per cent of the texts dealing with social sciences are published in English, which is nowadays functioning as a lingua franca in these fields 'although only 7% of our planet's population knows English' (Gajda 2001: 310).
12 Purists frequently bemoan the rise of English loans in Russian too (cf. Duličenko 1994). In the 'West', particularly French purism and the notion of Franglais is a well-known phenomenon.
13 'The rather forceful spread of English loans, especially after 1989 in certain spheres of life and among young people, raises concern (cf. the notions język anglopolski [Anglo-Polish language, M. M.], polangle) that English should not threaten the system of the Polish language and its position in public life' (Gajda 2001: 56).
14 The latter two only seemingly contradict each other.

Works Cited

Besters-Dilger, J. (2009) 'Language Policy and Language Situation in Ukraine. Analysis and Recommendations', INTAS Project, *Language Policy in Ukraine: Anthropological, Linguistic and Further Perspectives*, Frankfurt am Main: Peter Lang.

BHS (2003) Bosanski – Hrvatski – Srpski. Međunarodni skup 'Aktuelna pitanja jezika Bošnjaka, Hrvata, Srba i Crnogoraca', Beč, 27–28 Sept. 2002 / Bosnisch – Kroatisch – Serbisch. Internationale Tagung: Aktuelle Fragen der Sprache der Bosniaken, Kroaten, Serben und Montenegriner, Wien, 27–28 Sept. 2002, Neweklowsky, G. (ed)., Wien: Verlag Otto Sagner (Wiener Slawistischer Almanach, Sonderband 57).

Bilaniuk, L. (2005) *Contested Tongues. Language Politics and Cultural Correction in Ukraine*, Ithaca and London: Cornell University Press.

BM (1998) *Belaruskaya mova*, (eds) Lukashanec, A., Prigodzich, M. and Sjameshka, L., Opole: Wydawnictwo Uniwersytetu Opolskiego (Najnowsze dzieje języków słowiańskich).

——(2003) *Belaruskaja mova. Linhvistychny kampendyum*, (eds) Plotnikaŭ, B. and Antanjuk, L., Minsk: Intėrprėssėrvis, Knizhny Dom.

Czesak, A. (2008) *Mowa Górnoślązaków – nowe otwarcie*, in Tambor, J. (ed.), śląsko godka. Materiały z konferencji,śląsko godka – jeszcze gwara czy jednak już język?' z 30 czerwca 2008 roku, (Katowice, Wydawnictwo Gnome, Katowice 2008, 15–30).

ČJa (1998) Český jazyk, Kořenský, j. (ed.) Opole: Wydawnictwo Uniwersytetu Opolskiego (Najnowsze dzieje języków słowiańskich).

ČSU (2009) Český statistický úřad Obyvatelstvo podle národnosti podle výsledků sčítání lidu v letech (1921–2001) Available at: http://www.czso.cz/csu/2008edicniplan.nsf/publ/4032-08-2007 (accessed 19 November 2009).

116　*Michael Moser*

Del Gaudio, S. (2010) *On the Nature of Surzhyk: A Double Perspective*, München, Berlin, Wien: Verlag Otto Sagner (Wiener Slawistischer Almanach, Sonderband 75).

Duličenko, A. D. (1981) *Slavjanskie literaturnye mikrojazyki*, Voprosy formirovanija i razvitija, Tallin: Valgus.

——(1994) Russky yazyk kontsa XX stoletiya, München: Verlag Otto Sagner (Slavistische Beiträge. Bd. 317).

Gajda, S. (2001) *Język polski*, Opole: Wydawnictwo Uniwersytetu Opolskiego (Najnowsze dzieje języków słowiańskich).

Greenberg, R. (2004) *Language and Identity in the Balkans: Serbo-Croatian and its Disintegration*, Oxford: Oxford University Press.

Hentschel, G. and Tesch, S. (2006) 'Trasjanka: Eine Fallstudie zur Sprachmischung in Weissrussland', Stern, D. and Voss, C. (eds), *Marginal Linguistic Identities: Studies in Slavic Contact and Borderland Varieties*, Wiesbaden: Harrassowitz, 213–43.

Institutsberichte 2004–8 (2010) *Institutsberichte. Institut für Slawistik*, Wien: Universität Wien. Available at: http://slawistik.univie.ac.at/institut/institutsbericht/ (12 August).

Kamusella, T. (2002) 'Nation-Building and the Linguistic Situation in Upper Silesia', *European Review of History – Revue européenne d'histoire*, Vol. 9, No. 1, 37–62, Routledge.

——(2005) *The Triple Division of the Slavic Languages: A Linguistic Finding, a Product of Politics, or an Accident*, IWM Working Paper, Institut für die Wissenschaften vom Menschen – Institute for Human Sciences.

Katičić, R. (1992) *Novi jezikoslovni ogledi*, Zagreb: Školska knjiga.

Keller, R. (1994) *On Language Change. The Invisible Hand in Language*, London: Routledge.

Kirkwood, M. (2000) 'Language Planning in the Soviet Union and in the Post-Soviet Period', in Zybatow, L. (ed)., *Sprachwandel in der Slavia: die slavischen Sprachen an der Schwelle zum 21 Jahrhundert*, vol. 2, Frankfurt am Main: Peter Lang, 701–24.

Kitajgorodskaja, M. V.,Širjaev, E. N. and Zemskaja, E. A. (1981) *Russkaya razgovornaya retsh'*, Obshchie voprosy, Slovoobrazovanie, Sintaksis, Moscow: Nauka.

Language Change (2002) *Language Change: The Interplay of Internal, External and Extralinguistic Factors*, (eds) Jones, M. C. and Esch, E., Berlin and New York: Mouton de Gruyter (Contributions to the Sociology of Language; 86).

Magocsi, P. R. (2004) *Rusyn'skŷj jazŷk*, Opole: Wydawnictwo Uniwersytetu Opolskiego (Najnowsze dzieje języków słowiańskich).

Marti, R. and Nekvapil, J. (eds) (2007) Introduction, in *Small and Large Slavic Languages in Contact*, Berlin and New York: de Gruyter (*International Journal of the Sociology of Language* 183), 1–12.

Martin, T. (2001) *The Affirmative Action Empire: Nations and Nationalism in the Soviet Union 1923–39*, Ithaca: Cornell University Press.

Moser, M. (2000) 'Koexistenz, Konvergenz und Kontamination ostslavischer Sprachen in Weißrußland und in der Ukraine', *in Zeitschrift für Slawistik* 45 (2): 185–99.

——(2008) 'Slavische Regional-und Minderheitensprachen auf dem Gebiet der Republik Polen', in Duličenko, A. D. (ed.), *Slavyanskoe yazykoznanie: pokidaya XX vek ... K XIV mezhdunarodnomu s'yezdu slavistov*, Okhrid, Tartu: Tartu University Press (Slavica Tartuensia VIII), 123–53.

——(2009) 'Russischer Gaskrisendiskurs – Vladimir Putins Pressekonferenz vom 8. Januar 2009', *Studia Slavica Academiae Scientiarum Hungaricae*, 54 (2): 271–315.

——(forthcoming) 'Review of Magocsi 2004', *Harvard Ukrainian Studies*.

Nábělková, M. (2007) 'Closely-related languages in contact: Czech, Slovak, "Czechoslovak"', in Marti R. and Nekvapil, J., *Small and Large Slavic Languages in Contact*, Berlin and New York: Walter de Gruyter (*International Journal of the Sociology of Language* 183: 53–73).

The new linguistic landscape 117

Ostojić, B. (2006) *Istorija crnogorskog književnojezičkog izraza*, Podgorica: CID.

Polish Government (1999) Poland. Legislation. The Act on the Polish Language. U.S. English Foundation Research. Available at: http://www.usefoundation.org/view/477 (accessed 19 November 2009).

Porębska, M. (2006) *Das Kaschubische: Sprachtod oder Revitalisierung?, Empirische Studien zur ethnolinguistischen Vitalität einer Sprachminderheit in Polen*, München: Verlag Otto Sagner (Slavistische Beiträge 452).

Rannut, M., Vasiljeva, I., Zabarskaite, J. (2008) Multilingualism in the Baltic States, International Conference Everyday Multilingualism, Conference Report, Internationale Konferenz Lebensweltliche Mehrsprachigkeit, Konferenzbericht, Austrian Commission for UNESCO (Österreichische UNESCO-Kommission), Wien: Verlag des Bundesministeriums für Unterricht, Kunst und Kultur: 157–65.

Rautz, G. (2003) 'Politische Maßnahmen zur Förderung von Regional-und Minderheitensprachen in Europa. Aspekte ihrer Umsetzbarkeit, Kosteneffizienz und ihrer demokratischen Auswirkungen', in Besters-Dilger, J., de Cillia, R., Krumm H. J. and Rindler-Schjerve, R. (eds), *Mehrsprachigkeit in der erweiterten Europäischen Union*, Klagenfurt: Drava, 264–65.

Rehder, P. (ed.) (2009) Einführung in die slavischen Sprachen. (Mit einer Einführung in die Balkanphilologie von Wilfried Fiedler), 6th edition, Darmstadt: Wissenschaftliche Buchgesellschaft.

Sarnov, B. (2005) *Nash sovetsky novoyaz. Malen'kaya ènciklopediya real'nogo sotsializma*, Moscow, Èksmo (Dialogi o kul'ture).

SJa (1998) *Slovenský jazyk*, Bosák, J. (ed.), Opole: Wydawnictwo Uniwersytetu Opolskiego (Najnowsze dzieje języków słowiańskich).

Stabej, M. (2007) 'Size Isn't Everything: The Relation between Slovenian and Serbo-Croatian in Slovenia', in Marti, R. and Nekvapil, J., *Small and Large Slavic Languages in Contact*, Berlin, New York: Walter de Gruyter (*International Journal of the Sociology of Language,* 183: 13–30).

Šustek, Z. (1998) 'Otázka kodifikace spisovného moravského jazyka', in Duličenko, A. D. (ed.), *Jazyki malye i bol'šie. In memoriam akad. Nikita I. Tolstoi*, Tartu: Tartu University Press, 128–42.

Tošović, B. (2008) 'Die kroatische Sprachpolitik (mit einem Vergleich zu Serbien und Bosnien)', in Braselmann, P. and Ohnheiser, I. (eds), *Frankreich als Vorbild? Sprachpolitik und Sprachgesetzgebung in europäischen Ländern*, Innsbruck: Universität Innsbruck – University Press, 99–116.

UM (1999) Ukrajins'ka mova, in Jermolenko, S. (ed.), Opole: Wydawnictwo Uniwersytetu Opolskiego (Najnowsze dzieje języków słowiańskich).

Verschik, A. (2008) 'From Monolingualism to Bilingualism: Changing Identity and Linguistic Intuition', International Conference: Everyday Multilingualism, Conference Report, Internationale Konferenz Lebensweltliche Mehrsprachigkeit. Konferenzbericht, Austrian Commission for UNESCO (Österreichische UNESCO-Kommission) (ed.), Wien: Verlag des Bundesministeriums für Unterricht, Kunst und Kultur, 38–41.

Vince, Z. (1978) *Putovima hrvatskoga književnog jezika: Lingvističko-kulturnopovijesni prikaz filoloških škola i njihovih izvora*, Zagreb: SNL.

Zabarah, D. (2008) *Das Bosnische auf dem Weg zur Standardsprache: eine synchrone und diachrone Analyse der Sprachsituation in Bosnien und Herzegowina*, Saarbrücken: Verlag Dr. Müller.

Index

Abramov, Fiodor 89
Académie française 97
Adenauer, Konrad 32
Aeschylus 67
Aesop 81
Aitmatov, Chingiz 78
Alpe-Adria 27, 36–7n8
Aksionov, Vasilii 84, 89, 94
Akunin, Boris 8
Alexakis, Vassilis 97
Aleshkovskii, Iuz 89
Ali, Monica 53
Alme, Rolf 63
Americanization 33, 113
Anglopolski 115n
anti-Semitism 43
Arbatova, Mariia 81
Aristotle 59, 65
Arrak, Jüri 1–2, 10n2, n3, n4
Artaud, Antonin 66
Ash, Timothy Garton 35
Astaf'ev, Viktor 78
Auschwitz 48, 50
Austro-Hungarian Empire 4, 6,
    22, 25, 34

Babchenko, Arkadii 80
Balkans 14, 25, 26, 28, 36, 54–55
Baltic languages 107
Baltic Way 7, 75
Barba, Eugenio 66
Barroso, Jose Manuel 44
Barthes, Roland 65
Basho, Matsuo 89
Baška tablet 107
Bauhaus 56
Bavilskii, Dmitrii 85
Beckett, Samuel 65
    Waiting for Godot 65

Beethoven, Ludwig van 51
    Fidelio 51
Belarusian 108
Belov, Vasilii 89
Berberova, Nina 93
Berezovskii, Boris 87
Berlin Blockade 20
    East 19, 21, 40, 51
    Wall 2, 3, 5, 20, 40, 48, 49, 50, 51, 52,
        55, 58, 59, 60, 61, 64, 65, 78
    West 7, 19, 48–49, 52
Berliner Festspiele 64
Berlinguer, Enrico 40
Beyala, Calikst 97
Bezrodnyi, Mikhail 84, 90n12
Bibo, Istvan 37n13
Bolshevism 4, 76, 93, 100n3, 106
Bosnian-Croatian-Serbian 106
Brecht, Bertolt 7, 61, 62, 65
Brezhnev, Leonid 18, 90n4
Brix, Emil 34
Brook, Peter 60
Bruskin, Grisha 84
Buida, Iurii 88
Bunakov, I.I. 101n6
Bunin, Ivan 93
Busek, Erhard 27
Bykov, Dmitri 86, 90n16

Calderon, Pedro dela Barca 66
Cărtărescu, Mircea 43
Cartoucherie, la 66
Cassubian 110
Ceauşescu, Nicolae 26, 43
Censorship 8, 13
'Charta 77' 33, 45
Chekhov, Anton 60, 65
    The Cherry Orchard 65
    The Seagull 60

Index 119

Chernobyl 24
Churchill, Winston 2, 10n5
CIA 7, 48
Czech obecna čeština 112
Czechoslovakia 9, 22, 24, 25, 26, 27, 29,
  30, 31, 36n3, n4, 41, 43, 98, 105, 110
Chernobyl 86
Chisla 96
Čiurlionis, Mikolajus 73–74
Clinton, Bill 75
chernukha 80
Cold War 2, 7, 19, 36, 60, 109
Communism ix, x, 2, 3, 4, 5, 6, 13–14, 17,
  18, 21, 23, 26, 28, 33, 34, 35, 41, 42,
  43, 44, 46, 50, 58, 64
conceptualism 82
Conference on Security and Cooperation
  in Europe 18
Conrady, Karl Otto 56n7
Croce, Benedetto 42

Dalos, György 25
Deleuze, Gilles 90n5, 97
Demszky, Gabor 42
Denezhkina, Irina 87
Developing World 22, 35
Diderot, Denis 63
Dienstbar, Jiři 6
Dinescu, Mircea 43
Djebar, Assia 97
Dmitriev, Andrei 85
Draculić, Slavenka 10n11
Dreiser, Theodore 12
Dual Monarchy (see Austro-Hungarian
  Empire)
dystopian literature 86

Eastern bloc ix, 5, 8, 17, 19, 92, 104, 105,
  109, 110, 112, 113
Ermakov, Oleg 80
Erofeev, Viktor 78, 89
Est-Ovest 3
Esterhazy, Peter 6, 10n9, 42
Etkind, Aleksandr 84
Evseev, Boris 83, 84
European Union x, 5, 6, 7, 8, 22, 25, 28,
  29, 31, 33, 34, 35, 42, 45, 47, 52, 74,
  75, 95, 107
Euripides 67
  The Bacchae 67
Evans, Robert 10n10, 37n16

Fejtö, François, 37n10
Festival d'Avignon 64, 66

Foucault, Michel 2, 10n6
Franck, Julia 51
Franglais 115n12
French Revolution 66
Freud, Sigmund 90n10, 92, 100
Fukuyama, Yoshihiro Francis 41

Galician 111
Galkovskii, Dmitrii 90n12
Gandhi, Mahatma 42
Gandlevskii, Sergei 84
Gasparov, Mikhail 84, 90n12
Gastarbeiterliteratur 100
Gates, William 75
Gauss, Karl-Markus 52
Gdansk 54
Gellner, Ernest 71
Gendelev, Mikhail 95, 101n10
Genis, Aleksandr 84
Germany, East (GDR) 7, 17, 18, 19, 20,
  21, 40, 47n5, 49, 50, 51, 56
  West (FRG) 7, 17, 19, 21, 42, 44, 48,
  49, 51
Gippius, Zinaida 93, 101n6
glasnost' 20, 49, 105
Glotz, Peter 32–33
Goethe, Johann Wolfgang von 97
Goethe Institut 99
Gogol, Nikolai 81, 83, 85
Golovanov, Vasilii 88
Gonzales, Felipe 44
Goral 110–111
Gorbachev, Mikhail 20, 30, 34, 60
Gorenko, Anna 95
Gorky, Maxim 12
Gosteva, Anastasiia 88
Gramsci, Antonio 40
Grand Prix de l'Academie française, le 97
Grass, Günter 48
Greene, Graham 74
Grishkovets, Evgenii 86
Gropius, Walter 56n9
Grossman, David 52
Grossman, Vasilii 90n14
Grotowski, Jerzy 65–66
Grüber, Klaus-Michael 67
Guattari, Felix 97
Gulf War 40
Gusinskii, Vladimir 87
Gutenberg, Johannes 15

Habsburg Empire 4, 5, 18, 24, 25, 26, 27,
  28–32, 34, 35, 37n16, 53
  Franz Joseph, Emperor and King 28, 42

120 *Index*

Habsburg Empire (*Continued*)
  Karl IV, Emperor and King 6, 28
  Otto von, Archduke 6, 28, 37n9
  Zita, Empress and Queen 6, 28
Hacks, Peter 49
Handke, Peter 42, 55
Haraszti, Miklos 30
Hare, David 52
Havel, Vaclav 6, 74, 42
Hockney, David 16
Homer 98
  The Odyssey 98, 102n30
Honecker, Erich 18
Horn, Gyula 21, 28
Hungarian Revolution (1956) 17,
  25, 53
Hurt, Jakob 75
Hussein, Saddam 40
Huston, Nancy 97

Ibsen, Henrik 63, 64
  A Doll's House 63, 64
Ikonnikov, Aleksandr 85
Ingrao, Charles W. 37n16
Ionesco, Eugéne 6, 26
Iron Curtain ix, x, 2, 6, 7, 8, 17, 18, 21,
  23, 27, 28, 40, 49, 52, 55, 56, 58, 59,
  62, 63, 64, 65, 79, 92, 104, 105, 112
Iser, Wolfgang 65
Istituto per gli incontri culturali
  mitteleuropei 26–27, 35
Itinerari 34

Jahrhundertwende 34
Järvi, Neeme 73
Jaspers, Karl 56
Jelinek, Elfriede 49
Jelloun, Tahar Ben 97
Joyce, James 54, 56n8, 89
Jozsef, Attila 4
Judt, Tony 35
Jung, Carl Gustav 82, 90n10

Kaaplinski, Jan 76
Kabalov, Aleksandr 84
Kadar, Janos 34
Kafka, Franz 40, 42
Kaledin, Sergei 80
Kalevipoeg 72
Kaljuste, Tõnu 73
Kaminer, Wladimir 99–100, 102n33
Kaplinski, Joan 72
Kazakov, Iurii 78
Kende, Peter 29

Kenzheev, Bakh
Kiš, Danilo 6, 25, 28, 30
Klaus, Vaclav 43
Klimantovich, Nikolai 84
Kertesz, Imre 3, 6, 42
Kliuchariova, Natal'ia 87
Kojeve, Alexandre 41
Konrad, György 6, 25, 30, 31–32, 42
Koolhaas, Rem 76
Kreisky, Bruno 5, 6, 17–18, 25,
  33–34
Krytyka 30
Kristeva, Julia 97
Krleža, Miroslav 13
Kross, Jaan 72
  The Czar's Madman 72
Kucherskaia, Mariia 88
Kundera, Milan 3, 9, 14, 30, 31, 32, 92,
  98–99, 100, 102n24
Kunze, Reiner 50
Kureisi, Hanif 53
  The Buddha of Suburbia 53
Kuritsyn, Viacheslav 84

Lacan, Jacques 82
Landsbergis, Vytautas 73–74
Liehm, Antonin 31
Limonov, Eduard 87, 89–90n2, 94
Linhartova, Vera 99
Lippmaa, Endel 75
Lipskerov, Dmitrii 82
Lisbon Treaty 42
Lucas, Edward 74
Luxemburg, Rosa 40
Lyotard, Jean François 40–41, 46, 47n5

Mabanclou, Alain 97
Mahabharata 66
Magris, Claudio 6, 25, 27, 35, 54
Makanin, Vladimir 78, 81, 85
Makine, Andrei 97, 102n25
Mamleev, Iurii 80
Mandela, Nelson 42
Mann, Thomas 4
Manicheanism 85
Mareš, František Vaclav 105
Marinina, Aleksandra 83
Mark Aldanov Prize 96
Markish, David 95
Martynov, Vladimir 63
Marxism 35, 41, 48
Matzner, Egon 22
Mauerliteratur 53
McEwan, Ian 48, 56n2

Mečiar, Vladimir 23
Meri, Lennart 8, 74
Michnik, Adam 25, 30
Mitteleuropa 2, 4, 6, 26, 28, 29, 32, 33,
    34, 35, 36, 54
Mnouchkine, Ariane 66, 68
Mock, Alois 6, 21, 25, 28
Moliere, Jean-Baptiste de 63
Molodaia gvardiia 87
Molotov-Ribbentropp Pact 75
Montenegrin 106
Moravian 111–112
Müller, Heiner 50, 56
    Ajax zum Beispiel 50
Müller, Herta 46, 56n5
multiculturalism 14, 31, 54
Mussolini, Benito 42

Nadas, Peter 42
Narbikova, Valeriia 82
Narutowicz, Gabriel 10n6
Nash sovremennik 87
Nationalism x, 5, 6, 8, 13, 22, 25, 29, 31,
    43, 44, 45
national socialism (Nazis) 4, 29,
    35, 45, 51, 55
NATO 6, 17, 22, 24, 74, 7
Naumann, Friedrich 34
NDiaye, Marie 97
Nekrošius, Eimuntas 59
Neues Forum 33
Nemirovsky, Irene 96
Nemzer, Andrei 84
neo-Nazis 90n18
neo-Stalinists 90n18
New Review, The 96
Neumann, Peter-Horst 56n7
Nietzsche, Friedrich 50
Nikolaeva, Olesia 88
Nosov, Sergei 83
Nouvelle alternative, La
    37n12
Novalis 40, 42, 47n3

Oder-Neisse line 29
Odoevtseva, Irina 94
Old Rusian 107
Old Ukrainian 107
Olesha, Iurii 85
Õnnepalu, Tõnu 72
    Borderland 72
Osborne, John 64, 65
    Look Back in Anger 64, 65
Ostpolitik 34

Ottlik, Géza 53
    The School on the Border 53
Ovid 102n23

Palacký, František 29
Pan-European movement 6, 28
Pannonia 27
Pavlov, Oleg 80
Pärt, Arvo 73
Pelevin, Viktor 79, 82, 83, 90n8
Pen Club 25
perestroika 20, 49, 80, 105, 106
Peschel, Milan 63
Petrosyan, Mariam 101n15
Petrushevskaia, Ludmila 80
Pilsudski, Jozef 10n6
Pink Floyd 42
Pirandello, Luigi 62, 65
    Six Characters in Search of an Author
        62, 63
Pivovarov, Viktor 84
Pomeranian 110
post-communism x, 43, 44
postmodernism 41, 95
Post-Soviet Russia 77–91
Prague Spring (Czechosk Revlovaolution
    of 1968) 17, 18
Prilepin, Zakhar 80, 87
Prix Femina 97
Prix Goncourt 96, 97
Prix de Médicis 97
Prix Goncourt 96
Prokhanov, Aleksandr 86–87
Prokhorova, Irina 97–98, 101n22

racism 5
Rahimi, Atiq 97
Randviir, Tiina 10n1
Rasputin, Valentin 78
Reagen, Ronald 20, 60
red-brown fiction 86
Respekt 25
Ripka, Hubert 36n4
Robski, Oksana 86
Rolling Stones 42
Roma (Gypsies) 43, 45
Rossi, Francesco C. 34
Rozanov, Vasilii 90n12
Rybakov, Anatolii 90n14
Rubina, Dina 78, 95, 101n11
Rudiagina, Olesia 10
Russia 8, 9, 26, 29, 31, 36, 78, 79, 81, 82,
    83, 85, 88, 89, 93, 95, 96, 99, 100n4,
    107–108, 112

122 Index

Russia (*Continued*)
  Orthodoxy 2, 88
  Revolution (October 1917) 41, 81, 83, 93
Russian Berlin 100n3
Russian Award, The 96
Rumessen, Vardo 73
Rusyn 111

Sadulaev, German 80
Sadur, Nina 81, 82
St George 1–2, 70
Sajūdis 73
Schengen Agreement 7, 52
Schernikau, Ronald M. 49
  Kleinstadtnovelle 49
  Die Tage in L 49
  Legende 49
Schimmelphenning, Ronald 61
Schlesinger, Klaus 56
Schlögel, Karl 32–33, 54
Schneider, Peter 48, 50, 56n2
  The Wall Jumper 48, 56n2
Schnitzler, Arthur 28
Schönberg, Arnold 98
Schönbrunn, Svetlana 95
Schröder, Gerhard 45
Securitate 43
Semionova, Maria 83
Serbo-Croatian 105–106, 107
Sergeev, Andrei 84
Shakespeare, William 74
  Hamlet 59
Sharov, Vladimir 80, 84
Shirianov, Baian 82
Shishkin, Mikhail 78, 80
Siji, Daj 97
Silesian 110–111
Sinclair, Upton 12
Slapovskii, Aleksei 83, 85, 86
Slowacki, Juliusz 66
ialist realism 12, 77, 81, 89
Solzhenitsyn, Aleksandr 94
  The Gulag Achipelago 35, 72, 78
Sorbian 110, 114
Sorokin, Vladimir 82, 83, 86
Soros, George 72
Soviet Union ix, 1, 2, 5, 8, 9, 17, 18, 19, 20, 22, 24, 26, 28, 29, 31, 32, 33, 34, 35, 36, 40, 41, 43, 44, 48, 50, 51, 60, 74, 75, 76, 77–78, 79, 80, 81, 84, 85, 87, 88, 89, 92, 93, 94, 105, 106, 108–109
Spiegel, der 36n6, 99,

Srebrenica 55
Stalin, Joseph 40, 43, 78, 79
state socialism ix, 8, 9, 28, 51
Stasi 20
Strauss, Johann 47n6
  Die Fledermaus 43, 47n6
Strache, Heinz Christian 45
Strehler, Georgia 65
Stein, Peter 67
Suárez, Adolfo 44
Subcarpathian 111
Susi, Arnold 72
Surzhyk 108–109
Sydney, Sir Philip 4

Tarasov, Lev 96
Taylor, Frederick 50
Teutonic Order 2
Thatcher, Margaret 45
Theatre of the Absurd 1
Théâtre du Soleil, le 66
Third World (see 'Developing World')
Timatkova, Mariia 101n15
Tischner, Josef 110
Tito, Josip Broz 12, 13, 24, 42, 55
Tobias, Rudolf 73
Tatyana Tolstaya 10n10, 82, 86
Tönnies, Ferdinand 51
Tontić, Stevan 54–55
Tork, Aleksei 101n15
Tormis, Veljo 73
Transylvania 26
Trasjanka 108
Trieste 35, 54
Trifonov, Iurii 78
Troyat, Henri (see Lev Tarasov)
Tudman, Franjo 25
Tüür, Sven-Erik 73
Twin Towers 58, 59

Ugrešić, Dubravka 3, 5, 10n10, 12–16
  'The Culture of Lies' 5
Ulitskaia, Liudmila 84, 89
Ulbricht, Walter 50
UNESCO ixn, 75
USSR (see under Soviet Union)
Ustaša 25
Utkin, Anton 83

Varlamov, Aleksei 88
Vasiliev, Anatoly 62
Velvet Revolution 3, 6, 41, 42, 43, 45
Venclova, Tomas 76

Index   123

Verfremdung 58–69
Vīke-Freiberga, Viara 75
Vilar, Jean 64
Visegrád Group 24, 36n2
Vladimov, Georgii 85
Vojvodina 111
Völkerkerker 24, 29

Walser, Martin 48
Warsaw Pact 3, 6, 18, 42, 45, 109
Weigel, Helena 62
Westbindung 32
Wolf, Christa 50
Wolfrum, Edgar 50
  Die Mauer 50
World War I 4, 6, 33, 35,
  54, 100

World War II 2, 4, 12, 17, 62, 64
Weltliteratur 97

Xenophobia x, 5, 14, 43, 44

Yeltsin, Boris 74, 87
Yugoslavia 6, 9, 12, 14, 24, 25, 26, 27,
  28, 34, 35, 37n8, 42, 46, 55, 105–106,
  109, 111

Zaionchkovskii, Oleg 85
Zavtra 90n19
ZDF 100
Zentraleuropa 36
Zhvanetskii, Mikhail 90n3
Zweig, Stefan 28
Zwischeneuropa 36